What I like most about Dave and Scott Goudsward's Horror Guide series is that while they are informative and involved, they are - unlike many reference works - a lot of fun to read and easy to navigate. The newest installment, *Horror Guide to Northern New England: Maine, New Hampshire, and Vermont* (HGNNE) is, like its Massachusetts and Florida companion editions, an extensive and intensive display of research from the Goudsward brothers. It is especially sweet for me because I was born and raised in New Hampshire and had lived there for forty years, until 2002. I had spent my formative years traipsing between the three states that are the focus of this book and recognized many of the towns, sites, and sights covered within these pages. But you don't have to be native to these states to enjoy this book...or its predecessors.

For horror fans, non-horror fans, writers, researchers, or joy readers, HGNNE (and its companions) are a valuable and enjoyable guide and reference of all things fact and fictional related to horror (or "spooky" for the more sensitive reader), from the renowned to the obscure. It takes you on an alphabetical tour through each state, geographically correlating each town and site (both real and fictional) to works of popular fiction. As one would guess, the "Maine" section is loaded with Stephen King and Rick Hautala mentions, but for me - having read most of their works - it was a nostalgic trip that made me yearn to read these stories again. Thank you, Dave and Scott, for another fine Guide...now how about New York...or D.C.?

– John McIlveen – award-winning author of *Hannahwhere*

Horror Guide to
Northern
New England

Also in the Horror Guide Series

Horror Guide to Massachusetts
Horror Guide to Florida

Horror Guide to
Northern
New England
Maine, New Hampshire, & Vermont

David Goudsward &
Scott T. Goudsward

Introduction by
J.W. Ocker

POST MORTEM PRESS
CINCINNATI

To all those we lost in 2016 and 2017:

*The Droid, the Princess, and Prince. The Professor and the Stardust.
The Godfather of Gore, kind enough to blurb our second book. Those
that fought aliens and those that raised hell.*

*You enhanced our lives and distracted all of us from reality even if it
was only for two hours at a time.*

TABLE OF CONTENTS

FOREWORD

Horror Guide to Northern New England looks at Maine, New Hampshire, and Vermont in ways that the make the chambers of commerce a little uneasy. Think of it as a guide to geographical locations, real and fictional, utilized in horror tales and films set in the region. With a pinch of folklore and some actual, real facts tossed in for good measure. If your first impression is that this is simply a compilation of Stephen King and Rick Hautala, you're wrong. Yes, Rick and Uncle Stevie are in here, but so are those that blazed new trails into the dark scary woods of the genre - Sarah Orne Jewett, who came up with the concept of setting all her stories in one fictional town to tie them together; Frank A. Munsey, who created the pulp magazine; Harriet Prescott Spofford, who wrote the first haunted automobile story in 1916; Richard Potter, America's first stage magician – names that are not as familiar, but just as important to the development of horror as we know it today. And so this book also serves as an impromptu history of our accursed ancient land. And for the not so ancient part, there's a healthy slathering of Joe Hill and other modern authors and filmmakers.

This is not a comprehensive list of every horror story and film set in northern New England, but we think it's a fair representation. By the time you're finished reading this foreword, dozens of new stories will have been written and set to paper. We hope you come away from this project with at least one name, film or story you want to track down. Or inspired to write your own grisly tale. Or even better, get the urge to buy our other books.

One of John Greenleaf Whittier's later poems was "The Homestead." Written in 1886 after travels where he saw abandoned farms dotting the countryside, victims of the pursuit of steady jobs and better wages offered by the factories and mills. Whittier entreats the younger generation to return to the abandoned ancestral farms and by inference, their roots. Whittier's pleas went unheeded - traditional New England was in decline after the Civil War. The war had decimated the male population; their orphaned children, tired of sustenance farming in their late father's place, abandoned the farms for the long hours but steady work of the mills. This environment of change and instability gave birth to a new milieu for horror writers - isolated villages, declining blue-bloods, and hidden scandals. And it still works – About 90% of Maine, 85% of New Hampshire and 76% of Vermont are forested. So if you want an isolated village, New England is a good place to start. Haunted covered bridges? Check. Lake monsters? Check. UFO abductions? Check. You have Bigfoot in Maine, Shirley Jackson in Vermont, and sacrificial tables in New Hampshire. And if you don't believe location is vital to a horror story – imagine Collinwood located in the south – Barnabas Collins in a white linen suit? Now that's scary!

Scott T. Goudsward
Haverhill, MA

David Goudsward
Lake Worth, FL

Acknowledgements

The authors would like to thank …

Melinda Adams, Norman Williams Public Library
Stephen Bissette
Joseph A. Citro
John DiGeorge, Mutsu Crispin Productions
Rick Hautala & Holly Newstein
Diane Kachmar, Florida Atlantic University
Ari Kahan, swanarchives.org
Patrick Layne, Bangor Public Library
The New England Horror Writers
J. W. Ocker, OTIS
Charles Roxburgh, Motern Media
Susan M. Roy, Mad River Valley Chamber of Commerce
Michelle Souliere, Green Hand Bookshop
Dennis Stone, America's Stonehenge

On the Edge of Darkness, and Canada.

New England is the creepiest part of the United States. Seventeenth century numerals appear frequently on house plaques and grave epitaphs throughout the region, meaning its old enough to have gathered some serious rot in its cracks and corners. Its graveyards bristle with headstones covered with skulls, skeletons, coffins, even bats and snakes, as if they were fabricated out of foam and plastic specifically for a horror movie. You'll also find in those cemeteries vampire graves—semi-final resting places of tuberculosis victims who were disinterred and immolated by family to keep them from rising and attacking. Its city commons are full of dead witches, and generational curses are handed down like so many chintzy heirlooms. Too many major horror authors hail from New England for that to be at all coincidental—Poe, King, Jackson, James, Lovecraft, Wharton. I guess that's what you get when your founding fathers and mothers are witch hunters and vampire killers and devil resistors.

So, naturally, to me, the next question is, "What's the creepiest part of New England?" To answer that question, I'd lean forward and silently point upward, not wanting to name the devil: Vermont. New Hampshire. Maine. Northern New England.

See, Connecticut is a mere twilight zone between New York and New England. Rhode Island is too small and darling to be of any real threat, which is why Lovecraft had to find his monsters in Antarctica and the bottom of the ocean and in other dimensions. And Massachusetts is overly trod-upon territory, too well-known a quantity to be scary anymore. Salem witches are tourist draws. Danvers Insane Asylum is now condos. Lizzie Borden was squeezed into a nursery rhyme.

But in Northern New England, it's different. You're less safe there. More isolated. Easier prey. It's bookended at one end by Shirley Jackson and at the other by Stephen King. Even wholesome, grandfatherly poet Robert Frost, who lived in both Vermont and New Hampshire and whose homes in those states are museums dedicated to him today, had to turn eventually from lines about idyllic gambols along stone fences to much darker places. *The Witch of Coös. The Pauper Witch of Grafton. Ghost House. In a Disused Graveyard.*

Up north, murder and tragedy take on a stronger, stranger significance. Crimes haunt the towns longer. When schoolgirl Josie Langmaid was killed in Pembroke, New Hampshire, by an itinerant worker, the town erected a monument not so much to her, but to her murder. Inscribed upon its surface are the grisly details of the location where her body was found…as well as the separate site where her severed head was discovered.

Secrets are also easier to bury in the snow drifts up north. In the birch copses. It's a land of unknowns. Huge stretches of uninhabited spaces where Google just overlays shrug emojis on its maps. It might be the land of covered bridges, but those quaint wooden tunnels double in the dark as birdhouses for ghosts. Let's take Vermont. Don't let Ben and Jerry fool you about this place. It hides lake monsters. The Bennington Triangle. The ghost of Charles Dickens haunts there. They stone unlucky villagers there. Jack Nicholson turned into a wolf there. The guy who gave the world *Nosferatu* molders there.

And New Hampshire. It's the state you only think about once every four years, as if it were some kind of strange Shangri-La. That's why J.D. Salinger fled there to hide from the world. Why Sutter Cane holed up there to destroy it. Why Aleister Crowley magickly retired there to probe occult secrets. The Invisible Man was laid to rest there. Daniel Webster fought the Devil there. This is the spot aliens picked to start abducting and probing humans in the modern era. It gave the world one of the most prolific serial killers in recorded history: Herman Webster Mudgett, aka H.H. Holmes. Thanks, New Hampshire.

And then there's good old LL Bean-jacketed and Easton-booted Maine. Honestly, I believe there are only two states in the country where every single horror story—be it about a haunted house, backwoods cannibals, mutated creatures, evil aliens, supernatural serial killers, classic monsters of myth and movie—could be set with minimal suspension of belief. Those states are

West Virginia and Maine. In the case of Maine, too much of it is unexplored. Too much can hide there. It has every environment for housing horrors: ocean, mountain, forest, lake. Even a sandy desert. And, of course, its cold is a deathly cold. And all that was true even before the Collins family moved there. And before the Belasco House was built there. And before Stephen King utterly transmogrified the state.

And if you think I'm mixing the real and the fictional too much in the above paragraphs, well, let me introduce you to the authors of this book, the Goudsward brothers.

David and Scott aren't from Northern New England, but they do hail from Haverhill, Massachusetts, so they only missed being Northern New Englanders by mere inches. For instance, I live in southern New Hampshire, and just about all of Haverhill lies farther north than my house thanks to the rude way Massachusetts steals valuable coastline from the surrounding states. It also means that the shadow of Northern New England has hung above their heads almost their entire lives.

These two gents are tireless researchers and cataloguers of the odd and the macabre. In these pages, they have scraped down to the granite skeleton of Vermont, New Hampshire, and Maine, digging up horrors both real and imaginary. It doesn't matter if the murder is an actual tragedy or a plot point in a story, they record it, creating two landscapes in the process.

In one, you'll find real-life terrors and oddities. The skeleton of pedophiliac murderer at an Ivy League college. A mysterious arrangement of stones that inspired H.P. Lovecraft in writing *The Dunwich Horror*. A tiny lonely island off the coast where an infamous axe murder was committed. The burial site of an Egyptian mummy prince.

But where this book really stands out as unique is the other landscape it charts. The one Frankenstein'd together by movie makers and authors and artists. The imaginary Northern New England of our stories. The nightmarish Northern New England. In this book, you'll find just about every instance when a macabre storyteller used a Northern New England town in his or her art or book or movie. Sometimes the town is fictional. Other times the fictional events are set in a real town. In this landscape, you'll find sites that drew the attention of Mulder and Scully. Spots where Alfred Hitchcock buried a body or two. Rick Hautala's tireless efforts at wresting Maine from the King.

I don't care if you're a sepia-toned New England historian or a blood-drenched horror fan, you'll find something surprising in this guide. Because the Goudswards don't stop when they reach the casket. They keep digging.

J.W. Ocker
Nashua, New Hampshire
January 2017

MAINE

Detail from the wrought iron the fence outside Stephen King's home.
Photo courtesy of Norma J Fox.

Acadia National Park, Cadillac Mountain – Lisa and Arlan leave Bar Harbor to see the summer solstice sunrise on Cadillac Mountain in nearby Acadia National Forest. On the trail, they encounter a friend of Arlan's. Now Arlan has vanished. Lisa is traumatized, hospitalized, and getting a crash course in Celtic mythology. "The Gates of Dawn" by Rick Hautala was originally published in *The World of Darkness: The Splendour Falls* (1995), an anthology based on the "Changeling: The Dreaming" RPG system of White Wolf.

Acadia National Park, Newport Cove – Australian swimmer Annette Kellerman was as well known for her swimming and diving as she was as an actress. While filming *Queen of the Sea* (1918), a stunt was added to the plot to show off Kellerman's skills. As the mermaid, she is helping rescue a princess in the Tower of Knives and Swords. Without a stuntman, Kellerman proceeded to execute a dangerous tightrope walk away from the tower, constructed on Great Head, out over Newport Cove where she dove 65 feet into the water. See also **Mount Desert Street, Bar Harbor**.

Acadia National Park, Otter Cliff – Ashecliffe Sanitarium is missing a patient. U.S. Marshall Teddy Daniels (Leonardo DiCaprio) is sent to investigate how a patient can disappear from a heavily guarded island in the middle of Boston Harbor in the film version of *Shutter Island* (2010). Although filmed primarily in Massachusetts, for scenes where Daniels must descend a sheer rock face to investigate an abandoned lighthouse, director Martin Scorsese chose to film on the vertiginous edge of Otter Cliff.

Acadia National Park, Sand Beach – Annette Kellerman played the mermaid Merilla in the 1918 lost film *Queen of the Sea*. Merilla finds a book in a wreck at the bottom of the sea which contains a book prophesizing that she will save four human beings and be rewarded with a human body and soul. King Boreas (Walter Law), the master of the storms, is not happy that Merilla is cutting into the workload of his homicidally inclined sirens. The scenes of mermaids sunning on the rocks and scenes where the newly minted human Merilla arrives on the shore were filmed at Sand Beach. Now she must face the wrath of Boreas while helping a Viking prince (Hugh Thompson) return to his betrothed. See also **Mount Desert Street, Bar Harbor**.

Altonville – Fictional Altonville is a small agricultural town whose only claim to fame is that it is the location of a large medical research hospital. At the Maine State College of Surgery, medical student David Saunders chronicles the disappearance of Gideon Wyck, a controversial teacher whose embalmed remains are later discovered in the college dissection lab in *The Cadaver of Gideon Wyck* (1934) by Alexander Laing. Writers such as Karl Edward Wagner and Robert Bloch have credited this tale of murder, madness, and medical horror as an early influence on their own writings.

Amma Beach – In *X-Files* episode "Chinga" (5:10), FBI Special Agent Dana Scully takes a vacation in Maine and chances upon a bizarre situation where townsfolk appear to suffer from self-inflicted wounds, apparently on command of a child with a mysterious doll. The episode is "Chinga," which is also the name of the doll. Unbeknownst to screenwriter Stephen King, it is also a profanity in Spanish. When producer Chris Carter was informed, the episode name was changed to "Bunghoney" when it aired outside of the US.

Anson Beach – A pandemic has decimated the world. A small group of teen survivors congregates together on Anson Beach in the short story "Night Surf" which first appeared in *Night Shift* (1978). The super flu that has destroyed the world is strain A6, also known as "Captain Trips," which author Stephen King would later use to wipe out the world again in *The Stand* (1978).

4

Apex – Apex is a small town northwest of Portland, not much more than a church and a beer store at a blinking traffic light. The simple-minded giant Blaze kidnaps infant Joseph Gerard IV and flees to a cabin hideout buried in the woods of Apex in *Blaze* (2007) by Stephen King writing as Richard Bachman. See also **South Freeport**.

Appalachian Trail – See **Hundred-Mile Wilderness; Motton**.

Appledore Island – Poetess Celia Thaxter served as hostess at the family's hotel on the Isles of Shoals, which in turn became a legendary gathering place of the literary greats of the day, including her mentor, John Greenleaf Whittier. Her mentor's influence is particularly evident in Thaxter's "The Cruise of the *Mystery*," a poem of a ghost ship, reminiscent of Whittier's "The Dead Ship of Harpswell." In Thaxter's poem, slaves in the hold of a ship drown in a hurricane and the captain unceremoniously dumps the corpses overboard. The corpses beg to differ over their treatment. The poem was first published in *The Cruise of the* Mystery *and Other Poems* (1886). See also **Harpswell; Smuttynose Island**.
The ghost of Blackbeard's wife tells her version of the local legend of how she came to haunt the lonely cliffs. "Appledore" by David Bernard appeared in *Anthology: Year One* (2012).

Arcos – Audrey and Richard Bock's nine-year-old son Zach has been abducted. The stress of her missing child seems to have triggered latent psychic powers in Audrey. In order to find her son, she must control her new abilities, come to terms with some long-suppressed memories, and convince Sheriff Virgil Milche that she is not insane in *Night Terror* (2003) by Chandler McGrew.

Arden – In the novel *Follow* (2005), written by Rick Hautala as A.J. Matthews, Pamela Gardner crashes her car when the ghost of a murdered friend materializes next to her. She realizes that the ghost was warning her that she was next victim of a serial killer that they both know.

Arden, Camp Tapiola – Thirty-five years ago, the entire Arden Police Department was called to Camp Tapiola in the middle of Lake Onwego to investigate the death of little Jimmy Foster. This time, Jeff Cameron brings the crime to the Arden Police Department. He has escaped a vengeance-seeking psychopath on the island, which is more than his friends can say in *The Wildman* (2008) by Rick Hautala. See also **Westbrook**.

Assyria – Charles L. Grant, writing as Lionel Fenn, finds perpetually unemployed actor Kent Montana dealing with a vampire in his adopted hometown. Unfortunately, where there are vampires, there are also vampire hunters, who know vampires are always nobility. The idiot stake jockeys overlook the mysterious visitor Count Lamar in favor of Montana because he's descended from Scottish royalty. *The Mark of the Moderately Vicious Vampire* (1992) is the fourth book in the "Kent Montana" series.

Augusta – Stephen King's short story "Nona" first appeared in *Shadow I* (1979). In the story, the narrator joins forces with the deadly but alluring Nona at Joe's Good Eats on the outskirts of Augusta. As Maine's winter worsens, they continue down the Maine Turnpike, leaving a trail of bodies behind them as Nona drives him toward his childhood hometown. See also **Blainesville**.

Augusta, Juniper Hill Asylum – Stephen King's insane asylum of choice in named as an homage to writer Joseph Payne Brennan, whose stories often take place in the Connecticut village of Juniper Hill. It could be King simply renamed the State Hospital in Augusta, which King used by its real name in his Bachman story *Rage* (1977). However, the inclusion of "Hill" in the name has suggested to some fans that Juniper

Hill is the King version of Hepatica Hill in Bangor, where there is also an asylum. See also **State Street, Bangor**.

Miss Sidley is a primary school teacher who suddenly realizes that her students are not really human. The realization drives her to drastic measures in Stephen King's "Suffer the Little Children," first published in *Cavalier*, February 1972. Miss Sidley, in the aftermath of the carnage, is quietly sent to Juniper Hill.

The asylum is a pivotal location in Stephen King's *IT* (1986). Henry Bowers, who terrorized The Losers as children, was sent here after killing his father. He escapes with the assistance of Pennywise to help the evil clown thwart the adult Losers and their attempt to destroy the terror once and for all. See also **The Barrens, Derry**.

In King's *Needful Things* (1991), Nettie Cobb killed her abusive husband. After 5 years in Juniper Hill, she was released and became Polly Chalmers' housekeeper in Castle Rock.

While Jessie Burlingame is trapped in Stephen King's *Gerald's Game* (1992), she is visited by Raymond Andrew Joubert. Others claim the visit from the axe murdering, grave robbing, necrophiliac escapee from Juniper Hill was a hallucination, but Jessie's jewelry is still missing from the cabin. See also **Kashwakamak Lake**.

In King's *Insomnia* (1994), Charlie Pickering spent six months in the asylum for trying to firebomb a women's health clinic. Although released, he was not cured, as subsequent events in Castle Rock will demonstrate.

Augusta, State Hospital – After the events in Placerville, Charlie Decker is found not guilty by reason of insanity and remitted to Augusta State Hospital in *Rage* (1977) by Stephen King, writing as Richard Bachman. See also **Placerville**.

Augusta, Water Street – Mercer, Maine native Frank A. Munsey was the manager of the Western Union office on Water Street. Being in charge of the telegraph office that connected the news media to the major publishing hub that had sprung up in

Augusta, Munsey saw a niche that was not being filled and a way to make it profitable. In 1882, he moved to New York and began publishing inexpensive magazines on cheap wood pulp paper. Geared toward readers in specific genres, Munsey's "pulp magazines" spawned a new industry that launched the careers of authors ranging from Robert Bloch and H. P. Lovecraft to Jack London and Isaac Asimov.

Bangor – Stephen and Tabitha King permanently moved to Bangor in 1980. As early as 1983, in *Black Magic & Music: A Novelist's Perspective on Bangor*, King remarked that there were stories in Bangor that he could use to create a novel. That novel would be *IT* (1986) with Bangor fictionalized as Derry. See also **The Barrens, Derry**.
In the novella *The Eyes of the Carp* (2005) by T. M. Wright, we read the journal of narrator Kevin, who, with his wife Janet, has moved into a new home outside of Bangor. Kevin learns that their house includes parts of previous older buildings on the site, and he begins to suspect that the older components are slowly drawing the past over the present. Is this related to the ghosts that are Kevin's friends or is Kevin simply insane?

Bangor, The Barrens – Along Valley Avenue at the bottom of Nelson Street is The Barrens. Running diagonally through Bangor, King's fictionalized version in Derry is smaller but equally verdant in spite of the name. See also **The Barrens, Derry**.

Bangor, Civic Center – The real life version of the Derry City Center first mentioned in the Stephen King novel *IT* (1986), like its fictional counterpart, has a 30-foot statue of Paul Bunyan standing guard. Unlike Derry's version, both the building and the statue remain standing. See also **City Center, Derry**.

Bangor, Fairmont Park – Taduz Lemke relents under the "persuasion tactics" of Richie Ginelli and agrees to lift the curse on attorney Billy Halleck in Stephen King's 1984 novel *Thinner* (written as Richard Bachman). When they meet on a park bench for the counter-spell, the wily gypsy warns the attorney that there will be a cost to lifting the spell. See also **Elm Street, Camden**.

Bangor, Godfrey Boulevard – Steven King's novella "The Langoliers" was first anthologized in *Four Past Midnight* (1990). Boston's Logan Airport is the scheduled destination of American Pride Flight 29. However, something has happened, and most of the passengers and crew have vanished. Captain Brian Engle was a passenger aboard the plane, now he must land the jet. Without knowing what's happening on the ground and no radio contact with air traffic control, he opts to land the plane at an airfield better suited for unassisted landings – Bangor International Airport. "The Langoliers" was adapted as a two-part TV Movie for ABC in 1995. The movie was filmed almost entirely in Bangor International Airport and includes an appearance by King in a Craig Toomey (Bronson Pinchot) hallucination.

Bangor, Hammond Street Extension – Stephen King notes the inspiration for his novella "Fair Extension" occurred on a walk past the Bangor International Airport. A gravel patch along the airport fence on the Extension is home to various roadside vendors who have set up stands over the years. This evolved into the sinister George Elvid who peddles along a similar road in Derry. The novella "Fair Extension" first appeared in his collection *Full Dark, No Stars* (2010). See also **Harris Avenue Extension, Derry**.

Bangor, I-395 – After a tryst, adulterous Annie Lansing (Lois Chiles) is speeding to arrive home before her husband. She strikes and kills a pedestrian on the I-395 onramp in the "The Hitchhiker" segment of *Creepshow 2* (1987). Now a hit-and-run driver, Annie has bigger concerns, like the dead hitchhiker who won't leave her alone.

Bangor, Merchant Plaza – In 2015, the *Bangor Daily News* moved to Merchant Plaza from their former offices on Main Street. The previous location would have been where reporter Dana Bright (Kristen Dalton) worked. The journalist's first big break came from covering the exploits of "local psychic detective" Johnny Smith (Anthony Michael Hall) in the television series *The Dead Zone*, based on the characters created by Stephen King in the 1979 novel of the same name. Dana Bright was a recurring role for the first two seasons before being written out. She returned in season 5 episode "Articles of Faith" (5:04) where her disappearance was explained as having taken a television news job in Boston.

Bangor, Mount Hope Cemetery – The 254-acre cemetery is the nation's second-oldest garden cemetery and a frequent landmark in the world of Stephen King. It is the final resting places of Norma Crandall in the King novel *Pet Sematary* (1983) and George Denbrough in *IT* (1986). See also **The Barrens, Derry; Ludlow**.

The cemetery also appeared in the 1989 film version of *Pet Sematary*. Filmed on the State Street side of Cemetery Hill, look for Stephen King's cameo as a minister. See also **Hancock**.

Mount Hope is also the final resting place for Richard William Curless, Sr (1932-1995). Curless, a native of Fort Fairfield in Maine's Aroostook County, recorded twenty-two Billboard top-40 hits throughout his career, but none would replicate the success of his 1965 ballad to a dangerous stretch of road in the southern part of Aroostook County - the tale of the Haynesville Woods where there's a "Tombstone Every Mile." See also **Route 2A, Haynesville**.

Bangor, Mount Pleasant Cemetery – Mount Pleasant is the final resting place of actress Myrna Fahey (1933-1973). Born in Carmel, ME, her biggest film role was that of Madeline Usher to Vincent Price's Roderick in *House of Usher* (1960), Roger Corman's first Poe-based movie.

Actress Myrna Fahey with Vincent Price in House of Usher (1960).

Bangor, Ohio Street – Henry's Nite-Owl is a convenience store on Ohio Street. In Stephen King's short story "Grey Matter," first published in *Cavalier*, October 1973, Richie Grenadine's kid comes into the store for his father's beer, obviously terrified. It seems that Richie drank a tainted beer and isn't himself. In fact, he may not even still be human.

Bangor, State Street – The Dorothea Dix Psychiatric Center at 656 State Street opened in 1901 as the Eastern Maine Insane Asylum. The second of Maine's state-run mental health facility sits atop Hepatica Hill overlooking the Penobscot River with buildings that are a less dramatic version of Kirkbride architecture, a style thought to have a curative effect. But after a century of the design being associated exclusively with old asylums, the style just gives off a creepy vibe. See also **Augusta, Juniper Hill Asylum.**

Bangor, Stillwater Avenue – Darlene Bobich, through luck and her trusty Desert Eagle, has survived the initial onslaught of the zombie apocalypse. Leaving her home, she headed to the Bangor Mall on Stillwater. She was hoping for food and supplies. What she found was a handful of survivors. When the defenses were breached, Darlene headed south and kept going. Now she's the last snowbird, struggling for survival in Florida. *Dying Days* (2012) begins a series of novellas by Armand Rosamilia featuring Darlene and the ragtag band of humans in a world with rapidly evolving zombies.

Bangor, Thomas Hill – Thomas Hill Standpipe was built in 1897 to maintain water pressure downtown. Listed on the National Register of Historic Places, it holds 1,750,000 gallons of water in a riveted iron tank enclosed in a wood frame jacket. The standpipe's elevation provides enough pressure through gravity to supply the entire city with water. It is also the inspiration for the standpipe in Stephen King's Derry. Unlike Derry's standpipe, Bangor's is still standing. See also **Standpipe Hill, Derry.**

Bangor, Union Street – Psychic detective Phillip Vernon is investigating a murder in a seedy hotel on Union Street. The problem is the mystery he's unraveling is one with a personal connection. He just doesn't know it yet. Rick Hautala's "Hotel Hell," was originally published in *Cold Blood* (1991).

Bangor, Waterworks Road – Built in 1875, the old Waterworks Building once provided the city of Bangor with electricity and water. It was originally used to pump water from the Penobscot River to the standpipe on Thomas Hill but was abandoned in the 1950s. Beneath the buildings are a complex system of basements and tunnels; the perfect filming location for the labyrinth beneath the Bachman Mills in the Stephen

King film *Graveyard Shift* (1990). Look for the tunnels in scenes where fire hoses are used to combat the subbasement's rat infestation. In 2006, the buildings were sold and have been converted to apartments. Still surviving is the massive cast-iron Deane pump, restored and displayed in a common area. See also **Gates Falls**.

Bangor, West Broadway – West Broadway was the home of the lumber barons and gentry of Bangor in her glory days as "Lumber Capital of the World." Today, 47 West Broadway, an Italianate mansion with hip roofs and asymmetrical towers, is the home of Stephen King. Not sure which one it is? Look for the tour buses parked across from the wrought iron gates designed with spiders and bats.

King is convinced that he will be the next victim of a serial killer who has messily dispatched Danielle Steel, Sue Grafton, and Tom Clancy. So he reluctantly leaves his heavily fortified home to catch the killer before the killer catches him in the satire *Who's Killing the Great Writers of America?* (2007) by Robert Kaplow.

Bankerton – Taduz Lemke has refused to lift the curse he has placed on Billy Halleck in Stephen King's 1984 novel *Thinner*, so Billy has placed a curse on the gypsies. That curse manifests itself in the form of gangster Richie Ginelli who introduces himself in a spectacular way at the gypsy caravan camp in Bankerton. See also **Elm Street, Camden**.

Bar Harbor, Mount Desert Street – Home today to a series of small hotels and inns, Mount Desert Street was formerly home to one of the summer resort crown jewels – the St. Sauveur. In 1917, in addition to the bluebloods of society, the hotel played host to 125 Vikings, mermaids, and film technicians when the Fox Film Company arrived to use the "exotic shores" of Bar Harbor to film their next blockbuster, *Queen of the Sea* (1918). Ogling mermaids from the rocks along the beach became the main attraction that summer among tourists and locals alike.

See also **Newport Cove, Acadia National Park; Sand Beach, Acadia National Park.**

Barsham Harbor – At an isolated house at Setauket Point along the Kennebec River, Dr. Julian Blair seeks knowledge best left undiscovered. After the death of his wife, Blair's cutting edge research into human brain waves is redirected into making contact with the dead. With assistance from a phony medium who foresees a big payday when he succeeds, the project is threatened by greed in *The Edge of Running Water* (1939) by William Sloane.

The novel was filmed in 1941 as *The Devil Commands* with Boris Karloff as the grief-stricken mad scientist. Edward Dmytryk directed in his typical film noir style, making the film feel more like a mystery than a horror movie.

Baxter State Park – A camping trip at the base of Mount Katahdin by a troop of Wildlife Explorers is disrupted by a wild animal attack. Among those involved in the "baby bear" attack was Eddie Munster (Mason Cook). The family immediately moves cross-country to Mockingbird Heights, a suburb of San Francisco. There at 1313 Mockingbird Lane, Herman and Lily Munster (Jerry O'Connell and Portia de Rossi) attempt to avoid telling their son that he's a pubescent werewolf. Cousin Marilyn (Charity Wakefield) and Grandpa (Eddie Izzard) are not helping. *Mockingbird Lane* (2012) was a pilot for a reimagined series based on *The Munsters* (1964-66).

Beacon Point Lighthouse – See **Colby.**

Bedford – Bedford is a blighted mill town that some say is cursed. The rain can't wash away atrocities committed there, and the closing of the paper mill appears to finally be the end. No one sees the despair like Susan Marley, a former beauty queen turned skid row derelict. She walks the streets searching for something evil that begins to fill the dreams of the entire town in the 2006 novel *The Keeper* by Sarah Langan. Langan would return to Bedford at the start of her next book, *The Missing* (2007). See also **Corpus Christi**.

Belden – Austin Fletcher heads up to Maine to take possession of a house outside Belden. Willed to him by Maynard Whittier, an army buddy who died in combat, it is a picture-perfect refuge to convalesce. Fletcher learns that the house belonged to a witch who was hanged in the 1600s, one who never left. Between being haunted by the ghostly witch, stalked by the local wildlife, and the locals who don't like outsiders, Fletcher begins to have trouble differentiating between supernatural assaults and PTSD-triggered hallucinations. Either way, he may be very dead if he's not very careful in *Maynard's House* (1980) by Herman Raucher.

Berry's Peninsula – Rhonda Burke makes the mistake of double-crossing her crime lord boss. Now she and her boyfriend Kevin are on the lam, heading to a mysterious village on the Peninsula that empties out of residents each fall. As "The Cove" by Gregory L. Norris continues, Rhonda and Kevin are about to find out the very big reasons why the population clears out each year. Whether they'll survive is a different issue. The story appeared in *Monstrous* (2008).

Biddeford Pool – Off the coast of the Biddeford Pool are a number of islands, including the one known as Monument Island. Samantha Finnan and her friends have come to Biddeford Pool to celebrate their high school graduation. When a beach game goes wrong and a friend is dying, Samantha sees fires on Monument Island and valkeries beginning to gather. In Christopher Golden's novella "Pyre," first published in *Four Dark Nights* (2002). Samantha discovers that perhaps the rumors of the island being a Viking burial site might be true. Five years later, she returns to test her theory. See also **Monument Island**.

Black Lake – See **Indigo**.

Blainesville – In Stephen King's short story "Nona," the narrator battles the Maine winter as he cuts a bloody swathe toward his hometown of Blainesville. "Nona" first appeared in *Shadow I* (1979) – when the story was reprinted in King's *Skeleton Crew* (1985), the destination that Nona is goading the killer toward was changed to Castle Rock. See also **Gardiner**.

Blue Bay – A group of wealthy real estate investors has built an elite summer resort in Maine. Their investment may be doomed if word gets out about a terrible ailment plaguing their guests. The classic pulp villain Doctor Satan has devised a magical spell to paralyze guests in mid-stride and is blackmailing the resort. Now it is up to occult detective Ascott Keane to defeat his old foe and save Blue Bay. "Mask of Death" by Paul Ernst appeared in *Weird Tales,* August-September 1936. It was the eighth and final Doctor Satan story to run in the magazine.

Blue Harbor – In *The Lyssa Syndrome* (1990) by Christopher Fahy, a new strain of rabies is ripping through the island after animal-right activists break into a lab and release the test animals. Now the researchers at Jillson Labs are searching for a cure by testing on a new collection of animals and death row inmates. If they fail, nothing will stop the virus from reaching the mainland.

Bolton – Paranoid schizophrenic serial killer Greg Newman has driven to Maine to kill Angie Ross and her children, the surviving family of a previous victim in Rick Hautala's 1996 novel *Impulse*. See also **Clinton**.

Boxer Hills – The 1983 summer theater season ends on Cape Cod and some of the troupe decides to head north to Bar Harbor to relax before they head their separate ways. A storm forces them off the highway into a small town that worships a demonic creature. The troupe was planning to raise a little hell in Maine. Looks like they found it - now they must survive it in *Catching Hell* by Greg Gifune, a 2009 Cemetery Dance novella.

Brewster – The Pitney Lumber Mill uses mercury to treat lumber, dumping the waste into the river. Now hideous mutations are appearing and they have a taste for blood in director John Frankenheimer's *The Prophecy* (1979). See also **Ossipee River**.

Bridgton – In an interview promoting the 2013 start of the TV series *Under the Dome*, author Stephen King noted that, like his original 2009 novel, the TV version takes place in fictional Chester's Mill. Chester's Mill, it turns out was inspired by the geography of Bridgton. See also **Chester's Mill**.

Bridgton, Kansas Road – The first house Stephen King owned was RFD#2, Kansas Road in Bridgton, purchased with revenues from his writing. This may explain why King's fictional Kansas Street in Derry is not only the main road but also a focal point of the action. See **Kansas Street, Derry**.

The King house also served as a setting in *Song of Susannah* (2006), book 6 of the Dark Tower series. Gunslingers Roland and Eddie cross to the 'real world' in 1977 and visit the author Stephen King. The author's presence and some mysterious connection to the Dark Tower are causing the dimensional walls to grow thin and which allows allowing "walk-ins" to bleed through to torment Bridgton. They discover that King is a conduit for the tower to transmit its story. The gunslingers depart after making sure King will revisit the Dark Tower project that he had recently abandoned. See also **Center Lovell**.

Bridgton, Long Lake – A violent thunderstorm triggers a waterspout on Long Lake followed by an unnatural mist slowly moving across the small town of Bridgton. Not only is the town engulfed in zero visibility, the fog is home to tentacled creatures that attack anyone daring to enter the fog.

Stephen King's novella "The Mist" first appeared in the landmark anthology *Dark Forces* (1980). The 2007 film version was filmed in Louisiana; the 2017 TV series chose to film in Nova Scotia. See also **Main Street, Bridgton; Shaymore.**

Bridgton, Main Street – The grocery Store on Main Street is resilient. Back when it was Federal Foods, King had an idea for a story while waiting to check out. That idea led to the supermarket becoming the refuge of the townsfolk in Stephen King's 1980 novella "The Mist." See also **Long Lake, Bridgton.** The store later became part of the Food House chain. And like much of Bridgton, it was moved to Chester's Mill to be looted in King's 2009 novel *Under the Dome.* See also **Chester's Mill.**

Bridgton, Northern Cumberland Hospital – In Stephen King's novel *Cujo* (1981), Donna Trenton is sent to the hospital after the attack by the rabid dog. Her treatment includes the long and painful rabies vaccination. It is still a marked improvement over her ordeal on **Town Road #3, Castle Rock.** The hospital will feel the strain as the Castle Rock assault and homicide rates start to escalate under the tutelage of Leland Gaunt in King's *Needful Things* (1991).

When their newborn daughter Abra will not stop crying for hours, the panicked parents bring the baby to the hospital. After more hours of endless crying, she finally calms down. This was Abra's (and her parents) first introduction to her Shining. Her parents later realized the baby had foreseen the tragic events of the next day – September 11, 2001. The baby would prove to have formidable psychic powers, even greater than Dan Torrence in *Doctor Sleep* (2013), Stephen King's sequel to *The Shining* (1977).

Bristol Mills – In Rick Hautala's *Dead Voices* (1990), Elizabeth Meyer returns to her family home in Maine to mourn her daughter's death. But a rash of defiled graves and mysterious deaths seem to indicate her daughter is trying to contact her from the dead, regardless of the cost.

Brooklin – Elwyn Brooks White (1899-1985) is buried in Brooklin Cemetery. A prolific essayist and writer, he is better known as author and grammarian E. B. White. In addition to his children's books with a predilection for talking rodents such as *Stuart Little* (1945) and Templeton in *Charlotte's Web* (1952), White dabbled on the edge of horror and science fiction, often in thinly veiled morality stories such as "The Supremacy of Uruguay" (*The New Yorker*, November 25, 1933) where drones broadcasting a musical ditty have driven the world insane and ripe for conquering, or *"The Door"* (*The New Yorker, March 25, 1939) which leaves the reader to decide if the narrator's inability to leave the room is external torment or internal psychosis.*

Brownfield – On September 21, 2000, Bryan Edwin Smith was found dead in his mobile home on Bridgton Road. Smith had gained notoriety when, distracted by one of his dogs trying open a cooler with ground beef in it, his van struck Stephen King. King's injuries were serious enough (broken leg, broken hip, lacerated scalp and collapsed lung) to require multiple surgeries. King was far less forgiving than he could have been, due to Smith's nonchalance at the accident scene. King wrote of his accident in "On Impact" for the *New Yorker* (June 19, 2000), recalling Smith sitting nearby, casually eating the candy bars that had sent him to the store. King mocked him as "a character out of one of my own novels." In time, that would prove true. In *The Dark Tower* (2004), the seventh novel in the Dark Tower series, Smith and King are both characters. The story parallels the real accident except that Smith's stupidity and recklessness are exagerated. See also **Center Lovell; North Fryeburg**.

Bucksport – Bucksport appears in the cult classic gothic soap opera *Dark Shadows* (1966-1971), particularly in the 1840 time travel storyline, as the nearest large town to Collinsport. The town's history and reputation toward the supernatural are rumored by fandom to be the inspiration for the hometown of Barnabas Collins. See also **Collinsport**.

Bucksport, Buck Cemetery – Just east of Hinks Street along US Highway 1 is a small family cemetery. The most notable marker in the graveyard is an obelisk memorializing town founder Colonel Jonathan Buck (1719-1795). Buck would be a comparatively unknown, regional historical figure except for one thing – in 1852, his grandchildren decided the colonel deserved a more impressive monument. As the new monument weathered, a flaw in the stone appeared in the shape of a leg and foot. The heirs had the stone cleaned but the stain remains to this day, giving rise to an entire field of ghost stories explaining the stain as the result of a variety of curses, from a witch burned by Buck to his scorned mistress, all of which were created after the stain appeared, 50+ years after Buck's death.

Detail from Jonathan Buck's memorial showing the cursed leg.
Photo courtesy of Joseph A. Citro.

Adding to the body of lore, Robert P. Tristram Coffin wrote "The Foot of Tucksport," with Colonel Tuck having a witch tied to her house then burning down the house. Her malformed son rescued a leg bone from the fire, which the town recalled when the leg later appeared on the Colonels' grave. The poem first appeared in Coffin's collection *Ballads of Square-Toed Americans* (1933). See also **East Harpswell.**

Bucksport, Oak Hill Cemetery – A small white stone in the back of the cemetery marks the burial location of murder victim Sarah Ware (1846-1898). Technically, there is some question as to how much of Mrs. Ware is interred here. An unsolved bludgeoning attack, her skull was kept in an evidence locker for a century and only interred in 1998. It was assumed the rest of her was in the plot, effectively reuniting her parts, but there remains a persistent local rumor her headless remains, due to the notoriety of the case, were actually buried a mile north of her skull, at Silver Lake Cemetery in an unmarked grave.

Buford – The inimitable actor Conrad Brooks is cast as the creepy new owner of a failing ice cream shop who decides to rebrand the store as an adult ice cream parlor, with the buxom staff in low-cut half-shirts and white miniskirts. The new format is a success with everyone but the killer wearing a cardboard box as a mask, who is systematically killing off the Scoopettes one by one. With the employee roster plunging lower than their uniform's décolleté, it becomes a race to save the staff in *Ice Scream* (1997).

Buxton – An anonymous hay field in Buxton has a stone wall with a secret. In that wall, Andy Dufresne has hidden the key to a safety deposit box with a new identity, should he ever escape from prison in "Rita Hayworth and Shawshank Redemption," Stephen King's novella first published in *Different Seasons* (1982). See also **Shawshank Maximum Security Prison.**

Monette is a publisher's representative, selling books in northern New England. He lives in Buxton with his wife Barb and his daughter. While he's been on the road, his wife has led a second life. And the entire thing has unraveled in "Mute" by Stephen King. The story first appeared in *Playboy*, December 2007. See **Maine Turnpike**.

Buxton, Portland Road – Jess is on a bike tour of Maine when she decides it's not for her. She decides to break away from the group and head to Portland to visit friends. In Buxton, she turns on to the Portland Road and heads east. She decides to take a side road for the scenery and comes across an abandoned house. Naturally, she has to go explore it in "The Scenic Route" by Stuart Conover. The story appeared in *Snowbound with Zombies* (2015).

Cabot Cove – Considering how many murders Jessica Fletcher (Angela Lansbury) solved in this small fishing village over 12 seasons of *Murder, She Wrote*, it may be the deadliest place on earth. In the episode "The Legacy of Borbey House" (10:03), Jessica investigates the death of nocturnal newcomer Lawrence Baker (David Birney), who is found dead with a stake through his heart. Is it a murder or a vampire slaying?

Cadillac Mountain – See **Acadia National Park**.

Caesar Island – In *Flesh* (1990), a satire on the conspicuous consumption of the eighties, author Gus Weill introduces us to Justin Caesar, scion of a family wealthy enough to own a private island. Struggling musician Marion Anderson is invited to meet the family, oblivious to warning that when the Caesars have guests for dinner, they do so literally.

Calais – Harriet Elizabeth Prescott was born in Calais in 1835. She moved with her parents to Newburyport, Massachusetts, in 1849. By her early twenties, she began to write to supplement her parents' income. Her stories soon began appearing in the

Boston newspapers and in 1860, her first novel, *Sir Rohan's Ghost* was published. As noted author Harriet Prescott Spofford, her formative years in Newburyport are reflected in some of her genre tales, such as the maritime terminology in "The Moonstone Mass" (*Harper's Monthly*, October 1868), a tale of madness and obsession that takes place on a sailing ship in search of the Northwest Passage. Other genre tales include "The Amber Gods" about a gift with vampiress/Lilith undertones, first published in *Atlantic*, January-February 1860 and "Her Story," a story of a woman who is declared mad and institutionalized when she may actually be possessed, first published in *Lippincott's*, December 1872. It was Spofford who wrote the first haunted automobile tale, "The Mad Lady" (*Scribner's*, February 1916). Today Harriet Prescott Spofford remains a literary figure of note, with weird tales considered on par with Poe and Lovecraft.

Calais, North Street – John Dauphin, a Louisianan restaurant hygiene consultant, finds himself stranded in Calais when his car dies. With no money and no friends, he's forced to take a job as a breakfast cook at Tony's Gourmet Burgers on North Street. The adage warns its best not to know how laws and sausages are made. Ditto for Tony's burgers in "The Burgers of Calais." The story by Graham Masterton first appeared in *Dark Terrors 6* (2002).

Caliban Cove – Combat medic Rebecca Chambers joins a new STARS strike force when it is learned that the Umbrella Corporation has a genetic research lab at Caliban Cove. This strike force is unauthorized, has limited resources and no backup. A four-man team must work their way through a series of caves into an underwater genetic research facility, past an army of zombies and mutations, and stop a madman from unleashing a biohazard that would decimate the world in *Caliban Cove* (1998), book #2 of S. D. Perry's tie-in novels in the *Resident Evil* video game universe. See also **Exeter**.

Calico Island – Creepy Alan Swan is a big fan of actress Bliss Marshall. He's so big a fan that he abducts Bliss and brings her to his isolated home on remote Calico Island to save her from the Hollywood predators in *Eternal Bliss* (1998) by Christopher Fahy.

Camden – An aerial view of Camden stands in for Friendship, Maine in the film *Casper* (1995) in one of the few locations in the film version of the friendly ghost that was actually shot in Maine. See also **Friendship**.
In Erin Patrick's novel *Moontide* (2001), Melanie Gierek abandons her life in Chicago after her family's death in a car crash. She drives to Camden in a desperate attempt to reclaim happy memories of a summer on windjammers. Penniless and friendless, her car dies in a parking lot. It looks like she's hit rock bottom until she's offered a job on a schooner at a Shipyard in nearby Rockport. See also **Carleton Shipyard, Rockport**.

Camden, Belfast Road – Belfast Road is home to Beloin's on the Maine Coast, a series of small rental cottages overlooking the ocean. It was in one of these cottages that the scenes were filmed of Billy Halleck (Robert John Burke) and Richie Ginelli (Joe Mantegna) preparing to battle the gypsies in *Thinner* (1996). See also **Elm Street, Camden**.

Camden, Elm Street – The 1996 movie version of Stephen King's 1984 novel *Thinner* takes place in Fairview, Connecticut but Camden was chosen as the filming location for the upscale Connecticut community. The village green where Elm Street becomes Main is the location were the gypsies make their first appearance in the film before their carnival is rousted. See also **Freemont Park, Bangor; Bankerton; Belfast Road, Camden; Maine Street, Camden; Rockland; Technor**.

Camden, Main Street – The Boynton McKay Drugstore at 30 Main Street was the filming location in *Thinner* (1996) where one of the gypsies goes to fill a prescription with unfortunate results. Look for author Stephen King in a cameo as the pharmacist. The drugstore has been renovated and is now a cafe. See also **Elm Street, Camden**.

The new Goth girl in town is Cassie (Emily Osment). Bullied in school, harassed by her parents, and annoyed by her brother, she storms out of the house and finds a new Halloween shop where the creepy clerk (Tobin Bell) sells her a book. When she reads the book to her brother (Alex Winzenread) she summons a two-headed monster in R. L. Stine's *The Haunting Hour: "Don't Think About It"* (2007). Based on Stine's books, the film spawned a spin-off television series called *R. L. Stine's The Haunting Hour*. Filmed principally in Pennsylvania, aerial shots and street scenes were filmed in Camden. An early scene on Main Street, looking south toward the distinctive steeple of the Chestnut Street Baptist Church is particularly recognizable.

Camp Hiawatha – In August of 1981, at a summer camp along the New Hampshire-Maine border, a killer stalked the campers, picking them off one by one with a variety of sharp, pointy things. Twenty-four years later, a group of teens stumble across the camp and discover that the blood-soaked horror of that night in 1981 is still happening – the camp is trapped in time, endlessly repeating the day. Now the modern teens must deal with big hair, valley girls, and guys in short shorts while surviving long enough to break free of the cycle in *Camp Daze* (2005), released on DVD as *Camp Slaughter* in 2006. See also **Porter**.

Cape Harvest – Glenn Chadwick is a Cape Harvest lobsterman who ferries a reporter out to Nephews Island, where the ghost of a murdered wife supposedly haunts the lighthouse caretaker's house with sounds of her piano. When the reporter misses the rendezvous, Chadwick goes looking for him, but only finds an abandoned tape recorder and briefcase. He brings the recorder back to the mainland and surrounded by his friends in a bar, they listen to the tape in Rick Hautala's "The Nephews," originally published in *Lighthouse Hauntings* (2003).

Jeff Stewart is a recovery diver for the State with a bad feeling about a body 50 feet down in the bay. Pappy Sullivan thinks it's Old Man Crowther, but Jeff told him that the body's in too good of shape to have been there for decades. Pappy may be crazy, but he's not stupid. "Ghost Trap" by Rick Hautala first appeared in *The New Dead* (2010).

Cape Higgins – Rick Hautala's *Twilight Time* (1994) finds Jeff Wagner returning to his hometown to help his sister after her suicide attempt. His unwilling return is marked by a series of deaths and disappearances. Jeff's childhood was an endless blur of abuse at the hands of his fundamentalist guardians. Now, plagued by multiple personality disorder, he wonders if he unknowingly causing the tragedies or is someone trying to finish driving him insane?

Cape Tumbles – Derek Townsend is a Boston reporter doing a piece on the haunted lighthouses of New England. He ends up in Cape Tumbles where he and the town sheriff go to visit the abandoned lighthouse on Tumbles Point. Although the lighthouse is supposedly haunted, Townsend soon discovers there are worse things than ghosts in the lighthouse. "And the Sea Shall Claim Them ..." was written by Rick Hautala as A. J. Matthews with Matthew Costello. It originally appeared in *Lighthouse Hauntings* (2003).

Caribou – A ranger arrives to check on a hermit after the weather finally lets up. He's greeted by a broken window and the hermit's corpse, torn apart in the cabin. Closer examination reveals something inside that hermit really wanted out, and not just the cabin. The ranger finds the dead man's journal. Was he losing his mind, or was there really something out there in the snow trying to get his attention? "Northern

Lights" by Rob Smales first appeared in *Anthology: Year Three* (2015).

Casco – Hal Shelburn keeps throwing away a toy wind-up monkey but it keeps reappearing. Hal knows the toy well – each time it clangs its cymbals together, somebody dies. Now Hal has returned to his family home and his son has found the deadly toy in Stephen King's short story "The Monkey." The short story was first published in *Gallery*, November 1980 and then revised for King's anthology *Skeleton Crew* (1985).

Casco, Crystal Lake – In October of 1980, a large fish kill took place in Crystal Lake. The cause of the kill remains a mystery but seems to have been centered on Hunter's Point. Coincidentally Hal Shelburn had recently thrown a burlap sack into the lake at Hunter's Point in Stephen King's short story "The Monkey," revised for King's anthology *Skeleton Crew* (1985).

Casco Bay – Casco Bay is a deep-water inlet off the coast encompassing Portland on the south and north to Bath. It is a popular vacation destination for both humans and, apparently, sea serpents. Sightings of "Cassie" date back to 1751 and reports appear sporadically along the coast to 1958 (and possible later). Brown in color with lengths reported up to 100 feet, the sea serpent has been known to raise its head 10-feet out of the water. And since the sightings span centuries, we can probably assume that if Cassie does exist, she's part of a breeding colony.

Castine – Noah Brooks (1830-1903) was a journalist, editor, and Lincoln biographer. His birthplace and childhood home became Fairport, the setting for his regional short stories in *Tales of the Maine Coast* (1894), including several supernatural tales involving the local industries of fishing and farming. Brooks is buried in Castine Cemetery. See also **Fairpoint**.

Castine, Water Street – Although set on a fictional Massachusetts island, director Jeff Lieberman chose to use Maine coastal villages for exterior filming. Jenna Whooly (Katheryn Winnick) is home from college for Halloween. It will be more memorable than expected. Castine's Water Street can be recognized as the Whooly family drives home from picking her up at the ferry in *Satan's Little Helper* (2004). See also **Harpswell Neck Road, Harpswell**.

Castle County, Abenaki Lake – Alden McCausland and his Mama came into some money when his Daddy died, and now he and Mama spend most of their time drinking at their ramshackle cabin on Abenaki Lake. There's been a competition between the McCauslands and the out-of-staters across the lake in their fancy mansion. Each year, the Massimos show up for the holidays and embarrass the McCauslands with a fancier firework display. Each year, the McCauslands get drunker and the firework displays on both sides of the lake get more elaborate. Alden finally won the contest this year, and Castle County folks who saw the show will be talking about it for years – especially the volunteer fire department. "Drunken Fireworks" by Stephen King appeared in his collection *The Bazaar of Bad Dreams* (2015).

Castle Lake – Worth and Ophelia Todd have a summer home on Castle Lake and Homer Buckland is the caretaker. Mrs. Todd is obsessed with finding shortcuts to shave time off her trips from Bangor to Castle Rock. Homer admires her dedication, but is increasingly concerned as Mrs. Todd's mileage continues to drop. Ophelia finally convinces Homer to take one of her time-saving routes in "Mrs. Todd's Shortcut" by Stephen King, first published in *Redbook*, May 1984.

The summer home of author Thad Beaumont is on the edge of Castle Rock overlooking the north bay of Castle Lake. Thad, although a respected author, could not afford such a house. It was his alter ego George Stark, the best-selling, gritty crime writer, that paid for the house in Stephen King's *The Dark Half*

(1989). The 1993 film version of The Dark Half was written and directed by George Romero with Timothy Hutton as Thad Beaumont. See also **Ludlow**.

Castle Rock – Along with Derry, Castle Rock is a small mill town with big secrets. Located near Lewiston, it is the setting for a number of Stephen King's stories, starting with the novel *The Dead Zone* (1979) where John Smith identifies the serial killer known as the Castle Rock Strangler and culminating with the destruction of the town in *Needful Things* (1991). See also **Cleaves Mills**.

Castle Rock, Black Henry Road – Otto Schenck and George McCutcheon are wealthy Castle Rock businessmen, with some success in land speculation. When George's old Cresswell truck finally wears out, they abandon it along the Black Henry Road. Several years later, George is crushed beneath the derelict vehicle and Otto becomes fixated on the truck. He builds a one-room cabin across the road from the metal hulk and spends his days monitoring the truck. He insists that not only is the Cresswell creeping forward but it coming to kill him. Is it insanity or a guilty conscience? "Uncle Otto's Truck" by Stephen King was first published in *Yankee*, October 1983.

Castle Rock, Castle View Cemetery – In Stephen King's short story "The Body," first published in *Different Seasons* (1982), Gordie Lachance's older brother Dennis died in a jeep accident and is buried in Castle View cemetery.

Castle Rock, Homeland Cemetery – A hysterical Marie Brown imagined her son's tombstone in the graveyard the day he narrowly avoided being hit by a fuel tanker while sledding in Stephen King's *The Tommyknockers* (1987).
When best-selling crime novelist George Stark's real identity is discovered to be critically-acclaimed author Thad Beaumont, Thad stages a "funeral" in *People* magazine to confirm that he

is Stark and to announce he is done with Stark. Stephen King's *The Dark Half* (1989) was also inspired by the "death" of his Richard Bachman pen name. See also **Ludlow**.

Nettie Cobb and Wilma Jerzyck, never particularly friendly as neighbors, kill each other under the goading of Leland Grant in King's final Castle Rock novel *Needful Things* (1991). Now they are neighbors again, this time in the cemetery.

Castle Rock, Main Street – Pop Merrill's "Emporium Galorium" was on Main Street, a junk shop, a tourist trap or the devil's den, depending on whom you ask. Pop finagles a Polaroid Sun 660 camera away from Kevin Delevan in Stephen King's novella "The Sun Dog," first published in *Four Past Midnight* (1990). Kevin thinks the camera is defective, but Pop thinks there's profit in the camera, which takes pictures a brutish dog, regardless of what the camera is aimed at. And the dog seems to be drawing nearer to the camera with each photo.

After Pop meets an unfortunate end, a new shop opened across the street, one called "Needful Things." Proprietor Leland Gaunt used items in his shop to manipulate the hidden flaws in the citizens with increasingly deadly results in King's *Needful Things* (1991). The 1993 film version of *Needful Thing*s starred Max von Sydow as Leland Gaunt and Ed Harris as the one man who can stop him, Sheriff Alan J. Pangborn.

Castle Rock, Mellow Tiger – The Mellow Tiger is the only bar in Castle Rock, so needless to say, it appears in a number of Stephen King stories. Mailman George Meara is a regular there until he runs into *Cujo* (1981). Max Devore's toadies Dickie Brooks and Elmer Durgin are drinking buddies at the Tiger in *Bag of Bones* (1998). Ace Merrill did four years in Shawshank Prison for breaking into the Mellow Tiger, according to his father in "The Sun Dog" first published in *Four Past Midnight* (1990). Town drunk Hugh Priest and the Tiger play a pivotal role in the escalating problems in *Needful Things* (1991).

Castle Rock, Quik-Pik – Ray and Mary are unhappily married. She complains about his smoking. He complains about her weight. They stop at the Quik-Pik to pick up a kickball for Mary's niece. Ray wants her to pick him ups some smokes, even if it's the cheap Premium Harmony brand. He waits in the car while she goes in and immediately drops dead. Ray is grief-stricken, but also a little relieved in "Premium Harmony" by Stephen King. The story premiered in the November 9, 2009, issue of *The New Yorker*.

Castle Rock, Sugar Top Hill Road – In *Lisey's Story* (2006) by Stephen King, it is two years after the death of bestselling author Scott Landon. His widow Lisey begins to sort through her husband's papers. As she begins to clean out Scott's study, his notes and musings make her realize that she has forgotten parts of her life with Scott. Now she must recall what she has blocked out in order deal with a stalker after Scott's papers, a catatonic sister, and Scott apparently trying to reach her from beyond.

Castle Rock, Town Road #3 – The old Seven Oaks Farm at the end of #3 is now Joe Camber's Garage. Joe's dog chases a rabbit into a cave and is bitten by a rabid bat. Now a rabid two-hundred-pound Saint Bernard is loose in Castle Rock and the body count is beginning to rise in Stephen King's novel *Cujo* (1981). The 1983 film version kept the setting in Maine but was filmed in California with Dee Wallace as Donna Trenton, the neighbor trapped in her car by the killer dog.

According to King's 1993 short story "It Grows On You" (*Nightmares & Dreamscapes*), Castle Rock resident Joe Newall made his fortune in the Gates Falls mills and built his house on Town Road #3. The house was far too big for Joe and his family, which the locals took as Joe flaunting his wealth, especially when he added another unneeded wing. After Joe's death, the house remained vacant. Yet, each time a neighbor dies, the house seems to have a new addition.

Castle Rock, Verrill Farmstead – Stephen King himself stars in a segment of the movie *Creepshow* (1982). "The Lonesome Death of Jordy Verrill" features King as the titular dimwitted farmer, who discovers a meteor in his yard with results both tragic and verdant. The King screenplay was based on a previous short story "Weeds" (*Cavalier*, May 1976) but moved to Castle Rock for the film. See also **Cleaves Mills**.

Castle Stream – In the years before World War I, a young farm boy encounters a stygian stranger in the woods near Motton, where the Castle Stream divides into smaller streams heading into Castle Rock and Kashwakamak. Stephen King's "The Man in the Black Suit" was first published in *The New Yorker*, October 31, 1994.

Castle View – Just outside of Castle Rock is Castle View. In King's *The Girl Who Loved Tom Gordon* (1999), Trisha McFarland has gotten lost on the Appalachian Trail and her parents and brother stay in a Castle View hotel during the search operation. See **Motton**.

When eight-year-old George's Grandpa dies, his aunts and uncles get together and buy George's mother a house in Castle View so she can move back and become the caregiver for Gramma, who is blind, fat, and downright mean. George must battle his terror of Gramma when he must stay home alone with her in the short story "Gramma," Stephen King's nod to the Lovecraft mythos, first published in *Weirdbook #19*, 1984. See also **Central Maine Medical Center, Lewiston**.

Harlan Ellison converted the story into a screenplay for the 1985 revival of *The Twilight Zone* television series. The episode, also titled "Gramma" (1:18), originally aired in February 1986 with Barret Oliver as George and Frederick Long as Gramma.

Center Lovell – On June 19, 1999, Stephen King was walking on the shoulder of Route 5 in Center Lovell and was struck from behind by a van. The driver, Bryan Smith, had been distracted by one of his dogs and drifted onto the shoulder. King's injuries were serious enough to need multiple surgeries and require three weeks in a hospital bed. See also **Kansas Road, Bridgton; Central Maine Medical Center, Lewiston**.

King and his lawyers purchased Smith's van for $1,500. King was convinced it would become a collector's item and he would not allow that to happen. After his recovery, King destroyed the van with a baseball bat and had the remaining hulk crushed a junkyard. King similarly wanted to do damage to Smith and had his lawyers argue that Smith, who had multiple traffic citations, should be charged with aggravated assault, which would send Smith to jail. Instead, Smith received a suspended sentence and lost his driving license for a year. Ironically, that would prove more than long enough to keep Smith off the road. See also **Brownfield**.

King was able to use the accident in his work. Both King's miniseries *Kingdom Hospital* and his novel *Dreamcatcher* (2001) included major characters involved in similar serious auto accidents. See also **Kingdom Hospital, Lewiston; Jefferson Tract**.

In *The Dark Tower* (2004), the seventh novel in King's Dark Tower series, Smith actually kills King in the accident. This necessitates intervention from gunslingers Roland and Jake, who believe that King as a conduit for the Dark Tower series, must complete the series in order for their quest to succeed. They jump back to 1999 just as King about to be hit by Smith's van. Jake pushes King out of the way but is killed in the process. Roland, heartbroken with the loss of his true son, returns to the quest alone.

Chamberlain – Margaret White is a questionably sane widow, a fundamentalist zealot who lives on Carlin Street, with her daughter Carietta. Carrie White must endure both her irrational home life and the cruelties of being an outsider at school. The combination explodes with deadly results in Stephen King's first novel, *Carrie* (1974). See also **Thomas Ewen Consolidated High School, Chamberlain;**

Chamberlain Center; Sugg Drive, Lisbon Fall; North Chamberlain.
Ray Brower was a runaway from Chamberlain in 1960. His body was found by Castle Rock teens. Now a group of Castle Rock boys set out to see the body in "The Body," a novella by Stephen King originally published in the 1982 collection *Different Seasons*. See also **Harlow.**

Chamberlain, Thomas Ewen Consolidated High School – In Stephen King's *Carrie* (1974), when Carrie White finally snapped and lashed out, her hometown died. Carrie's rage resulted in 440 dead including most of the Ewen High School senior class. See also **Chamberlain.**
In the 1976 film version directed by Brian De Palma, California schools stood in for Chamberlain's Ewen High, which was renamed Bates High School for the film. Sissy Spacek starred as Carrie White, whose revenge on her classmates all but destroyed the tiny western Maine town.
It is 20 years after Carrie White's rampage. Rachel Lang (Emily Bergl) is an outcast at the new high school. And her guidance counselor Sue Snell (Amy Irving) is experiencing déjà vu. Sue survived the original telekinetic terror of Carrie, and she sees events beginning again. She learns that Rachel's father was Ralph White, making her Carrie's half-sister. To try and prevent disaster again, Sue takes Rachel to the ruins of the old high school to show her the danger of her unchecked abilities. Sue fails in her attempt in *The Rage: Carrie 2* (1999).
A 2002 TV movie version starred Angela Bettis as the world's worst prom date. The end was changed so that Carrie survived, theoretically making the film a pilot for a weekly series that never came to fruition. Chloë Grace Moretz would subsequently star as the telekinetic in a 2013 unnecessary remake.

Chamberlain Center – In Stephen King's *Carrie* (1974), Margaret White worked at the Blue Ribbon Laundry, an industrial laundry in Chamberlain Center. The Blue Ribbon Laundry uses a Hadley-Watson Model-6 Speed Ironer and Folder, nicknamed "The Mangler." The infernal device also appears in the Wisconsin laundry in the Richard Bachman novel *Roadwork* (1981) and the King short story "The Mangler" (first anthologized in *Night Shift*, 1978). A 1995 film version starring Robert Englund moved the setting. See also **Chamberlain; Riker's Valley**.

Chamberlain Lake – The short story "The Last Time I Saw Harris" by Galad Elflandsson first appeared in *Shadows 9* (1986) and tells of college pals Harris and Edward. Harris meets Jessica and leaves school to travel while Edward becomes an architect. Years later, at a construction site in the backwoods of Maine, Edward understands his friend's motivations and why Jessica still haunts him.

Channel Islands – The coldest winter in 50 years has created an ice bridge between the Channel Islands and Steel Harbor, ME. The last time this happened, there was a series of vicious killings in Steel Harbor and it's happening again. The islands were formerly known as "Wolf Neck" based on local legends of ghostly wolves that wander the islands. The legends are beginning to look very real in *Winter Wolves* (1989) by Earle Wescott. See also **Riverston**.

Chester's Mill – One day, with no warning, Chester's Mill was suddenly sealed off from the rest of the world by an invisible force field in Stephen King's *Under the Dome* (2009). No one can understand what this dome is, where it came from, or if it can be breached. Dale Barbara and a small band of citizens must unravel the mystery of the dome while struggling to maintain the town against Big Jim Rennie, a power-mad politician. A 2013 TV series adaptation featured Mike Vogel as Barbie and Dean Norris as Rennie. See also **Bridgton; Main Street, Bridgton**.

Chesuncook – According to H.P. Lovecraft in "The Thing on the Doorstep" (*Weird Tales*, January 1937), Chesuncook is part of "the wildest, deepest, and least explored forest belt in Maine." Edward Derby wanders out of these woods, hysterical and bedraggled. Daniel Upton drives to rescue his old friend, who babbles on about his wife taking him to an unholy pit where ancient protoplasmic horrors known as Shoggoths dwell. Author Stephen Mark Rainey returns to Chesuncook after the modern horror of suburbia has caught up with the area. A beautiful three bedroom colonial on a secluded lake is available, but it comes with a little something that the realtor neglected to list in "The Pit of the Shoggoths," first anthologized in *The Azathoth Cycle* (1995).

In James Wade's "Those Who Wait," first appearing in *The New Lovecraft Circle* (1996), a Miskatonic University student narrowly escapes becoming a sacrifice to Cthulhu cultists. Now he joins a desperate attempt to prevent the summoning of the Old One called Ithaqua the Wind Walker in the Maine woods.

Clear Lake – One of Black Lake's giant crocodiles is captured by a thug (Stephen Billington) and Betty White's hook-armed son Jim (Robert Englund). They are poachers working for a team of dubious scientists experimenting on crocodile and snake DNA. Since this is a crossover film with the Anaconda franchise, both species escape and head to nearby Clear Lake. Now the local wildlife officer (Corin Nemec) and poacher-turned-EPA agent-turned-sheriff Reba (Yancy Butler) have twice as many killing machines to deal with and twice as many devoured civilians in *Lake Placid vs. Anaconda* (2015). See also **Indigo**.

Cleaves Mills – In the Stephen King novel *The Dead Zone* (1979), teachers John Smith and Sarah Bracknell live in the small town near Haven. An auto accident plunges Smith into a coma for four years. When he awakes, Sarah has married Walter Hazlett and Smith has psychic powers. The 1983 film version was directed by David Cronenberg and featured Christopher Walken as John Smith and Brooke Adams as Sarah. The 2002 television series The Dead Zone continues the story of John Smith, with Anthony Michael Hall as John Smith and Nicole de Boer as Sarah. See also **Castle Rock; Gate Falls; Birches Cemetery, Pownall**

Lisa Debusher moved out of her family home in Lisbon Falls into an apartment in Cleaves Mills. It was here she would meet and later marry author Scott Landon in King's *Lisey's Story* (2006). The newlyweds would move to **Sugar Top Hill Road, Castle Rock**.

Cleaves Mills, Verrill Farmstead – Hapless Jordy Verrill sees a meteor crash and goes to investigate. When he touches the rock, he is infected with something that is quickly turning him into a plant. "Weeds" is a short story by Stephen King, first published in *Cavalier*, May 1976. King would turn "Weeds" into a segment of the movie *Creepshow* (1982) as "The Lonesome Death of Jordy Verrill," moving the Verrill Farm westward to Castle Rock for the film. See also **Verrill Farmstead, Castle Rock**.

Cliffport – The final episode of Irwin Allen's 1967 TV series *The Time Tunnel*, "Town of Terror" (1:30), finds Doctors Tony Newman (James Darren) and Doug Phillips (Robert Colbert) exiting the tunnel in the near future (1978). There they discover reptilian androids have captured the town as a base to steal the Earth's oxygen. Now Doug and Tony must avoid alien doppelgangers of the town folk and stop the aliens.

Clinton – Homicidal stalker Greg Newman finds his way to intended victim Angela Ross's secluded camp, leaving a trail of sadistic killings and horrific torture behind him in Rick Hautala's novel *Impulse* (1996). See also **Bolton**.

Colby – Jimmy had two goals in life: marry his childhood sweetheart Kate and become the keeper at the Beacon Point light. Neither looks likely until Kate's husband is killed and Jimmy lands the job. The short story "Ghost of a Chance" by

Ed Gorman, first published in *Lighthouse Hauntings* (2002), explores what happens when the only thing between having dreams and fulfilling them is a ghost.

Collinsport – Collinsport is a fishing village on the coast near Frenchman Bay, first settled in the early colonial era by the Collins family. The village's primary industry is the Collins Cannery, run by the descendants of the original founding family. The Collins family controls major land holdings in and around Collinsport, but the family remains isolated from the town, both because of their wealth and because of strange things that are whispered about the family – rumors of supernatural events, curses, and mysterious strangers. The fictional town is the setting for cult classic gothic soap opera *Dark Shadows* (1966-1971). The series created spawned two films, *House of Dark Shadows* (1970) and *Night of Dark Shadows* (1971), a short-lived revival in 1991, and a 2012 comedy with Johnny Depp futilely attempting to replace Jonathan Frid as the vampire Barnabas Collins. See also **Bucksport; Saint Eustace Island**.

Thirty-two Dark Shadows novels were published during and after the show's initial run. All were written by Marilyn Ross as Gothic suspense novels and were all set in Collinsport at various points in history starting with *Barnabas Collins* (1968) and ending with *Barnabas, Quentin and the Vampire Beauty* (1972).

Lara Parker, the actress who portrayed the witch Angélique in the original series has launched a new line of novels based on the series: *Angélique's Descent* (1998) and *The Salem Branch* (2006).

Collinsport, Eagle Hill Cemetery – Eagle Hill is the original cemetery of Collinsport. One of the most recognizable landmarks is the massive Collins family mausoleum, where the colonial members of the town's founding family were placed. The most famous inhabitant of the crypt is not actually listed as being interred in the crypt – it was in a hidden room that the vampire Barnabas Collins (Jonathan Frid) was imprisoned in *Dark Shadows* (1966-1971).

In the 2012 film, Barnabas is buried underground and is discovered by construction workers. The Collins Mausoleum does appear when Angélique (Eva Green) chains Barnabas (Johnny Depp) in a coffin.

Coventry – Dr. Sam Beckett (Scott Bakula) leaps into second-rate horror novelist Joshua Ray on Halloween, 1964 in "The Boogie Man" (3:05) episode of *Quantum Leap*. Strange things begin to happen immediately - masked figures, mysterious deaths, goats, threatening animals, all in a house haunted by the ghost of a witch burned at the stake. Now Sam/Joshua must find the source of the evil phenomena, aided by his (possibly telekinetic) fiancé Mary (Valerie Mahaffey) and Stevie, a teenage protégé (David Kriegel). All ends well, especially when Sam and Al (Dean Stockwell) realize Stevie's last name is King, and he's picked up a lot of story ideas recently.

Corinna – The Eastland Woolen Mill was used for scenes of mill equipment in operation in the film version of *Graveyard Shift* (1990). In 1996, the mill closed as part of the cleanup of one of the state's worst Superfund sites. The EPA subsequently removed the mill, the entire length of Main Street and a good chunk of the riverbed. See also **Harmony; Gates Falls**.

Stephen King returns to Corinna in *Insomnia* (1994). May Locher worked half of her 40 years as a textile worker in the dye house at the mill. Suffering with "textile lung" and going through 2 oxygen cylinders a day, she would die in Derry soon after a visit by the creatures her neighbor Ralph Rogers calls "The Bald Doctors." See also **Harris Avenue, Derry**.

Corpus Christi – The remote and affluent town of Corpus Christi was untouched by the events leading to the destruction of the neighboring mill town in author Sarah Langan's previous book, but the evil of Bedford takes many forms. In *The Missing* (2007), a third-grade teacher takes her class on a field trip to

Bedford. There, one of the children discovers something buried in the woods, triggering a virus that changes the victims into something inhuman, angry and carnivorous. See also **Bedford.**

Crowley – Jake Crowley returns home for the funeral of his uncle, whose brutal murder mirrors that of Jake's mother in the past. Suddenly, murders and assaults rock the town. Has the Crowley curse returned to claim more victims or does something else stalk the streets of Crowley? The novel *In Shadows* (2005) was written by Chandler McGrew.

Cumberland County – Although it is the most populous county in Maine, the county encompasses 835 square miles, making it easy to live in isolation as you head away from the coast. Mary Portman (Naomi Watts) is a child psychologist who lives in a remote part of the county. Her husband died in a horrific car accident that also left her 18-year-old son Stephen (Charlie Heaton) in a catatonic state, making Mary his full-time caregiver. One of Mary's young patients (Jacob Tremblay) arrives at her home as a runaway, only to disappear again in the middle of a blizzard. The sheriff presumes the boy has died in the storm, but Mary is convinced that the boy's ghost is now haunting both her and Stephen. Trapped by the worsening storm, things are about to come to a head in *Shut In* (2016).

Cumberland County Airport – CCA is a small regional airport located north of Portland, between Falmouth and Jerusalem's Lot. Tabloid reporter Rick Dees flies into the airport to begin his search for the Cessna Skymaster 337 belonging to a vampire with a pilot's license in "The Night Flier" by Stephen King, first published in the anthology *Prime Evil: New Stories by the Masters of Modern Horror* (1989). Miguel Ferrer starred as Rick Dees in the 1997 film version.

Dark Score Lake – Located in western Maine's Township Region 90 thirty miles from Rangely, Dark Score Lake is loosely based on Kezar Lake. Dark Score Lake is where novelist Mike Noonan's summer cottage is located in Stephen King's *Bag of Bones* (1998). After his wife dies unexpectedly, he leaves their home in Derry and moves into "Sara Laughs," their cottage on Dark Score Lake. There he finds he must battle personal demons, insane millionaires, and something supernatural that has festered in the area for decades. See also **Benton Street, Derry; Kezar Lake**.

Jessie Burlingame is handcuffed to a bed and trapped in King's *Gerald's Game* (1992). She recalls viewing the 1963 eclipse at Dark Score Lake as a child and being abused by her father. In the aftermath of the abuse, she has a vision of Dolores Claiborne, peering at someone she has pushed into a well during the same eclipse. See also **Kashwakamak Lake; Long Tall Island**.

The Red Arrow Lodge is a vacation spot nestled in the woods on the secluded lakefront. It is here that Danny and Wendy Torrance convalesce and visit with head chef Dick Halloran after the events at the Overlook Hotel in Stephen King's *The Shining* (1977). Dark Score is not mentioned by name in *The Shining*, but the location of the lake matches where King would introduce Dark Score Lake 15 years later in *Gerald's Game*. Halloran had been a cook in the Army, stationed at the Derry Air Base in 1930 as chronicled in *IT* (1986). See also **Army Air Corps Base, Derry**.

Darkfield – When Ben Dane skids off the road in a snowstorm, he takes refuge at Harp Ryder's farm. Soon, both men are locked in a struggle against a sasquatch-like creature that no one else in town will accept as real. "Longtooth" by Edgar Pangborn first appeared in *The Magazine of Fantasy & Science Fiction*, January 1970.

Dawson Corner – The demon known as Hellboy is sent to Maine on a simple job – investigate a strange fog that has enveloped the town. The problem turns out to be not as simple as expected and he must stop the dead who walk again in "From an Enchanter Fleeing" by Peter Crowther in *Hellboy: Odder Jobs* (2004).

Dead River – Dead River is a coastal town where the primary industry is summer tourism. Carla opts to visit off-season. Soon, she and her fellow New Yorkers discover that in addition to the locals, the area is home to a tribe of primitive, inbred, cave-dwelling cannibals in Jack Ketchum's *Off Season* (1980). The cannibal horde returns in *Offspring*, Ketchum's 1991 sequel, seeking fresh meat for supplies and women for breeding stock.

Dead River, Crouch Place – Dan is a local and justifiably bored. When he meets bored college kids Casey, Kim, and Steven, the summer gets more interesting for all of them. Their thrill-seeking culminates in an ill-advised game in the local haunted house in *Hide and Seek* (1984) by Jack Ketchum.

Deephaven – The prototype "isolated New England village" was created by New England regionalist Sarah Orne Jewett for her stories in *Atlantic Monthly* and collected in book form in *Deephaven* (1877). The village of Deephaven, a fishing village dying of attrition, provides an underlying framework for Jewett's short stories. The supernatural elements are in tales by old sea captains, but more significant is Jewett's concept of a fictional village as the connection between of a series of stories. Deephaven, and Jewett's later creation Dunnet Landing, are the forerunners of such staples of the genre as Lovecraft's Dunwich, Massachusetts, Grant's Oxrun Station, Connecticut, and King's Derry, Maine.

Deephaven Post Office – When Carl Ledderer dies, his widow takes over his daily routine of walking his dog Enoch to Harris's General Store, which doubles as Deephaven's post office. Her devotion to Enoch is reciprocated later after the dog dies and his ghost saves her from freezing to death. The existence of the dog's spirit convinces her to go on living. Jessica Amanda Salmonson's homage to Sarah Orne Jewett, "A Mirror for Eyes of Winter" was first published in *Gothic Ghosts* (1997).

Deer Isle – In the earliest version of Stephen King's "Home Delivery," anthologized in *Book of the Dead* (1989), Maddie Sullivan is a Deer Island native. When she marries Jack Pace, she moves to neighboring **Gennesault Island**.

Derry – Stephen King's Derry is located thirty miles west of Bangor, the model for the town with landmarks often interchangeable between the two. The primary difference is Bangor is a lumber town and Derry is a nexus where King's Dark Tower pantheon bleeds into our reality on a murderously frequent level. The town was introduced in the novel *IT* (1986) (whose working title was simply *Derry*) and is liberally mentioned throughout the body of King's work.

In 1990, the novel *IT* was adapted for television as a two-night TV mini-series. John Ritter, Harry Anderson, Richard Thomas, Tim Reid and Annette O'Toole are the adult Losers Club members who must reunite to defeat Tim Curry as Pennywise in the sewer pipes beneath Derry.

The 2017 film version of *IT* is the first of a two-film series based on the book. The first chronicles the Losers Club and their first encounter with Pennywise as children.

Derry, Army Air Corps Base – In 1930, as chronicled in *IT* (1986), the black soldiers on the base have been forced to open their own club. When it becomes the local hot spot both on and off the base, it is burned to the ground. Is it another tragedy in the cycle of evil that haunts Derry, or is it merely a normal act of racial intolerance? See also **The Barrens, Derry**.

Derry, The Barrens – In spite of the name, The Barrens is a small tract of land off Kansas Street along the Kenduskeag Stream that is overgrown with foliage. The Barrens appears most prominently in the novel *IT* (1986) with the Losers using it as their home away from home, building a clubhouse with old doors and scrap wood salvaged from the neighboring town dump. More importantly, the sewer pipes dumping into the Barrens lead to the monster's lair. See also **Juniper Hill Asylum, Augusta; Bangor; The Barrens, Bangor; Civic Center, Bangor; Mount Hope Cemetery, Bangor; Dark Score Lake; Army Air Corps Base, Derry; City Center, Derry; Costello Street, Derry; Harris Avenue, Derry; Kansas Street, Derry; Kitchener Ironworks, Derry; Neibolt Street, Derry; Outer Central Street, Derry; Standpipe Hill, Derry; Up-Mile Hill, Derry.**

Derry, Benton Street – A stately Edwardian house at 14 Benton Street was the home of novelist Mike Noonan and his wife Jo in Stephen King's *Bag of Bones* (1998). After her unexpected death at a local strip mall, Mike develops writer's block, finally moving to their summer lake house to recapture his muse. A 2011 TV mini-series featured Pierce Brosnan as Mike Noonan. See also **Dark Score Lake; Up-Mile Hill, Derry.**

Derry, City Center – The original City Center and the 30–foot tall Paul Bunyan statue that stood in front of it were destroyed in the storm at the end of the Stephen King novel *IT* (1986). See also **City Center, Bangor.**

The new Civic Center first appears in *Insomnia* (1994). It was designed by Ben Hanscom, one of the Losers who defeated Pennywise the Clown. The new Civic Center appeared doomed to be a short-lived endeavor when anti-abortion fanatic Ed Deepneau attempted to crash an explosive-laden small plane into the parking lot in the climax of *Insomnia* (1994). See also **Harris Avenue, Derry.**

Derry, Costello Street – The library at Kansas and Costello Street was originally built in the 1890s when Derry was flush with lumber money. The massive stone building has a smaller children's library behind it, connected by a glass passageway that did not survive the onslaught at the end of Stephen King's *IT* (1986). *IT* has the library playing a pivotal role in the lives of two of the Losers. It is Ben Hanscom's favorite childhood haunt and aspects of it appear in his designs as an award-winning architect. Mike Hanlon grows up to become the town librarian, where he researches the haunted past of the town and realizes the senseless violence and tragedy that rip through the town is actually cyclical in nature. His manuscript *Derry: An Unauthorized Town History* documents the tragedies brought by Pennywise the clown; the manuscript remains locked in the library vault. See also **The Barrens, Derry**.

In King's *Insomnia* (1994), Mike Hanlon is still the librarian, and he gives battered wife Helen Deepneau a job at the library.

Derry, Harris Avenue – Ralph Roberts quietly lives out his golden years in his house on Harris Ave. Since his wife died, Ralph has been having trouble sleeping. As his insomnia progresses, he begins to perceive things not evident to other people, such as madness, auras and trans-dimensional beings in Stephen King's *Insomnia* (1994). It could be sleep deprivation, but it could also be the beginning of a battle whose outcome will affect King's *Dark Tower* multiverse. See also **Corinna; City Center, Derry; High Ridge, Derry; Outer Central Street, Derry; Old Orchard Beach**.

Stephen King's 2011 novel *11/22/63* starts with high school teacher Jake Epping's journey back to 1958 through a mysterious wormhole in Al's Diner in Lisbon Falls. He has a mission, to determine how malleable the past is. To test if past events can be modified, he elects to go to Derry and prevent the murder of school custodian Harry Dunning's family. He rents a furnished apartment on Harris and spends seven weeks in Derry, awaiting the opportunity to change the chain of events. He learns to loathe the town, still recovering from the events in King's earlier book *IT* (1986). See also **The Barrens, Derry; Lisbon Falls**.

Derry, Harris Avenue Extension – Dave Streeter is suffering from aggressive cancer. While driving past the Derry airport, he experiences a wave of nausea and pulls over to the side. Across the intersection, he sees George Elvid, a pudgy man selling all sorts of extensions. Streeter quickly deduces who he is talking to and agrees to a life extension that requires transferring his bad luck to someone he hates. He chooses his old best friend Tom. Now Dave is healthy and successful and Tom is watching his happy life fall apart piece by piece in "Fair Extension." The novella first appeared in his collection *Full Dark, No Stars* (2010). See also **Hammond Street Extension, Bangor**.

Derry, High Ridge – Out near the Newport town line is the former Barrett's Orchards. When the family sold the property, the house became High Ridge, the women's shelter and halfway house owned and operated by WomanCare, Derry's women's healthcare center. In Stephen King's *Insomnia* (1994), it is attacked by Ed Deepneau's anti-abortion thugs, led by the insane Charlie Pickering. See also **Harris Avenue, Derry**.

Derry, Kansas Street – In Derry, Kansas Street is the main road, at least as far as Stephen King is concerned. In Stephen King's novella "The Road Virus Heads North," first anthologized in *Everything's Eventual* (2002), King notes that once outside the city limits, Kansas Street becomes Kansas Road, then Kansas Lane. Kansas Lane eventually ends at the home of Richard Kinnell, a horror writer living outside Derry. Kinnell is on the receiving end of the terror for once, for a painting he purchased is following him, cutting a bloody trail up the coast. See also **West Broadway, Derry**.

In Stephen King's novella "Secret Window, Secret Garden," first published in *Four Past Midnight* (1990), writer Mort Rainey moves out of the stately Victorian at 92 Kansas Street when he divorces his wife. Soon after, the house burns to the ground. Is it arson or is Rainey's antagonist John Shooter starting to make good on his threats? See also **Tashmore Glen**.

The Tracker Brothers trucking depot was also on Kansas Street. In 1985, Eddie Kaspbrak encounters Pennywise the Clown at the abandoned depot as he reminisces about playing baseball behind the depot in 1957 in King's *IT* (1986). This is the same depot where, in 1978, Jonesy, The Beav, Henry, and Pete first meet Duddits in *Dreamcatcher* (2001), rescuing him from bullies. The depot was among the casualties in the storm at the end of *IT* (1986). See also **The Barrens, Derry.**

Derry, Kitchener Ironworks – In 1906 the Ironworks on Pasture Road exploded without warning, killing 88 of the town children who were there for an Easter egg hunt. The tragedy was caused by the monster known as "IT" and the terrible loss of life sated the creature, which started its 27-year hibernation cycle. According to Stephen King in his novel *IT* (1986), the ironworks lay abandoned until the mid-1980s when the Derry Mall was built on the site. See also **The Barrens, Derry.**

Derry, Mary M. Snowe School for the Exceptional – Douglas "Duddits" Cavell attends Derry's special education school in Stephen King's novel *Dreamcatcher* (2001). Jonesy, Henry, Pete and The Beav would meet him at 7:45 am and walk him to the school each morning.

Derry, Municipal Country Club – Howard Cottrell keels over during a game of golf in Stephen King's "Autopsy Room Four" first published in *Robert Bloch's Psychos* (1997). Now he's on an autopsy table. Problem is, he's not dead. See **Outer Central Street, Derry.**

Derry, Neibolt Street – Stephen King's *IT* (1986) finds the Losers at 29 Neibolt Street; an abandoned house near the train yards that even the hobos have deserted. A confrontation on the property in 1957 sends Pennywise fleeing into the sewers. Because of this, the gang decides to enter the sewers for the final showdown with the demon clown in 1985. See also **The Barrens, Derry.**

Derry, Outer Central Street – Every case of abuse, assault, and murder in Derry, some inexplicably committed by good people, ends up at Derry Home Hospital in King's *IT* (1986). Small wonder that by the time Bill Denbrough returns as an adult to reunite with the Losers, the hospital he drives past on Outer Central Street is an unrecognizable, sprawling complex with state of the art equipment. See also **The Barrens, Derry**.

As Ralph Roberts circle of friends grow older, the Derry Home Hospital becomes a more frequent destination in Stephen King's *Insomnia* (1994). His wife dies here, Helen Deepneau is admitted after being beaten by her husband, and Ralph himself comes here after being stabbed by religious nutcase Charlie Pickering. See also **Harris Avenue, Derry**.

Howard Cottrell keels over during a game of golf in Stephen King's "Autopsy Room Four" first published in *Robert Bloch's Psychos* (1997). The EMTs pronounce him dead at the scene and send him to the hospital for an autopsy. There's just one problem: Howard's pretty sure he's still alive. In the 2006 Turner Network Television series *Nightmares & Dreamscapes*, Richard Thomas plays Howard Cottrell, the first person to view their own autopsy. See also **Derry Municipal Country Club, Derry**.

c.1925 postcard of the Bangor Standpipe, the inspiration for Derry's landmark.

Derry, Standpipe Hill – The hill was home to the standpipe, a 1,750,000 gallons iron tank enclosed in a wood frame jacket, used to control water pressure downtown, based on the standpipe on Thomas Hill, Bangor. In Stephen King's *IT* (1986), a "freak storm" causes the collapse of the tank. It rolled down Standpipe Hill, flooding the downtown area and leveling sections of the town. Previously, Stan Uris of The Losers had encountered IT at the standpipe where IT terrorized Stan in the form of drowned children. See also **The Barrens, Derry; Standpipe Hill, Bangor**.
In Stephen King's novel *Dreamcatcher* (2001), Mr. Gray drives Jonesy to Standpipe Hill looking for Derry's water supply using his limited access to Jonesy's stolen memories. When he discovers the tank is gone, he sets his sights on a larger prize – infecting the Quabbin Reservoir, the water supply of Boston, Massachusetts.

Derry, Up-Mile Hill – In Stephen King's *IT* (1986), the flood water from the collapsed standpipe rolls down Up-Mile Hill in a wave of destruction. See also **The Barrens, Derry**.
In front of the Derry Rite Aid in the strip mall at the intersection of Witcham and Jackson Streets on Up-Mile Hill, Johanna Arlen Noonan collapsed and died. Her tragic death would be the catalyst for the events that envelope her grieving husband in Stephen King's *Bag of Bones* (1998). See also **Dark Score Lake**.

Derry, Voigt Field – Ben Richards has survived longer than any other runner in the Games Network's "The Running Man," but his time is running out. He has made his way up the coast of Maine toward the Voight Field Jetport. He's a hero now, with the media following him, so he is protected from the hunters by both his hostage and the throngs of fans. As far as Ben is concerned, his end game has begun. Games Network will be next to discover his plan in *The Running Man* (1982) by Stephen King writing as Richard Bachman.

Derry, West Broadway - Horror author Richard Kinnell (Tom Berenger) arrives home in Derry after buying a painting of a demonic youth in a sports car at a yard sale in New Hampshire. He is convinced the image is changing, dogging his trail with carnage in its wake. His home in Derry is an Italianate mansion with hip roofs and asymmetrical towers, very similar in architecture and look to a certain other horror writer's house on West Broadway in Bangor. When Stephen King's story, "The Road Virus Heads North" was made into a 2006 episode of *Nightmares & Dreamscapes* TV series (1:05), Kinnell's address was switched to create the inside joke. See also **West Broadway, Bangor; Kansas Street, Derry.**

Derry, Witcham Street – Stephen King's *IT* (1986) begins in 1957 at a storm drain on Witcham near the intersection with Jackson Street. Georgie Denbrough is playing in the puddles after a storm. First, he loses his paper boat down the drain, and then, his arm to Pennywise the clown. Poor Georgie does not survive the ordeal and is buried in **Mount Hope Cemetery, Bangor.**

Desert of Maine – see **Freeport**.

Dexter – Billy (Domenick John) is waiting at the newsstand for the delivery of his *Creepshow* comic book. The truck arrives and the scene changes into the four-color animation that ties together the segments of the film *Creepshow 2* (1987). The newsstand was built exclusively for the scene, shot on Dexter's Main Street.

Dog – The old Graag house is 15 miles beyond the hamlet of Dog, a settlement so small it barely has a name. It is at this house that a trio of writers goes on vacation. It is here they find the old book of Wizard Graag and seal their doom in "The Mantle of Graag" by Paul Dennis Lavond. The author's name is an alias used by Frederik Pohl, Harry Dockweiler, and Robert A. W. Lowndes when the story was published in *Unique Magazine,* October 1941.

Dowrie – Dowrie is the most recent fictional town created by Stephen King, making its debut in the December 2007 issue of *Playboy* in King's story "Mute." Barb Monette is the administrative secretary for Maine School Administrative District #19 located in Dowrie. Also in Dowrie is the Grove Motel, where unbeknownst to her husband, Barb has been meeting her boyfriend for the last two years. See also **Maine Turnpike**.

Dredmouth Point – In J. Michael Straczynski's novel *Demon Night* (1998), Eric Matthews is drawn back to his hometown by nightmares. There he discovers that demons have possessed townsfolk and their strength is growing. Now he and a small band of friends must find and close the portal to Hell before it's too late.

Dry Falls – *Incubus* by Ann Arensberg (1999) takes place in the summer of 1974. Dry Falls is a typical small town, except for the excessively hot weather, the unusual lack of rain and the arrival of an incubus.

Dunnet Landing – At the turn of the century, the most famous non-existent town in New England was Dunnet Landing, the imaginary community created by New England regionalist Sarah Orne Jewett. Introduced in *The Country of the Pointed Firs* (1896), Jewett created the mythic archetype of an isolated, decaying village between "the rocky shore and the dark woods" with a rich past and no future prospects, populated by mysterious and haunted characters of old Yankee stock. As with her previous book *Deephaven* (1877), *The Country of the Pointed Firs* is a series of sketches, short stories and vignettes woven into a novel – the village itself is the unifying theme.

Her decaying coastal fishing village, long past its prime, where the supernatural is a facet of day-to-day life became the ancestor of such towns as Lovecraft's Dunwich, Brennan's Jupiter Hill and King's Castle Rock.

Dunphy – Budding musician Winslow Leach leaves Dunphy for NYC to seek fame and fortune. Evil music producer Swan steals Leach's songs and frames him. Swan plans to use Leach's Faustian rock opera to open his new theater in NY. By that time, Leach is a disfigured, insane escaped prisoner and not the least bit happy with Swan. Bjarne Rostaing's novelization of *The Phantom of the Paradise* (1975) is based on Brian De Palma's screenplay. The book version was apparently based on an early draft of the screenplay as the novel excludes the supernatural aspects of the film.

Durham – From age 12 until he went to college, Stephen King lived with his mother and brother in a small house on Runaround Pond Road. Just down the road from the house is the Harmony Grove Cemetery, the inspiration for Harmony Hill Cemetery in *Salem's Lot* (1975). The fictional counterpart is where Mike Ryerson exhumed the undead Danny Glick. See also **Jerusalem's Lot; Sugg Drive, Lisbon Falls**.

Dutch Island – Known as Sanctuary in colonial times, Dutch Island is a small island in Casco Bay, cursed by the spirits of those betrayed and slaughtered by one of their own in 1693. In the modern day, Edward Moloch is an escaped death row convict. Driven by dreams of slaughtering colonists, he and a gang of escaped felons are carving a bloody path toward Dutch Island in *Bad Men* (2003), a novel by John Connolly. But violent men are about to meet the phantoms of the past that will tolerate no more violence on Sanctuary.

Dutton's Wharf – Heiress Judith Gold owns thousands of acres of woodlands, accessible only by pontoon plane. She arrives at Dutton's Wharf to be flown to her estate with Dr. Berg and

Nathan King. Dr. Berg had kidnapped Nathan for his experiments. When Judith, the daughter of Berg's foundation sponsor arrives, she soon becomes Nathan's cellmate. Judith adapts to captivity, and it becomes difficult to tell who is controlling who. Berg realizes he's become a participant but it's too late for him. As *The Captives* (1971) by Michael Fisher progresses, Judith and Nathan take Dr. Berg to Maine to turn the tables and see how he likes having his regressed animal instincts used as the test subject.

Dyer – Dale Harmon comes to Dyer to investigate the death of his friend. All trails lead to the local funeral director. Soon Harmon finds himself battling zombies, down east style, in *Moon Walker* (1989) by Rick Hautala.

East Harpswell – Cranberry Horn Cemetery is the final resting place of Pulitzer Prize Prize-winning poet and novelist Robert P. Tristram Coffin (1892-1955). Noted for his poems celebrating the locations and citizens of New England, he includes the occasional foray into the supernatural. "The Warning," his short poem of an owl's suggestion to stay inside at night, first appeared in *Commonweal* (April 6, 1932). The poem is probably better remembered from its inclusion in *Dark of the Moon: Poems of Fantasy and the Macabre* (1947), Arkham House's first poetry anthology where it shared space with the likes of Poe, Lovecraft, and Robert E. Howard. See also **Buck Cemetery, Bucksport; Merrymeeting**.

Echo Lake – Philadelphia Mafioso Tony Vincenza has a cabin on Echo Lake. It's where Angelo Martelli shot him. For such a simple hit, why is Angelo having so much trouble leaving Maine? Rick Hautala's short story "Hitman" first appeared in *Night Screams* (1996).

Eden – Gate Battons, a retired FBI profiler has a new mission – destroying the fallen angels that didn't land in Hell. He follows a powerful fallen angel into Maine where a recently reopened storage facility is somehow is a focal point of the gathering evil. Now Batton must battle for mankind's destiny in *Siege of Eden* (2002) by J. Dak Hartsock.

Exeter – David Trapp, Captain of the Special Tactics and Rescue Service's Exeter branch, has uncovered an Umbrella base in Maine where illicit biological experiments are taking place. Umbrella has successfully bribed a number of high-ranking STARS leaders to end the investigation, and Trapp fears members of his own team have been compromised by the evil pharmaceutical mega-corporation. So he recruits a team he can trust to investigate in *Caliban Cove* (1998), book #2 of S. D. Perry's tie-in novels in the *Resident Evil* video game universe. See also **Caliban Cove**.

Ellsworth – The film version of *Pet Sematary* (1989) used Ellsworth as its base of operations, and while the crew filmed predominantly in Hancock, Ellsworth does appear. On Dr. Louis Creed's (Dale Midkiff) first day at the clinic, he loses a patient, Victor Pascow (Brad Greenquist), but gains a ghost whose warnings go unheeded. The scene where Pascow and most of his skull is carried up the stairs and into the infirmary was filmed at the front entrance and on the stairs leading into Ellsworth City Hall. See also **Hancock**.

Fairfield – At the Fairfield rest area on the Maine Turnpike, two groups are about to have a memorable if tragic encounter. Brenda and Jasmine are single moms, impoverished and unloved. Brenda has rented a van to take their combined seven children to visit their parents in their shared hometown. Meanwhile, septuagenarian poets Phil and Pauline, heading to an appearance at a poetry festival, have stopped for a picnic lunch. As they reminisce, Brenda's van makes an explosive intrusion into the tranquility of the rest area in "Herman Wouk is Still Alive" by Stephen King. The story first appeared in the May 2011 issue of *The Atlantic*.

Fairington – Fairington elementary school teacher Emily Young is afraid to express her fondness of her coworker, Aaron Jackson. Jackson is still fighting a childhood fear of drowning. Such fears will pale when a psychotically angry serial killer takes a shine to Emily as his next victim in "Things We Fear." The novella first appeared in print in Glenn Rolfe's collection *Where Nightmares Begin* (2016).

Fairport – Noah Brooks (1830-1903) was a journalist, editor and Lincoln biographer. His 1894 collection *Tales of the Maine Coast* featured stories set in the dying seaport of Fairport. Several supernatural stories are included in the anthology, including a study in the psychology of ghosts in "The Hereditary Barn," first published in *Overland Monthly*, October 1886 and "The Phantom Sailor," where a seaman comes to Fairport and visits each house with a missing sailor family member, claiming to be that lost sailor, first published in *The Century*, August 1882. Fairport, as Brooks readily admits in the foreword, is a thinly disguised version of Brook's hometown of **Castine**.

Fairwater – A small town with a tragic past, Fairwater is horrified to discover the killings that plagued the town in the past have started again. Frank Bannister (Michael J. Fox) is a con man that sees ghosts and gets them to haunt houses long enough for Frank to be hired to eradicate them. Unfortunately for Fairwater, Frank is their best defense against a mass murderer back from Hell to continue his work in the 1996 film *The Frighteners*.

Falmouth – In the middle of a blizzard, Jerry Lumley staggers into Tookey's Bar on the northern fringes of Falmouth. He has walked 6 miles through the storm in search of help in Stephen King's "One for the Road," part of the *Night Shift* (1978) collection. His car is stuck in a snow bank with his wife and daughter still inside. Unfortunately for the Lumleys, the car is stuck in the ruins of **Jerusalem's Lot**.

Falmouth, Pine Grove Cemetery – Actor Gary Merrill (1915-1990) is buried in his adopted hometown. As a leading man, he added gravitas to roles on both television and the big screen, whether he was battling alien monsters underwater in *Destination Inner Space* (1966), unsuccessfully disposing of his wife in *The Woman Who Wouldn't Die* (1965), or battling giant crabs with Captain Nemo in *Mysterious Island* (1961). He was equally in demand on television, appearing in episodes of *The Outer Limits*, *The Twilight Zone*, two episodes of *The Alfred Hitchcock Hour*, and five episodes of *Alfred Hitchcock Presents*. He also appeared in the pilot episode of Irwin Allen's *The Time Tunnel* and appeared in "The Menfish" (2:24) episode of *Voyage to the Bottom of the Sea* as an admiral battling an underwater monster, cast as a possible replacement for an ailing Richard Basehart.

Fingus – A federal highway is being built along an isolated stretch of Maine when a mass grave is accidentally uncovered. The remains have apparently been cleaned and moved to this new location to be buried beneath the new highway. And The Foundation seems very interested in the site in the "Skull & Bones" (3:06) episode of *Millennium*.

First Landing – Diane Whitehead is visiting Maine from her native England. Her distant ancestors were among the original settlers here in 1788, and she has come to learn of her lineage. Strange things have started to follow her – poltergeists, deaths, and destruction – all accompanied by eerie music. Has Euclid Wrencott returned from the dead to torment the descendent of one of those who maimed and killed him over a piano or does the music foretell something else? *Deathsong* (1989) was written by Jack Scaparro.

Forest Lake – Temp worker Jack agrees to take a job as a companion to convalescent Roger Lannisfree. He will live in an isolated cabin in the woods with Mr. Lannisfree for a month until his wife joins him. The cabin is located 10 miles from the coast, on a fresh water lake. So why does Jack keep finding wet footprints that reek of salt water in the house each morning? August Derleth's "Mrs. Lannisfree" first appeared in *Weird Tales*, November 1945.

Freeport, Desert of Maine – Poor farming practices in the late 1800s and early 1900s exposed a 40-acre deposit of glacial sand. So, they created a tourist attraction out of it. Roland Turner explores the site in his quest for American follies in Thomas Tessier's "In Praise of Folly," first anthologized in *MetaHorror* (1992).

Freeport, Woolman's Free Trade Center Market – For the first 300 miles of Stephen King's *The Long Walk* (1979), Ray Garraty has focused on this building, where he hopes to see his mother and girlfriend in the crowd. Based on how he feels after the endless miles, it could be the last time he sees them. See also **Pownal**.

Friendship – Friendship is the location of Whipstaff Manor, home of Casper the Friendly Ghost in the movie version *Casper* (1995). Friendship was not actually used for filming – neighboring towns up the coast were used for establishing shots of the village and harbor. The Friendship Lighthouse is actually the Point Reyes Light near San Francisco. See also **Camden; Rockport**.

Frenchman Bay – See **Collinsport**.

Fryeburg – Reuben Bourne was wounded at Lovewell's Fight, a famous battle on the banks of Saco Pond in what is now Fryeburg. Bourne was convinced to abandon his fatally injured companion Roger Malvin after Malvin convinced him it was the only chance one of them might survive. Bourne departs after promising to return to bury Malvin. Nathaniel Hawthorne's "Roger Malvin's Burial" was first anthologized in *Mosses from an Old Manse* (1854) and tells how guilt over broken promises can lead to fatal consequences.

Gardiner – Stephen King's short story "Nona" first appeared in *Shadows* (1979). Norman Blanchette picks up a hitchhiker outside Augusta on the Maine Turnpike. At the Gardiner off-ramp, the hitchhiker gets dropped off and Norman gets a nail file in the neck for his troubles. See also **Blainesville**.

Gates Falls – Gates Falls is a small mill village in Cumberland County, north of Portland, and according to Stephen King in *'Salem's Lot* (1975), is near enough to Jerusalem's Lot and Castle Rock that residents of both towns work at the mills. King's short story "It Grows On You" in *Nightmares & Dreamscapes,* (1993) elaborates on the mills. Castle Rock resident Joe Newall owned the Gates Falls Mill, single-handedly turning the mill into a profitable operation. At the height of his career, he owned three mills and was a wealthy man. See also **Town Road #3, Castle Rock; Gates Falls Mill, Lewiston, MA**.

The sheriff of Gates Falls is Tom Harrison. Prior to this job, he was a deputy in Castle Rock. King's *The Dead Zone* (1979) further notes that Deputy Harrison attended a Rural Law Enforcement Course with fellow deputy Frank Dodd, aka the Castle Rock Strangler. See also **Cleaves Mills**.

Pete Riley, in danger of flunking out of the University of Maine in *Hearts in Atlantis* (1999), tries to console himself with the thought that he can always return home to Gates Falls and his father's old job at the Gates Falls Mills.

King brings us inside the mill in his short story "Graveyard Shift," first published in *Night Shift* (1978). Gates Falls Mills and Weaving was founded in 1897 and a century of accumulated junk has made the mill a haven for rats. A team of employees spends Fourth of July weekend cleaning the basement in hopes of deterring the rats. They discover a trapdoor leading to a sub-basement that predates the mill and is a very bad place to be, especially if you hate rats.

Outside of Gates Falls, Alan Parker is hitchhiking along Ridge Road. He gets a ride from George Staub. Unfortunately for Alan, George is already dead and delivering souls to the afterlife. Alan is given a choice: his mother's life or his own in Stephen King's novella "Riding the Bullet." See also **Harlow**.

Gennesault Island – The Island, usually just referred to as "Jenny" by the locals, appears in Stephen King's revised version of the short story "Home Delivery" as published in *Nightmares & Dreamscapes* (1993). Jack Pace is killed in a lobster boat accident off the coast. When the "Star Wormwood" appears in the sky, it heralds the beginning of the biblical End of Days, and the rising of the dead. The island is soon overrun with the walking dead, and pregnant Maddie Pace finds herself face to face with her zombified drowned husband, returned from the sea.

Gilson Creek – Sheriff Joe Fischer's worst nightmare has returned. There's a local legend about a mystery creature that mauled wild animals and terrorized the town. Fischer thought he finished off the beast years ago. Looking at the fresh damage, Fischer knows the carnage is going to start up again and continue each full moon in *Blood and Rain* (2015) by Glenn Rolfe.

Glendale – When he comes stumbling out of the woods into Glendale at sunrise, the narrator learns why the locals never enter the Mayfair Woods on the night of the full moon. They tell a tale of ghosts, lycanthropy, and mayhem, which seems to fit with the narrator's experience in "The Ghost-Eater" by C. M. Eddy, Jr., first published in *Weird Tales*, April 1924. See also **Mayfair**.

Glooscap Island – In Rick Hautala's novel *Winter Wake* (1989), John Carlson and his family arrive on Glooscap to care for John's father Frank. Frank is partially paralyzed after a stroke and the relationship between father and son, not good to start with, deteriorates rapidly. Especially after a local construction crew uncovers bones that appear to be one of John's old girlfriends. A deleted scene from the novel, "Sleigh Ride," the story was later published as a short story in *Footsteps 9*, July 1990.

Mark Stover returns to Glooscap Island after 10 years away in Rick Hautala's "Iron Frog," originally published in *Murders for Mother* (1994). There, with his widowed mother, he confronts the demons of his past.

Goat Island – "The Reach" is a Stephen King short story, first published in *Yankee*, November 1981 under the title "Do the Dead Sing?" The re-titled story was first anthologized in *Skeleton Crew* (1985). Elderly Stella Flanders, dying of cancer, sees "The Reach," the stretch of open water between the island and mainland, freeze for the first time since 1938. She also sees departed family, urging her to cross the reach.

Goat Mountain – In the 1960s, Goat Mountain was an exclusive resort. Now it's the increasingly shabby home of Charles "Dan" Jacobs. When his wife died, the minister cursed God from the pulpit, necessitating a new career. Decades later, as a sideshow act in a traveling carnival, Jacobs would find an aging, strung out Jamie Morton. Jacobs would use his electrical inventions to detox and cure Jamie's addiction. Jacobs took to tent evangelism to mask his electrical-based healing. Years later, Morton comes to assist Jacobs in his last, and greatest electrical experiment – to pierce the barrier and see beyond death. As one might expect, it does not end well in *Revival* (2014) by Stephen King. See also **Harlow**.

Godsville – Dennis is a school librarian who explains we all have flaws we learn to hide and deal with internally. Unfortunately, Dennis's flaw is no longer hidden – he has an increasingly angry urge to make animals and people around him dead. "Flaws" appeared in *Slush*, a 2015 short story collection by Glenn Rolfe.

Gorham, University of Southern Maine – The library on the Gorham campus has a facsimile reprint of an ancient grimoire. It turns out that's good enough for an English Professor to summon the Devil and trade his soul for a foolproof way to commit murder. As always, the devil's in the details. "Colt .24" by Rick Hautala first appeared in *Devils* (1987).

Gray Haven – When your buddy has as bad a track record with life choices as Max, getting set up on a blind date is a disaster waiting to happen. This time, the only way Max could have made this double date worse would have been to wait until a full moon. "Microbrew" by David Bernard appeared in *Something Funny IV* (2017).

Great Diamond Isle – See **Great Diamond Isle, Portland**.

Gull's Peak – Seth, his brother Raymond, and their friends are vacationing in a remote cabin when a blood-covered teen named Christy staggers into camp. She claims she has just killed the man who abducted her and forced her to his cabin in the woods. They give her refuge for the night, but in the morning, she has disappeared and all the men find gaps in their memories. A year later, the event still haunts them and they all suffer from increasing terrifying flashbacks of something they can't quite recall. Something is pursuing them and to save their families, friends, and sanity, they must return to the cabin and relive the night in order to conquer the demons Christy released in each of them. *Deep Night* (2006) by Greg F. Gifune asks the question of how to stop an evil inside yourself when you don't understand your enemy.

Haddock Harbour – Zeb Perkins has had four dreams of ancestor Sara Perkins, and those he tells the dreams are haunted by them, just as Zeb is still haunted by his grandmother in "Four Dreams of Gram Perkins" by Ruth Sawyer, first published in *The American Mercury*, October 1926.

Hancock – The location of the new home of Rachel and Louis Creed (Denise Crosby, Dale Midkiff) is in Ludlow, but the primary filming location of the new Creed home for the film version of *Pet Sematary* (1989) was Point Road in Hancock. The red-roofed, yellow-sided house used for exteriors remains a private residence. Across the street, the production company built the façade of the house of Jud Crandall (Fred Gwynne). The façade was built six feet in front of a real house, meaning later scenes when the Crandall house burns to the ground was done in one take and was staged very carefully. See also **Ludlow; Mount Hope Cemetery, Bangor; Ellsworth**.

Harlow – Ray Brower was a runaway from Chamberlain in 1960. His body was found by teens on the Back Harlow Road, some 30 miles from Chamberlain. Now a group of Castle Rock boys set out along the Great Southern and Western Maine train tracks to see the remains. "The Body," a novella by Stephen King, was originally published in the 1982 collection *Different Seasons*. Rob Reiner made the story into the 1986 film *Stand by Me*.

"Riding the Bullet" is a novella by Stephen King that was originally published as an e-book. Later collected in *Everything's Eventual* (2002), tells the story of Alan Parker, who hitchhikes from college to visit his mother who has been hospitalized after a stroke. Outside of Gates Falls, Alan is picked up by George Staub. As the ride goes on, Alan discovers George is a courier for the grim reaper and he wants Alan or his mother. The 2004 movie version moved the film from 2000 to 1969, with Jonathan Jackson as Alan and David Arquette as the demonic driver George Staub. See also **University of Maine, Orono; Central Maine Medical Center, Lewiston; Gates Falls**.

Charles Jacobs is Harlow's new minister with a fascination with building electrical gadgets in his spare time. When Jamie Morton's brother loses his voice in a freak skiing accident, Jacobs tries one of his inventions – the "Electrical Nerve

Stimulator" to bring the boy's voice back. Divine Intervention succeeds with a little help from science. *Revival* (2014) by Stephen King is equal parts homage to Machen's *The Great God Pan* (1894) and Shelley's *Frankenstein* (1818), with a little Lovecraft tossed in for good measure. See also **Goat Mountain**.

Harmony – In the 1990 film version of Stephen King's *Graveyard Shift*, the Gates Falls Mills have been renamed the Bachman Mills. For the exterior shots, the 200-year old Bartlett Yarn Mill in Harmony was called into service. See also **Gates Falls**.

Harpswell – In the ship building communities around Harpswell, there was a legend about a ghost ship named *Dash*, a locally built privateer that disappeared in 1815 with all hands. Since then, the ship appears out of the fog, and heads toward shore, regardless of the wind. Under full sail with no hands, the ship then disappears back into the fog before it can run aground. The appearance of the ship foretells a death in the Harpswell community. John Greenleaf Whittier was inspired to immortalize the *Dash* as "The Dead Ship of Harpswell" after a Maine schoolteacher wrote him, bemoaning that the local folklore was fading away. See also **Appledore Island; Merrymeeting; Commercial Street, Portland**.

Harpswell, Harpswell Neck Road – Ten-year-old Dougie Whooly (Alexander Brickel) is obsessed with a video game called Satan's Little Helper to the point that he wears a "Satan's Little Helper" costume for Halloween. Dougie meets a serial-killer that is wearing a Satan costume and becomes a groupie in *Satan's Little Helper* (2004). Although the film is set on a fictional Massachusetts island, director Jeff Lieberman used Maine coastal villages for exterior shots. A familiar Harpswell landmark, Estes Lobster House on Harpswell Neck Road, can be recognized in the background as Dougie's sister Jenna (Katheryn Winnick) races home after discovering a serial killer in their midst. See also **Water Street, Castine**.

Harpswell Neck – Hannah Stover is to be buried in unconsecrated ground, a Quaker whose faith made her an outsider. Now that outcast status forced upon her by the bigoted townsfolk has transformed her into a witch, and the aftermath of the funeral divides the town in "The Witch of Harpswell" by Arlo Bates, first published in *The Cosmopolitan,* October 1886.

Harrington, Flint Island – The 170-acre, Nature Conservancy managed Flint Island in Harrington maintains no trails through its lush spruce and fir forest, making it a great filming location for director Katie Aselton's *Black Rock* (2012), but a bad place to be a woman fleeing for your life from homicidal hunters. See also **Milbridge**.

Haven – The Stephen King-created town of Haven poses a problem for King purists because of its conflicting locations. It first appears in *The Tommyknockers* (1987) as a land-locked community southwest of Bangor, where writer Bobbi Anderson uncovers something buried in the woods near her home. She discovers it is an ancient alien spaceship piloted by aliens that Bobbi names Tommyknockers. Exposure to the spacecraft has mixed effects – it gives you technical skills not found on earth, but the gift slowly kills you in Stephen King's *The Tommyknockers* (1987). The book was made into a 1993 miniseries with Marg Helgenberger as Bobbi.
When FBI Agent Audrey Parker (Emily Rose) travels to Haven to track down an escaped prisoner in the first episode of the 2010 TV series *Haven,* it is now a coastal fishing village. What should be a routine case becomes anything but routine when she discovers that Haven is periodically afflicted with "The Troubles," where residents develop supernatural abilities. Over the course of the five seasons, Parker quits the FBI and joins the Haven Police Department as she and her partner, police detective Nathan Wuornos (Lucas Bryant) must deal with problems caused by those who are "troubled" as well as citizens who want to take a proactive approach to the threat

through violence. Parker begins to suspect her arrival in Haven was not a coincidence and begins to question everything, including herself. *Haven* was loosely based on the Stephen King crime novel *The Colorado Kid* (2005).

Haven, Nista Road – "The Revelations of `Becka Paulson" is a short story written by Stephen King and originally published in the July/August 1984 issue of *Rolling Stone*. The story has never been included in a collection of King's stories other than a limited edition 1000 copy release of *Skeleton Crew*. 'Becka Paulson accidentally shoots herself in the head. The bullet lodges in her brain and now the picture of Jesus on the TV talks to her. 'Becka and Jesus decide that her husband Joe is a worthless cheater and the Lord helps her rewire the TV to electrocute him.

Three years later, a revised version of the story was incorporated into the novel *The Tommyknockers* (1987). 'Becka and Jesus are still planning to kill Joe, but it's the influence of the uncovered alien space ship, not small caliber weapon induced schizophrenia.

The original, non-alien, version of the story was made into an episode of the revived *Outer Limits* in 1997. 'Becka Paulson (Catherine O'Hara) and the model's headshot that came in the picture frame (Steven Weber) still plan to dispose of her husband (John Diehl).

The 1993 TV mini-series *Tommyknockers* again finds Joe Paulson (Cliff De Young) on the receiving end of a doctored TV, courtesy of the brain power of his alien-enhanced wife 'Becka (Allyce Beasley).

Haynesville, Route 2A – Maine native Dick Curless's truck-driving song "Tombstone Every Mile" became a national hit in 1965. The tale of the Haynesville Woods and its high fatality road, most notably along a 90° curve where the road crosses the Mattawamkeag River mentions the truck drivers that died on the road, but neglects to mention the road's reputation as a hotbed of hauntings by ghostly hitchhikers looking for a lift, presumably from truckers still of this mortal coil. See also **Mount Hope Cemetery, Bangor.**

The walkers in Stephen King's *The Long Walk* (1979), would also follow the road between Houlton and Macwahoc. They too would also leave bodies behind, but not because of the immortalized treacherous driving conditions. See also **Pownal.**

Hermon – Since 1967, Coldbrook Road off I-95 has been home to Dysart's Truck Stop and Restaurant. The venerable truck stop is believed to have been the inspiration for Stephen King's short story "Trucks" which features a small group of strangers trapped in a roadside diner when trucks suddenly come to life with a dislike of humans. The story was first published in the June 1973 issue of *Cavalier*.

The story was the basis of the film *Maximum Overdrive* (1986) starring Emilio Esteves and set at a truck stop in Wilmington, North Carolina. The film was King's first (and only) attempt at directing. He and his wife Tabitha made a cameo at an ATM. The story was adapted again in 1997 as *Trucks* starring Timothy Busfield.

Hilton – The small mill town of Hilton is the nearest town to Mount Agiochook, the second highest point in Maine and a popular destination for climbers in spite of the legends of the summit being a sanctuary for Sasquatch in Rick Hautala's novel *The Mountain King* (1996). See also **Mount Agiochook.**

In "Served Cold" by Rick Hautala, the narrator has Roy Curry, an old war buddy, over for dinner. He was just a green kid from Hilton when he was sent to Nam 30 years ago. He panicked, ran and didn't warn Roy when a grenade landed nearby. Whether Roy knows it or not, tonight is the night he gets even. The story first appeared in *Deathrealm* (Summer 1994).

Hilton, Earl's Diner – When hunting season rolls around, it means the special breakfast menu at Earl's diner is back. Rick

Hautala's short story "Breakfast at Earl's" was originally published in *After the Darkness* (1993).

Hilton, Laymon House – Rick Hautala's short story "Crying Wolf" first appeared in *Cemetery Dance*, Summer 1990. Billy Lewis convinces Sarah to accompany him to the deserted house in the swamp behind his house. Billy's known for his practical jokes, but is he serious this time?

Hilton, Moulton's Field – Rick Hautala's short story "The Voodoo Queen" (*Overlook Connection*, Summer 1989) tells the tale of Dennis Levesque's ill-fated trip to the traveling carnival and how revenge can be as simple as a literal interpretation.

Hilton, Pine Haven Trailer Park – Rick Hautala's "Speedbump," first anthologized in *Bedbugs* (1999), tells the tale of Lester Croix, a boss mean enough to make his crew pave roads in August. Lester is about to learn how unpleasantly hot asphalt is in August.

Hilton, Ridge Road – Tim Harris brings his family to Hilton to restore his ancestral family home. Tragedy has struck the family and Tim feels the change of scenery will help his wife recover. But the house is haunted by unspeakable crimes of the past, and when bones are unearthed nearby, spirits demand answers in *The White Room* (2001) by Rick Hautala as A.J. Matthews.

Hilton, Story Street – The abandoned Pingree School on Story Street holds terror for Pete Garvey. Haunted by his nightmares, he has returned to Hilton to face his fears and discovers repressed memories in Rick Hautala's short story "Schoolhouse," which first appeared in *Thunder's Shadow*, August 1995.

Hilton, Watcher's Lake – In the shadow of Watcher's Mountain is Watcher's Lake. Bobby's father, plagued by nightmares calling him back to the lake all his life, finally returns to the lake with his son for the first time in years. There Bobby sees the horror that has tormented his father's dreams and will now plague Bobby. "The Call" first appeared in the Rick Hautala collection *Occasional Demons* (2007).

Hilton, Watcher's Mountain – Merit Parker's farm sits at the foot of the mountain. Behind the barn is a compost pile where Merit has just killed and dismembered his cloying wife Lydia. It would be the perfect murder if the compost would just stay put in Rick Hautala's "The Compost Heap," originally published in *Night World*, Winter 1991.
Just up Route 25 towards Watcher's Mountain is a haunted house. Tom Martin brings reporter Ed Marlboro out to the house to scare him. It turns out there's a good reason to be scared in that house. "Setup" by Rick Hautala was originally published in *100 Vicious Little Vampires* (1995).

Hocomock Island – Callie Trask finds herself in the unfortunate position of reminding Charles Sprague of his long lost Millie. Women who remind Charles of Millie end up dead. Callie flees back to Hocomock, the only place she's ever considered home. But the small island quickly becomes a trap, not a haven. Good thing Callie has a secret weapon – the guardian spirit of an ancient Native American in *The Burying Point* (1991) by Ann Brahms.

Holland – David Logan returns to his childhood home in Holland to administer the estate of his late grandmother and reconnect with his estranged uncle. On the first night of his return, he discovers the mutilated body of a missing child. The longer he stays in town, the more rumors fly about his possible guilt. When a second child turns up assaulted and mutilated, the town is convinced he is the dreaded Moonbog Killer in *Moonbog* (1982) by Rick Hautala.

Houlton, Timber Lake – Henry Duryea reunites with his son Arthur after 20 years apart. There, in an isolated cabin in northernmost Maine, Arthur learns of the *vrykolakas* curse on the Duryea name. Unfortunately for Arthur, it involves fathers feeding on their male kinfolk in "Doom of the House of Duryea" by Earl Peirce, Jr. in *Weird Tales*, October 1936.

Hundred-Mile Wilderness – The Appalachian Trail Conservancy warns that the Hundred-Mile Wilderness, the notorious final stretch of the Appalachian Trail from Monson to Mount Katahdin is fraught with hazards such as drowning, falling, and lightning. They neglect to mention that in the center of the vast wilderness is an exit portal from Purgatory. As envisioned in seasons 6, 7, and 8 of the TV series *Supernatural*, Purgatory is an endless forest in perpetual gloom. It serves as a prison and the final destination of the souls of monsters. The portal was designed as an emergency escape hatch for humans trapped in Purgatory. But as we learn in *Supernatural*, other things have been known to occasionally slip out as well.

I-95 – Ricky and his big brother were always competing with each other – bike races, sports, and of course, cars. Ricky got a Porsche, his brother an Impala. His brother is driving along an icy stretch of I-95 between Augusta and Bangor, trying not to think of the night Ricky was killed while they raced. He starts hallucinating the black Porsche tumbling end over end and Ricky ripped apart in the accident. So, he and Ricky have a chat and then Ricky steals the Impala. "Dark Highways" by Dan Foley first appeared in *Anthology: Year Three* (2015).

Indigo – Picturesque Black Lake has a large, aquatic, carnivorous problem in the 1999 comedy/horror film *Lake Placid*. A Fish & Game Ranger (Bill Pullman) and a New York paleontologist (Bridget Fonda) must figure out to stop a giant crocodile from using the townsfolk as hors d'oeuvres while Betty White roots for the reptile.

A 2007 made-for-basic-cable-TV movie, *Lake Placid 2*, returned to the lake where the offspring of the original beast matches wits with the local sheriff (John Schneider), Fish and Wildlife officer (Sarah Lafleur), and Betty White's sister (Cloris Leachman). In the similarly produced *Lake Placid 3* (2010), Cloris Leachman's nephew (Colin Ferguson) has inherited the house on Black Lake, and his son (Jordan Grehs) continues the family tradition of feeding crocodiles, much to the vexation of the sheriff (Michael Ironside) and a local poacher (Yancy Butler). *Lake Placid: The Final Chapter* (2012) finds the government has surrendered to the reptiles, and turned Black Lake into a crocodile sanctuary surrounded by an electric fence. When the fence is left open by mistake, a bus of high-school swim team members due at Clear Lake arrives at the wrong lake. Now a new sheriff (Elisabeth Röhm) has the same old problem but has help familiar with the situation: poacher-turned-EPA agent Reba (Yancy Butler) and Betty White's son Jim Bickerman (Robert Englund). See also **Clear Lake**.

Isles of Shoals – When Maine became a state in 1820, they took the Massachusetts-owned parts of the Isles of Shoals with them, making the state border with New Hampshire pass in between the islands. The Maine territories are Appledore, Cedar, Duck, Eastern, Malaga, Mingo, Shag, and Smuttynose Islands. See also **Appledore Island; Smuttynose Island**.

Islesboro – See **Lincolnville**.

Jefferson Tract – In Stephen King's novel *Dreamcatcher* (2001), childhood friends reunite each year for a week of deer hunting. Their cabin, "Hole in the Wall" is about twenty miles east of the local landmark, Gosselin's Market in Jefferson Tract. This year, the reunion will not be the same, starting with the UFO reports in the area. See also **Kineo**.

Jenny Island – See **Gennesault Island**.

Jerusalem's Lot – Stephen King's primary contribution to the Lovecraft mythos is the shunned town of Jerusalem's Lot, founded by a splinter group of Puritans in 1710. Led by a religious zealot who used the legendary tome *De Vermis Mysteriis* as a primary religious text, the town has been a problem spot ever since. In the novella "Jerusalem's Lot" first anthologized in *Night Shift* (1978), the entire population disappeared in October 1789, leaving the town abandoned until 1850 when Charles Boone moved into the family house in nearby Preacher's Corners. Boone soon discovered that "appearing abandoned" and "being abandoned" are not the same. See also **Durham; Preacher's Corners**.

Jerusalem's Lot, Marsten House – In King's novel *'Salem's Lot* (1975), Ben Mears returns home to Jerusalem's Lot. A successful writer, he has returned to write a book about Hubert Marsten and the Marsten house that overlooks The Lot. The Marsten house has haunted Ben's dreams since a childhood visit. Now the house has been rented to a stranger and people seem to be disappearing again.

Two film versions of *'Salem's Lot* have been made, a 1979 TV miniseries directed by Tobe Hooper with David Soul as Ben Mears and a two-part TV movie in 2004 with Rob Lowe as Ben Mears. There was also a nominally related sequel *A Return to Salem's Lot* (1987) with Michael Moriarity as an anthropologist who inherits a house in The Lot and ends up being forced to write a vampiric history.

Two years after the events at the end of King's novel *'Salem's Lot* (1975), a tourist is trying to drive through a blizzard and gets stuck in a snow bank on Jointner Ave, which goes through The Lot and out to Route 295. It is also the road that passes nearest the old Marsten House. He walks six miles through the Nor'easter back to Falmouth for help, only to learn that freezing to death may be the best thing that could happen to the family he left in the car in Stephen King's "One for the

Road" (*Maine Magazine,* March/April 1977). See also **Falmouth.**

Kashwak – Although known as a town in northern Maine where a large state fair is held, Kashwak is also a cell phone dead zone, useful in the post-apocalyptic world of Stephen King's *Cell* (2006). On the fairgrounds, Clay Riddell and his ragtag survivors of The Pulse are trapped by the Raggedy Man and the phone-people. See also **Kent Pond.**

Kashwakamak Lake – Gerald Burlingame suffered a heart attack and died in his secluded cabin on the lake. Unfortunately, his wife happened to be handcuffed to a bed at the time. Now she is trapped in *Gerald's Game* (1992). As she struggles to escape, she begins to remember repressed memories of a past summer. See also **Dark Score Lake.**

Keeler's Point – Luke Sinclair (Chris Sarandon) is a best-selling novelist of a series of graphically violent books about serial killers. He has developed writer's block on his latest book, one that is past due at the publisher. To avoid his clamoring publisher and agent, he drives to the randomly selected small town of Keeler's Point. His hopes of peace and quiet are shattered when a girl is found murdered the morning after his arrival. The sheriff (Vlasta Vrana) brings in detective Sonya Lehrman (Catherine Mary Stewart), a sex crimes specialist. Sinclair becomes a party of interest when a page from one of his novel is found near the body, describing the same style of murder. Another body appears that was killed in a manner described in another of Sinclair's books. The detective must determine if someone is using Sinclair's book as a how-to manual or if Sinclair has taken a more hands-on approach to his research in *Reaper* (1998).

Kent Pond – Although graphic artist Clay Riddell lives on Kent Pond, at the time of the Pulse, he is in Boston in Stephen King's *Cell* (2006). Clay cannot determine the fate of his family, so he begins a treacherous journey by foot from the smoldering ruins of Boston back to Kent Pond. See also **Kashwak**.

Kennebec River – See **Barsham Harbor**.

Kennequit – Douglas Murdoch and his daughter Janna come to Kennequit to convalesce after the horrific accident that killed his wife and left him barely alive. Off the coast, he sees a small island that calls to him through the fog. He is warned away from Silk Island and the shoals that destroy boats. Then he sees the ghost of his wife on the island. Elizabeth A Lynn's short story "The Island" first appeared *in Fantasy & Science Fiction,* November 1977.

Kezar Lake – The narrator and his twin brother Derrick are both artists. Derrick just happens to be more talented and more successful. Needless to say, Derrick must die. The narrator drives up to Derrick's luxurious house on Kezar Lake, shoots him, cuts his hands off, and fashions a pair of gloves so he can make art through Derrick's hands. Derrick's hands disapprove of the plan. "The Back of My Hands" by Rick Hautala first appeared in *More Phobias* (1995).
Stephen King's summer home on this secluded lake in western Maine was the basis for his Dark Score Lake, moving the fictional version further north in the state. While summering at the lake in June 1999, King was critically injured after being struck by a car. He would discuss his recovery in an autobiographical essay "On Impact" in the June 19-26, 2000 issue of *New Yorker*. Coincidentally King had recently finished *From a Buick 8*, a novel where Ned Wilcox's father dies in an automobile accident. The book's release was delayed until 2002. See also **Dark Score Lake**.

Kezar Notch – In Stephen King's *The Girl Who Loved Tom Gordon* (1999), Trisha McFarland strays from the Appalachian Trail at the point where an abandoned trail to Kezar Notch forks off the main trail, west of TR-90. See **Motton**.

Kineo – In Stephen King's novel *Dreamcatcher* (2001), Richard McCarthy is a Skowhegan lawyer who has a hunting camp in the unincorporated township of Kineo, thirty miles to the west of Gosselin's Market, the nearest outpost of civilization. A stranger comes to the camp – is he just a lost hunter who has somehow wandered over 50 miles in a storm to "Hole in the Wall" cabin or is he somehow associated with mysterious lights and disappearances reported in Kineo? See also **Jefferson Tract**.

Kincairn Island – Kincairn is the island sanctuary of John Leland Ransome. It is here that he goes to create the portraits that have brought him international acclaim. He produces five portraits every three years because he takes a year to know and understand his model before any painting begins. His latest model is Echo Halloran, a budding painter and art historian. But as she settles into her life on the island, her fiancé in New York has discovered a horrifying truth about the previous models of Ransome, at least those that survived, in the John Farris novella *The Ransome Women*.

Kittery – Elderly spinster Mary Ann Jenness has a ghost story, one she'll share if you ask. Forty years before, she befriended a ghost while house-sitting in New York. Mary Ann was alone in the world and so was Norvle, the ghost of a young boy from New Hampshire. Together, the two expatriate Yankees pass the lonely hours in "A Speakin' Ghost" (*Harper's Magazine*, December 1890) by Annie Trumbull Slosson.

Kittery, Foreside – Carrie is a normal housewife and mother, juggling the chores and the family in the Foreside neighborhood. She also happens to be a witch, and her talkative friend has started sending folks to her for supernatural assistance that Carrie is too rusty to actually do in "Just Another Working Mom" by Patricia B. Cirone, which first appeared in *Yankee Witches* (1988).

Lake Androscoggin – See **Wayne**.

Lambardton – The waters of the Sagadahoc River moved as if a living thing, rushing to the sea. In 1764, settlers come to the banks of the river and established Lambardton. A prosperous lumber mill may not be enough to prevent the river from discouraging the colony. "Sagadahoc" by Scott Thomas appeared in *Quill & Candle* (2010).

Lancaster County – Anna Ivers (Emily Browning) doesn't remember the night she witnessed her terminally ill mother's death in a boathouse fire. Now after a year in a psychiatric hospital, Anna returns home to her father (David Strathairn) and her sister Alex (Arielle Kebbel). Her convalescence is complicated when she discovers her father's new girlfriend (Elizabeth Banks) was her late mother's nurse. Now she's seeing ghosts that warn her about her father's new girlfriend in *The Uninvited* (2009). The film is a remake of the South Korean film *Janghwa, Hongryeon* (2003, A Tale of Two Sisters).

Land's End – In a reversal of traditional gender roles in a gothic ghost tale, Painter Judd Pauling marries Rachel Daimler after a whirlwind romance. Rachel's mother is dying and her last request is to see her estranged daughter again. So Rachel brings her new husband and stepdaughters to the isolated Maine mansion where Rachel grew up. Immediately Judd and his daughters find themselves bewildered by the family's reaction to their arrival. Soon they are besieged by the ghost of a little girl as Rachel grows increasingly nervous in the house. This is a house of secrets and madness, and Judd's new wife seems to be at the center in Diane Guest's *Lullaby* (1990).

Land's End Island – Peter Thorpe, devastated by the brutal murder of his wife, moves to the remote island of Land's End. The tiny fishing village is home to barely fifty families with roots on the island that date back to the earliest settlers. Soon

Peter learns that in isolation, the old ways never went away and that the only alternative to following the status quo is rather unpleasant in *Land's End* (1985) by Anne Leclaire.

Landor's Bay – Sandra and Paul return to the ocean-side cabins where they honeymooned 10 years before. Now, beneath a single star, one has disappeared. The question is which one? "Cabin 13" by Scott Thomas appeared in the author's collection *Over the Darkening Fields* (2007).

Lewiston, Central Maine Medical Center – Alan Parker's mother has been admitted to CMMC after suffering a stroke. Now Alan is hitchhiking from college to his mother's side in Stephen King's "Riding the Bullet," which may place his mother in even greater jeopardy. See **Harlow**.

Prior to the 1976 name change, the CMMC was known as Central Maine General Hospital. George's older brother Buddy is taken there when he breaks his leg. With his mother at the hospital with Buddy, that leaves George with the onerous task of tending to the titular "Gramma" by Stephen King (*Weirdbook* #19, 1984). See also **Castle View**.

Lewiston, Gates Falls Mill – An 1869 fire in the Lewiston plant of Gates Falls Mills resulted in the destruction of the textile mill with numerous deaths, mostly child laborers. The Kingdom Hospital was built on the site, but the property's past bleeds into the present in Stephen King's *Kingdom Hospital* TV mini-series of 2004.

Lewiston, Kingdom Hospital – Kingdom Hospital was the setting of Stephen King's *Kingdom Hospital*, a thirteen-episode miniseries based on the Danish TV mini-series *Riget* (1994). It is the second hospital of that name on the site, and it is haunted by the ghosts of dead mill children, victims of "experimental surgery" at the previous hospital, as well as earthquakes and manifestations of Anubis. The series ran in 2004 on ABC.

The miniseries included a version of the accident that nearly killed King. In the script version, one of the main characters, Peter Rickman (Jack Coleman), is hit by a van driven by a man who is distracted by a dog in the back of the vehicle. See also **Center Lovell**.

Lewiston, Saint Peters Cemetery – New Hampshire-born actor Lew Cody (1884-1934) died unexpectedly in Hollywood at the height of his career as a leading man. Among his roles in melodramas and light comedies was the drama *The Grinning Skull* (1916), set in San Francisco on the eve of the 1906 earthquake. Audiences were amazed at the special effects of the city shaking apart in one of the earliest disaster films.

Lewiston Rest Area – Pete isn't allowed to play with the older boys, so he sneaks off to the back of the closed Turnpike rest area to prove he's just as brave as them. Sneaking into the abandoned building, he steps into a world of old needles, empty beer bottles, and something eating commuters in "Mile 81," a novella by Stephen King, originally published as an e-book in 2011. In the print version that appeared in *The Bazaar of Bad Dreams*, (2015), King added several more characters to be get eaten by the station wagon from Hell. Today, the buildings are gone. Southbound vehicles can, however, still glimpse the brush-littered parking lot where it stood.

Limestone – Stephen King's *The Long Walk* (1979), published as Richard Bachman, starts north of Limestone. As the first town the walkers pass through, they are still fresh and upbeat. The full realization that most of them will die will not set in until the first gunshots. See also **Pownal**.

Lincolnville – A lawyer (Alan Rickman) and his trophy wife (Polly Walker) are driving through the rain to catch the last ferry out of Lincolnville to Islesboro and from there on to their private island vacation home. They spot a young man collapsed by the road (Norman Reedus) and reluctantly stop to help, missing the ferry. Arriving the next day, they venture out in a sailboat only to run aground in the fog on a neighboring island where the same drifter has set up camp. They all return to the island home where tension begins to grow between the three in *Dark Harbor* (1998). See also **Northport**.

Lisbon Falls – Teacher Jake Epping, is a regular at Al's Diner. Al is dying, seemingly overnight, of advanced lung cancer. It turns out Al's pantry has a time warp that has been allowing Al to leap through time to 11:58 A.M. on the morning of September ninth, 1958. No matter how much time has passed in the past, he returns two minutes after he left. Al is convinced that if he can stop Kennedy's assassination, it would improve the modern world, but after the most recent five-year stay, he developed the disease that will kill him in days. He convinces Jake to take his place and try to stop the assassination. Jake will try, but Al neglected to mention that when you try to try to change the past, the past tries to stop you in Stephen King's novel *11/22/63* (2011). See also **Harris Avenue, Derry**.

In 2016, Hulu created an 8 part mini-series of *11/22/63* with James Franco as Jake Epping. Hespeler, Ontario stood in for Lisbon Falls and the producers did their own time warp, changing the date of the portal from 1958 to 1960.

Lisbon, Catherine Street – Ronnie and Lorna are having a garage sale - just an ordinary day of haggling over prices. All that changes when Leon Hickey shows up and proves to be simultaneously creepy and scary. And now he's back looking for a refund on his purchase and it does not appear he will take no for answer. "The Garage Sale" by Peter N. Dudar appeared in his collection *Dolly and Other Stories* (2013).

Lisbon Fall, Sugg Drive – Stephen King attended Lisbon High School, graduating in 1966. King and his family were living in neighboring Durham, a town small enough to only have four students attending high school. Rather than pay for a school bus to transport the four, the town hired Mike's Taxi to handle transportation. The taxi in question was actually a converted hearse, and one of his fellow students was one of the two LHS girls that King used as the inspiration for the telekinetic Carrie White in his first published novel, *Carrie* (1974). See also See also **Chamberlain**; **Durham**.

Lisbon Falls, Worumbo Mill – Demolished in 2006, the Worumbo Mill, built in 1864, had been a major force in textile manufacturing up through World War II. By the time Stephen King took a summer job at the mill, those glory days were in the past. As he eloquently phrased it in *On Writing* (2000), it was "a dingy fuckhole overhanging the polluted Androscoggin River like a workhouse in a Charles Dickens novel." It did give him a story idea, however. One of the full-time staff told him about the rats in the basement, giving King the seed for "Graveyard Shift," first published in *Cavalier*, October 1970.

Little Goat Bay – Growing up, Meg Kendricks felt like a prisoner in her own home. Her mother was dead and her father was cold and unforgiving. Desperate to escape her father and the town, she elopes. Soon after her marriage, Meg discovers her mother is still alive, hidden away in a sanitarium in the Florida Keys. Now she has rescued her mother, only to discover they must return to her hated hometown in *The Home* (1984) by David Lippincott.

Little Sebago Lake – Rick Hautala's short story "Late Summer Shadows" first appeared in *Maine,* September/October 1989. It tells a story about two young boys who find an old headstone in the woods down off Campbell Shore Road where Kimball's Brook drops down to the lake. Is it something really scary, or just is it just the shadows?
Hautala returns to Campbell Shore Road in his novel *Ghost Light* (1993). After fleeing Portland, Cindy Toland goes to a cabin on

Little Sebago with her niece and nephew. There, she is finally forced to confront her psychotic brother-in-law, who has cut a bloody swath cross-country in pursuit. There may be only one chance to stop Alex Harris's rampage - the ghostly blue lady that her niece Krissy claims has been following them. See also **Coyne Street, Portland**.

Dave and Beth flee the city and head to their cabin on Lake Sebago. The world is going mad because of an underlying hum that fills the air, first causing sleep loss, and now fraying nerves. Here, away from civilization, the noise is almost bearable. Of course, it now appears that the noise is merely a symptom of something much worse that is happening. "The Hum" by Rick Hautala was first published in *Man vs. Machine* (2007).

Little Tall Island – Little Tall is a sleepy fishing village in the rugged Outer Islands off the coast of Maine. The eponymous *Dolores Claiborne* lives on the island and is accused of murder in the 1992 Stephen King novel. However, she confesses to a murder that occurred during the 1963 eclipse, not the one she is currently accused of committing. Kathy Bates portrayed the islander in the 1995 film version.

Maddie Sullivan is also a native of Little Tall, but moves to nearby Gennesault Island after her marriage to Jack Pace in the short story "Home Delivery," anthologized in *Nightmares & Dreamscapes* (1993). See **Gennesault Island**.

In King's *Storm of the Century* (1999), the islanders' thin veneer of civility wears through when a nor'easter isolates them with Andre Linoge, whose intimate knowledge of hidden sins rips apart of the tight-knit community. See also **Southwest Harbor**.

Long Lake - See Bridgeton.

Ludlow – In Stephen King's 1983 novel *Pet Sematary*, Dr. Louis Creed moves to Ludlow after taking a job with the University of Maine, Orono. He learns of a local pet cemetery located atop an ancient Indian burial ground. Dead pets buried here come back, changed and evil. See also **Mount Hope Cemetery, Bangor; University of Maine, Orono; Orrington**.

King adapted his novel into the screenplay for the 1989 film version featuring Dale Midkiff as Louis Creed and Fred Gwynne as neighbor Jud Crandall. See also **Hancock**.

A sequel film, *Pet Sematary II* (1992), continued the carnage in Ludlow without the involvement of Stephen King. Filming it Georgia didn't help either.

Ludlow is also the winter home of Thad Beaumont. Under his real name, he's a highly regarded, impoverished author. Under the pen name George Stark, he's a successful crime writer. When Stark's real identity is uncovered, Thad stages a "funeral" to confirm that he is Stark and to announce he is done with Stark. However, it appears that Stark may not be done with Thad in Stephen King's *The Dark Half* (1989). See also **Homeland Cemetery**, **Castle Rock; Castle Lake**.

Lugar Island – Dr. Ian Sanders has returned to his childhood home on the isolated island just as a series of killings rock the town, just as they did in the past. As residents begin to flee in *Wolffile* (1988) by Jack Woods, Ian decides to stay, as does Maeve Adams. As Maeve seeks why her sister and her family were brutally slaughtered, Ian tries to decipher a centuries-old diary. Both are drawn to the secrets of the Luna Coven and local legends of the loup-garou.

Luketown – Tara (Lindsey Pulsipher) and a mute named Johnny (Jesse Haddock) are locked in the cellar of Ruric International Music Academy, an isolated conservatory run by a deranged couple (Lori Petty and William Samples). The couple has made a pact with a demon to resurrect their dead son in exchange for twelve teenage sacrifices and Tara is scheduled to be the last victim. Johnny also has his own problem - he intermittently turns into a bloodthirsty demon. It's going to be a long night in the basement in "Fair Haired Child," an episode of the *Masters of Horror* television series.

Mackerel Cove – Captain Peter Crum decides to sail his sloop to the Paris Exhibition. The trip was a failure from the start due to Captain Crum swearing that even Beelzebub couldn't stop them from reaching Paris, a statement just begging for trouble. The ample supply of rum onboard probably didn't help either. "The Terrible Voyage of the Toad" by Edward Page Mitchell was first published in the New York City newspaper *The Sun*, October 20, 1878.

Maine State College of Surgery – See **Altonville**.

Maine Turnpike – The Maine Turnpike is now a section of I-95 running from exit 3 near Kittery to exit 109 in Augusta. I-95 itself then continues north to the Canadian border near Houlton. See also **Augusta; Fairfield; Gardiner; Lewiston Rest Area; Stillwater River**
Monette is a publisher's sales rep whose life is in complete disarray. Not only has his wife been having an affair, she's going to jail. Getting on the turnpike at Portland en route to a sales call, he picks up a deaf, mute hitchhiker. Now on the 160-mile drive to Derry, Monette tells his tale of woe, relieved to finally vent out loud about his wife's treachery and comforted knowing the hitchhiker can't actually hear of his personal life. Or can he? "Mute" by Stephen King first appeared in *Playboy*, December 2007. See also **Buxton; Dowrie**.

Marsden – Li'l Ron meets Sweet Kate under Abram's Bridge. When he realizes she's the ghost of a local woman who disappeared in 2000, he decides to make things right so she can cross over. Li'l Ron had no idea how dangerous delving into small town secrets can be. If he's not careful, he may cross over before Sweet Kate in "Abram's Bridge." The novella first appeared in print in Glenn Rolfe's collection *Where Nightmares Begin* (2016).

Matawaskie Valley – Emeric Belasco's mansion is considered the "Mount Everest of Haunted Houses," and like the mountain has a legacy of broken and dead adventurers. Richard Matheson's iconic *Hell House* (1971) tells of the most recent attempt by a group of psychic investigators to conquer Hell House and exorcise the demons within. Dr. Lionel Barrett, a physicist who believes in a scientific explanation of parapsychology and his wife Edith are joined by two mediums, Florence Tanner and Benjamin Franklin Fischer. They were hired by dying millionaire William Reinhardt Deutsch to determine if there is life after death. Previous scientific explorations of the Belasco house have resulted in death, mutilation, and madness. This trip isn't looking much better. *The Legend of Hell House* (1973) was Matheson's film adaptation of his own novel, with the setting moved to England.

In the original novel, Benjamin Franklin Fischer was hired both because of his psychic abilities and because he was the only survivor of the 1940 investigation. In the Richard Matheson tribute anthology *He Is Legend* (2009), author Nancy A. Collins tells the story of the doomed 1940 expedition and psychic prodigy Ben Fischer's narrow escape in "Return to Hell House."

Mattawamkeag River – See **Route 2A, Haynesville**.

Mayfair – The narrator needs to get from Mayfair to Glendale for a business meeting the next day, and when no one from Mayfair will drive him there so late in the day, he decides to walk. He gets lost on the abandoned trail and as night closes in, he encounters a house in the woods where he is invited to spend the night in "The Ghost-Eater" by C.M. Eddy, Jr., first published in *Weird Tales*, April 1924. See also **Glendale**.

Merrymeeting – John Dawn is a shipmaster and a ship-builder in Merrymeeting in Robert P. Tristram Coffin's novel *John Dawn* (1936), the story of four generations of his family. The Dawns' lucky drinking mug is counterbalanced by the family's uncanny knack of encountering the "dead ship of Harpswell," the legendary harbinger of death and doom that follow the Dawn ships across the globe. See also **East Harpswell; Harpswell**.

Milbridge – Actress, writer, and director Katie Aselton returned to her hometown to film *Black Rock* (2012). Sarah, Lou, and Abby (Aselton, Lake Bell, and Kate Bosworth) attempt to reunite by renting a boat and camping on the deserted island where they spent much of their youth. The attempt to reconnect is interrupted by three local hunters. A shared campfire meal turns into an attempted rape and the violence escalates. Now the three friends must fight for their lives and make it back to their boat to escape. See also **Flint Island, Harrington**.

Monmouth – Gove Cemetery on Academy Street is the final resting place of the William Drake family, including his daughter Florence Hazel Drake Heald (1896-1961) better known as author Hazel Heald. Through mutual friend Muriel Eddy, Heald was introduced to, and became a regular revision client of, H.P. Lovecraft with at least five published stories credited to her that involved revision work by Lovecraft.

Monson – See **Hundred-Mile Wilderness**.

Monument Island – Stage Island has a 19th-century daymark, a 40-foot stone tower for ship navigation during the daytime that gives the island its more common name, Monument Island. Christopher Golden transforms this modern monument into a more ancient and sinister stone circle in "Pyre," first published in *Four Dark Nights* (2002). Samantha brings her father's corpse to the island to burn on a pyre in hopes of summoning his spirit to find out why if he loved her, he left her. The problem is that the Vikings who built the monument consider it blasphemy and return, very angry and very undead.

Moody Point – While fishing at Miller's Bend, Avery Ludlow is held up at gun point. When he has no money to give, the three boys kill his dog Red out of spite. Jack Ketchum's novel of class warfare, Downeast style, *Red* (1995) was made into a 2007 film with Brian Cox as Avery Ludlow.

Motton – In Stephen King's *The Girl Who Loved Tom Gordon* (1999), the McFarlands originally planned to hike the Appalachian Trail from Motton in TR90 to North Conway, New Hampshire. That was before Trisha McFarland wandered off the trail. See also **Castle View; Kezar Notch; Sanford**.
In King's first novel *Carrie* (1974), Carrie's mother Margaret White was born and raised in Motton. Fire engines from Motton were later among those sent to help extinguish the fire at the high school prom. See also **Chamberlain**.
The main character in Stephen King's short story "The Man in the Black Suit," anthologized in *Everything's Eventual* (2002), is an octogenarian named Gary who tells a tale from his youth of when he encountered a demonic stranger in the pre-WWI woods between Motton and Kashwakamak.

Mount Agamenticus – The weathered remains of an old farm on the southern slope of Agamenticus became the home of a somber stranger in Sarah Orne Jewett's "The Gray Man." The story first appeared in *A White Heron and Other Stories* (1886) and explores the different manners in which a house can be haunted.

Mount Agiochook – In Rick Hautala's novel *The Mountain King* (1996), Mark Newman and Phil Sawyer are trapped on the slopes by a snow squall. Phil is injured and Mark can only watch as his friend is carried off by a Sasquatch. Making his way back to town, no one believes he has seen the legendary mountain monster. Now Mark must return to the mountain alone to rescue his friend. See also **Hilton**.

Mount Crag – In Ray Garton's sequel *The Folks 2: No Place Like Home* (2008), Andy has had plastic surgery to hide the scars on his face. He still lives with the Bollingers and their assortment of deformed children, now thriving in a loving environment. He falls in love with Roxanne, a normal girl who works at the bowling alley. Andy is justifiably concerned how his ex, Amanda Bollinger, will take the news. See also **Pinecrest**.

The mountain village awakens the day after a meteor shower to find a new type of flower blooming across the area. It is so beautiful it's unearthly. And when the blossoms start dropping off their stems and hunting prey, the whole unearthly thing takes on new meaning in *Crawlers!* (2006) by Ray Garton. In 2016, Garton released a revised ebook edition with a less upbeat ending, a new forward and no exclamation point in the title.

Mount Desert Island – In 1947, Saxon Faraday returns to her ancestral home Roquefort Manor after a five-year stay at an insane asylum. Now she must battle her personal demons as well as the external ones that haunt the Faraday women in *Ghosts of Eden* (2005) by T. M. Gray.

Lawson heads to Maine to seek the aid of Belladonna, a lycanthrope elder in deciphering an ancient text with the location of a lycanthrope artifact in *The Destructor* (2003), the third book in the "Lawson Vampire" series by Jon F Merz.

Mount Katahdin – See **Baxter State Park; Hundred-Mile Wilderness**.

Mount Olive – The Simpson House has a bad reputation. It seems that ever since 1692, whenever a member of the Simpson family moves into the house, the man of the house tends to go mad and kill off the entire family. Since the last massacre in 1949, the house has remained abandoned. Ian Donovan and Caly St. John come to Mount Olive for a vacation. There they meet Patrick Simpson, the last of the "Mad Simpsons" who must unravel the curse on his family before it claims one last victim in Sharon Combe's *Caly* (1986).

Naples – Luke Howard and his mother move to Naples. His new friends have a game they call "chasing ghosts," that involves visiting abandoned houses out in the woods. Unfortunately, the boys decide to play in the old Cobb place. Unfortunately, there may some error in the town's belief that the Cobbs died out years ago. *Chasing Ghosts* (2016) is a novella by Glenn Rolfe.

*A 6th-century Chinese temple statue guards the
Naples Historical Society Museum.
Photo courtesy of Joseph A. Citro.*

Naples, Village Green – Among the standard historical society acquisitions of town artifacts, antiques, and photos in the Naples Historical Society Museum is a somewhat incongruous display – a 6th-century guardian statue from a Chinese Temple. Seven foot tall, carved from wood, covered in plaster, and decorated in gold leaf, it also was apparently cursed. Local brothers Charles and Ruben Hill were merchants in the lucrative Chinese tea trade who used the mayhem of the Boxer rebellion to steal the statue and two additional, smaller pieces. Bringing them home to Naples, they discovered a secret stash of jewels in a hidden cavity. The money was used to build a mansion above the town with the statue on display. The statue was apparently unamused at its absconsion and both brothers died soon after. The heirs, now believing in cursed idols, tossed the two small statues into the lake. The house was destroyed by fire, but its curse lingered on, not only plaguing the Hill heirs but subsequent property owners and businesses on the location of the house. The large statue somehow survived and ended up in the basement of the Boston Museum of Fine Arts. The statue was returned to Naples in the 1970s where he contentedly guards the museum.

Needland – In Chandler McGrew's *The Darkening* (2004), Dylan Barnes is a martial arts instructor plagued with sleepwalking and odd mental lapses two years after his wife's death. When his wife's grave is vandalized and her coffin stolen, he finds himself drawn into a cross-country flight from a secret society somehow tied into Lovecraft's Old Ones. But are they trying to stop their return or advent it?

Nephews Island – See **Cape Harvest**.

New Briarcliff – A minister is sent to convalesce at the New Briar Sanitarium. He discovers a farmhouse around the bend, exactly as he had imagined it. Soon he is falling in love with the farmer's daughter, in spite of local claims that the house was destroyed decades before. Add claims of ghosts and loup-garou and it could shape up to be a deadly courtship in "The Phantom Farmhouse" by Seabury Quinn (*Weird Tales*, October 1923).

New Sharon – New Sharon Teachers' College is introduced in Stephen King's short story "Strawberry Spring," first

anthologized in *Night Shift* (1976). In 1968, an unseasonably warm "strawberry spring" brought a thick fog to the campus at night, as well as a serial killer named "Springheel Jack."
The New Sharon Teachers' College also appears in Stephen King's short story "I Know What You Need" first anthologized in *Night Shift* (1976), where Elizabeth Rogan falls under the spell of Edward Hamner, romantically and possibly literally.

Newaggen – The first and only 3-masted schooner launched from the shipyard at Newaggen was the *Flying Sprite*, a ship with a mind of its own and a nose for trouble. So difficult was the ship, that in a fit of despair, Captain Trumbull Cram had her rechristened as the *Judas Iscariot*. Captain Cram finally decided to sink her but even that wasn't the end of her in "The Last Cruise of the Judas Iscariot" by Edward Page Mitchell, first published in the New York City newspaper *The Sun,* April 16, 1882.

Newbridge – Elderly spinster Florence Willowby is the town's reclusive eccentric. But the town doesn't know that she has been secretly preparing a ritual to resurrect the man she loved, lost, and murdered. All Hell is about to break loose in Newtown because of Florence's obsession in *Resurrexit* (1986) by Leona C. Ross.

Nodd's Ridge – Tabitha King's contribution to Maine's fictional landscape appears in a five of her novels, most of which are romances. None the less, they are indelibly connected to horror through her novel *Pearl* (1988). Pearl Dickinson arrives in Nodd's Ridge to close out her late uncle's estate and decides to stay. Pearl hails from Key West, Florida, where she learned to cook from Dick Hallorann, the cook from the Overlook Hotel in Stephen King's book *The Shining* (1977).
Olivia Russell's marriage is in trouble, so she and her son head out to the family's cottage in Nodd's Ridge in the dead of winter. But the rules change after the tourists leave at summer's end and she is soon in a battle to survive against a

trio of local hoods. Tabitha King's *The Trap* (1985) was also released as *Wolves at the Door*.

North Chamberlain – Irwin Henty owns a farm in North Chamberlain. Billy Nolan's gang kills Henty's pigs and collect the blood for a prom surprise in Stephen King's *Carrie* (1974). Wait until Billy sees the surprise Carrie has for him in return. See also **Chamberlain**.

North Fryeburg – Riverside Cemetery is the burial location of Bryan Edwin Smith (1957-2000). His death brought him a second wave of notoriety, second only to the first when his van slammed into Stephen King. His death was fodder for the media - not only did he die on King's birthday, this passing was mysterious. Until a toxicology report later found he had accidentally overdosed on painkillers, it was looking very much like King's supernatural powers weren't limited to the written page. See also **Brownfield**.

North Manchester – The North Manchester Meetinghouse was built in neighboring East Readfield in 1793 and moved to Scribner Hill Road in North Manchester in 1839. The picturesque cemetery next door is surrounded by the typical stone wall, but with a difference – one of the stones in the wall includes the cloven footprint of the devil himself. The story goes that a construction crew was building Scribner Hill Road when they came upon a boulder too big to move. One of the workers climbed up on the rock and swore he'd sell his soul to the devil if that rock could be moved. The next day, the rock had been moved to its present location and the construction worker had disappeared. All that was left were two imprints on the boulder, the triangular mark of a cloven hoof and a second mark that appears to be a pair of overlapping human footprints.

North Waterford – In 1820, woodcutter Elijah Pike was lost in a blizzard. He took refuge in an isolated cabin, where a hermit offered him a hot drink that infected him with a form of vampirism. Two centuries later, the woodcutter has reinvented himself repeatedly in his search for a cure, this time as a hematologist in Texas. He is drawn into the investigation of a serial killer leaving drained corpses across the city of Houston in *Night Blood* (2001) by James M. Thompson, the first of a trilogy that spans the continent.

Northbrook – During Spring Clean-up Week, Jeremy McCough finds a window frame with the glass intact which might work when he remodels his shed. When he looks through it, he discovers that he can see people as their spirit animal. His wife, for instance, appears as a cat. Too bad he looked through the glass into a mirror in "True Glass" by Rick Hautala, published in *Shivers V* (2009).

Northbrook, Spear Street – After the death of his wife, Ben Skillings is so grief-stricken that he cannot sleep. He leaves his formerly happy home on Spear Street each night to be alone in a secluded park along the river. But he soon discovers that things happen late at night along the river in the novella *Cold River* (2003) by Rick Hautala. Only he can see these creatures, and they are actively recruiting Ben to join them.

Northport – Sprawling across 128 acres of woodland along the rugged coast of Northport, the Crow's Nest is a private estate that was used as the primary filming location for *Dark Harbor* (1998). Built in 1920 in the Federal style, the Crow's Nest served as the private island summer home of Alexis Chandler Weinberg (Polly Walker). Already bickering with her lawyer husband (Alan Rickman), the bad situation is exacerbated by the presence of a mysterious drifter (Norman Reedus). And things are getting worse.

Ocoma Heights – Clayton Blaisdell and his partner George Rackley planned the heist of the century. In the black of the night, they would visit Portland's wealthy suburb, kidnap the infant heir of the Gerard fortune and retire on the ransom. George was the brains of the operation but he's dead. Now the mentally challenged Blaze is determined to go ahead with the plan, using the voice of George in his head for guidance in *Blaze* (2007) by Stephen King writing as Richard Bachman. See also **South Freeport**.

Ogunquit – Frannie Goldsmith's life was turned upside down when she learned she was pregnant. That quickly becomes the least of her troubles when a weapons lab accidentally releases a rapidly mutating virus that wipes out most of the world's population in Stephen King's *The Stand* (1978). One of the few survivors, Frannie and fellow survivor, the odious Harold Lauder, decide to head west in search of other survivors. King's epic novel was turned into a six-hour miniseries, premiering in 1994 with Molly Ringwald as Frannie Goldsmith and Corin Nemec as her creepy companion.

Ogunquit, Main Street – Venerable Ogunquit Playhouse on Main is the setting for the W. E. D. Ross gothic ghost tale *The Yesteryear Phantom* (1971). Joyce Wales is a new arrival at the theater and is immediately plunged into terror paralleling the nightmares she has suffered all her life. Now the August heat brings a murderous ghost dressed as a Model T driver of yesteryear. The show must go on, but that could be difficult if no one in the cast is still alive.

Ogunquit, Oceana's By the Sea – An employee at the restaurant releases a deadly virus on the customers. It is a field test. His real target is a small college in Massachusetts, where Jenna Blake's soon-to-be stepmother is the first victim. Jenna Blake, college student and budding forensic scientist must put the pieces together before the death count rises in *Throat Culture* (2008): a Body of Evidence novel by Christopher Golden and Rick Hautala, the tenth book in the "Body of Evidence" series.

Old Orchard Beach – In Stephen King's *Insomnia* (1994), Ralph has a dream that someone has buried his late wife Carolyn up to her chin in the sand and he cannot dig her out fast enough to save her from the tide. All the while, Carolyn seems to be warning Ralph about something unrelated to her predicament. See also **Harris Avenue, Derry**.

After an afternoon jog on the beach, Bill Wheeling starts receiving crank calls from a young woman with a vaguely familiar voice. Even as he has dinner with friends, he dwells on the call, building a fantasy image of the woman. During a moonlight walk on the beach with his wife, he suddenly remembers the woman from a visit to the beach 20 years before and sees her beckoning him to follow her into the waves. "I've Been Thinking of You" by Rick Hautala was originally published in *Terminal Fright*, Summer 1996.

Old Town – See **Stillwater River**.

Orono – Rick Hautala's short story "Karen's Eyes" (*Footsteps #9*, July 1990) takes place near the University of Maine, in an off-campus apartment at College Ave and Main Street, where a college student takes revenge on her roommate and her former boyfriend.

Orono, University of Maine – Stephen King's alma mater repeatedly appears in his works. Both Jo and Mike Noonan were English majors at the university in *Bag of Bones* (1998) before their marriage and move to Derry. See also **Benton Street, Derry**.

It is also where Chicagoan Dr. Louis Creed accepts a position at the Cutler Health Center in the novel *Pet Sematary* (1983). The Creeds take up residence in nearby **Ludlow**.

In the second and titular novella in King's *Hearts in Atlantis* (1999), Pete Riley is a 1966 freshman on Chamberlain Dorm's third floor. There, he falls in love with Carol Gerber and joins a game of hearts that becomes a metaphor for the Viet Nam war.

UMO student Alan Parker learns that his mother has had a stroke and is now in the hospital; in Lewiston. Alan has but one way to reach his mother's side in Stephen King's "Riding the Bullet" – hitchhike. See also **Harlow**.

Rick Hautala uses the campus in his novel *Cold Whisper* (1991). Sarah Lahikainen is a freshman when Alan Griffen gets a job as a janitor. Officially working as part of his parole, he is actually there to stalk Sarah, waiting for the right moment to kill her, just like he killed her mother. See also **Waterville**.

Orrington – In 1978, Stephen King moved to Orrington, renting a house for his year as the writer in residence at University of Maine, Orono. While there, the King's pet cat Smucky was struck and killed in the heavy traffic along Route 15. The cat was buried with other neighborhood road kill in a small local pet cemetery. Smucky would return as Church, the family cat similarly killed in traffic on Route 15 in the novel *Pet Sematary* (1983). He would also have a posthumous cameo in the 1989 film version – a grave marker is dedicated to him in the opening credits. See also **Hancock; Ludlow**.

Orrs Island – Dr. Ben Cahill (Thomas Calabro) leaves his post at a Boston hospital to renovate a cabin on a small fishing village on an isolated Maine island in the TV movie *They Nest* (2000). A body washes up on shore, infested with a rare breed of carnivorous cockroaches. The film was released to DVD as *Creepy Crawlers*.

Ossipee River – At Mary's Bend, near where the Ossipee joins the Saco River, EPA medical investigator Robert Verne (Robert Foxworth) rescues a mutated bear cub from fishing nets. Now a very angry, very large mother bear mutant is in hot pursuit in director John Frankenheimer's *The Prophecy* (1979). See also **Brewster**.

Passamaquoddy – A young orphan (Sean Marshall) named Pete comes to the small fishing village with his only friend, a dragon named Elliott (voiced by Charlie Callas). Elliott is usually visible only to Pete, which causes endless problems for the runaway orphan who now must juggle evil foster parents, a conniving patent medicine salesman, and a village of superstitious fisherman in *Pete's Dragon* (1977). The 2016 remake moves the setting to Oregon.

It's November 1938 and Professor Paul Harding has come to the coast to study common surf shoggoths during their "blooming stage," when the shoggoths go dormant on the rocks and exude tendrils that bear "fruit." Harding discovers the unexpected truth about shoggoths. Now, with reports of *Kristallnacht* on the radio, the professor must make a decision that affects both mankind and the shoggoths in "Shoggoths in Bloom." The story by Elizabeth Bear first appeared in the March 2008 issue of *Asimov's Science Fiction*.

Pastor's Bay – Anna Kore, a young girl from Pastor's Bay is missing. Randall Haight served 18 years in prison for the murder of a young girl when he was 14. And someone is taunting him with that knowledge, and if word gets out, he'll be lynched, guilty or not. He hires Charlie Parker, a private detective, to find out whose stalking him and hopefully find Anna alive. Parker has always walked a fine line between criminal cases and paranormal investigations. This time, even he's not even sure where the line is, in *The Burning Soul* (2011) by John Connolly.

Pendleton University – In the 1998 film *Urban Legend*, Robert Englund is a folklore professor at a remote university in Maine. Someone in his class is killing students in manners similar to famous urban legends, and everyone still alive is a suspect, although the list is getting shorter.

Pepperell – In 1952, Diana Chilton rebels against the patriarchal order of magicians that raised her. She abandons the order and heads to Maine in search of another former member of the order, the legendarily reclusive Thomas Morgan. The two devise a plan for a new order of magicians, one that will utilize magic to catalyze social and political change by creating a reservoir of power. The fact Morgan was cursed by the Fae and is now a vampire just complicates things. *The Longer the Fall* (2010) by Inanna Arthen is book 2 of her "The Vampires of New England" series.

As book 3 of the series, *All the Shadows of the Rainbow* (2013), opens, the aftermath of the project continue to resonate. It is 1955, and Diana's encounter with the Fae have elicited a similar result – she too is now a vampire. She returns to Pepperell to assess her life and realizes she must leave Maine. She will attempt again to manifest political and social change, this time on a smaller scale.

Phillipsport – Phillipsport is a picturesque seaport village that is a tranquil haven, right up until waves of over-sized venomous crabs start flooding the village. It's "Creature Feature" meets Splatter Gore as the town must battle an onslaught of homicidal crabs in *Clickers* (2005) by J. F. Gonzalez & Mark Williams.

J. F. Gonzalez returned with co-author Brian Keene in a 2007 sequel *Clickers II: The Next Wave*. The Clickers are back in the wake of a major hurricane and this time, they're winning.

Gonzalez and Keene would do two more books on the killer crustaceans – *Clickers III: Dagon Rising* (2011) and *Clickers Vs Zombies* (2012) which move the setting away from the ruins of Phillipsport.

Phipp's Cove – A group of bored dilettantes decides to visit the long-abandoned home of Jeremiah Phipps, pirate. Now boredom is the least of their problems in Thorp McClusky's "Dark Mummery" a short story first appearing in *Weird Tales*, November 1944.

Pinecrest – Pinecrest is a remote village on isolated Mount Crag. Andy avoids the locals, not only because they shun his fire-scarred face but the fundamentalist mentality of the town.

One day he meets Amanda Bollinger of a local mysterious but wealthy family. Amanda's family is a collection of outsiders with physical deformities and mental disorders. Because of his scarred face, the Bollinger clan believes Andy is the Chosen One, ordained to lead the family in *The Folks* (2001) by Ray Garton. See also **Mount Crag**.

Placerville – Charlie Decker attends the local high school. He is expelled after a yelling match with the principal. He goes back to his locker, pulls out a weapon and goes on a shooting spree. *Rage* (1977) was Stephen King's first novel written as Richard Bachman. Because of subsequent real world school shootings King has chosen to let *Rage* go out of print. See also **State Hospital, Augusta**.

Pocock Island – The population of Pocock is 311 or 312, depending on whether you include John Newbegin. John actually died in 1870, but 4 years later, decided to come back and again become a respectable member of the community in "Back from That Bourne" by Edward Page Mitchell, first published in New York City newspaper *The Sun*, December 19, 1874.

Porter –Maine Teen Camp in Porter has the dubious distinction of being the filming location for Camp Hiawatha in the 2005 film *Camp Daze*. Back in 1981, a killer stalked the woods, killing the campers in the proud slasher film tradition. See **Camp Hiawatha**.

Portland – Andy Campbell's response to problems with the IRS are not government sanctioned, especially for the auditor in his basement in Rick Hautala's short story ". . . from a Stone" first anthologized in *Bedbugs* (1999).

Portland, Brighton Avenue – The Portland city hospital on Brighton was replaced by a municipal nursing home in 1982. After Clayton Blaisdell, Sr. disciplined his son by repeatedly tossing him down a flight of stairs, the child was sent to Portland General Hospital to convalesce. There it is discovered that Clayton Blaisdell, Jr. had brain injuries from which he will never recover, as well as a distinctive furrow in his skull in *Blaze* (2007) by Stephen King writing as Richard Bachman. See also **South Freeport**.

Portland, Civic Center Square – In Rick Hautala's short story "Winter Queen" (*Dark Destiny*, 1994), rock star Alex VanLowe's plane crashes in the deeps woods of Maine. Now as his fans hold a candlelight vigil outside the Civic Center, he struggles to survive against cold, hunger and lycanthropes.

Portland, Commercial Street, Andy's Old Port Pub – Rom-zom-com *Night of the Living Deb* (2015) begins at a girls' night out when Deb Clarington (Maria Thayer) hooks up with Ryan Waverly (Michael Cassidy). When they sober up the next morning in Ryan's apartment, Deb's walk of shame is cut short when they realize Portland has developed a severe case of zombies. See also **High Street, Portland; India Street, Portland; Western Prom, Portland**.

Portland, Commercial Street, Flatbread Company – Jim thought the age of ghost ships was long past. Then one night, he was sitting on a restaurant deck on Commercial Street and saw the Dead Ship of Harpswell silently passing the Maine State Pier. "Whose Dead Ship" by Michelle Y. Souliere debuted in *Snowbound with Zombies* (2015). See also **Harpswell**.

Portland, Congress Street, Canal Building – Caribou Records is run by Louis Phillips, who can make or break careers. He's also notorious for screwing over musicians with his contract fine print. Abigail recorded her album at Caribou and Lou legally owns it. Good thing she tweaked the first track. "Master Tape" by Rick Hautala first appeared in *100 Wicked Little Witch Stories* (1995).

Portland, Congress Street, Green Hand Bookshop – Hidden behind the stacks of books at the Green Hand bookstore is owner Michelle Souliere. In addition to serving as a guardian of the works of such local notable authors such as Rick Hautala and Glen Chadborne, Souliere is the author and editor of the award-winning Strange Maine blog and the *Strange Maine Gazette*, its print offshoot. Souliere has also published the crème de la crème of odd from her blog as the book *Strange Maine: True Tales from the Pine Tree State* (2010).

Portland, Congress Street, Monjoy Hill – Manda Simoneau lives on Congress in the Monjoy Hill area and works for a bookstore chain. She has special ordered an expensive book that her boss demands she either buy it or send it back. Manda returns *Psychic Black Holes* to the publisher only to have it repeatedly sent back to the store. Now different aspects of Manda's life seem to be disappearing. "Non-returnable" by Rick Hautala was originally published in *Shelf Life*, 2002.

Portland, Coyne Street – In *Ghost Light* (1993) by Rick Hautala, Cindy Toland flees Nebraska with her murdered sister's children, pursued cross-country by her psychotic brother-in-law Alex Harris. Their first attempt at a normal life in Portland is cut short by the arrival of Alex. In the middle of the night, they flee to a cabin in the woods. See also **Little Sebago Lake**.

Portland, Deering Park – Marie is an art student who comes upon an old woman feeding crows in the park. Marie begins to paint the charming scene but the old woman is not amused, accusing Marie of stealing her image. As Marie packs up, the old woman levels a curse on her. Later, as Marie continues work on the painting, the image seems to change. And when bad things happen to Marie, they are mirrored on her son Conner. When the curse is complete, it's not the old woman in the painting. "Portrait of an Old Lady with Crows" by Peter N. Dudar appeared in *Wicked Witches* (2016).

Portland, Evergreen Cemetery – Author and playwright Charles W. Goddard (1879-1951) is buried in a family plot in Evergreen Cemetery. He is best remembered for writing the play that would become *The Perils of Pauline* (1914) the archetype "damsel in distress" film that proved serials could be successful. But before Pauline was hanging off cliffs, Goddard and co-writer Paul Dickey premiered *The Ghost Breaker* on Broadway. The play was not successful, closing at the Lyceum in May 1913 after a two-month run. It would prove far more successful as a film script. The film version of *The Ghost Breaker* (1914), directed by Cecil B. DeMille, was one of the first films in the "haunted house" genre. The film was remade several times. First in 1922, then again in 1940 as *Ghost Breakers* with Bob Hope and Paulette Goddard, and then as *Scared Stiff* (1953) with Dean Martin and Jerry Lewis.

Portland, Exchange Street – As the sun sets in Portland, a woman is recounting a horrible incident in a local restaurant. She was at a table with her husband when she recognized a deceased friend at a nearby table. To her horror, she realizes all the other patrons are people she knew that are deceased. Only after she has fled the bistro does she recall her husband is also dead. "Worst Fears" by Rick Hautala first appeared in *Gothic Ghosts* (1997).

Portland, Great Diamond Island – Great Diamond is an island in Casco Bay, across from Portland but considered within city limits. Great Diamond was the final home of actress Nancy Hsueh (1941-1980). To horror aficionados, she will always be remembered for her role as Jenny, the straight-talking personal assistant to aging horror star Byron Orlok (Boris Karloff) in *Targets* (1968). As Orlok prepares to make his final public appearance at a drive-in showing his final film, he bemoans to Jenny that he is an anachronism – monster movies are tame compared to the real-life violence of the modern world. As Orlok arrives at the theater, old school horror and real-life monsters collide in the guise of Bobby Thompson

(Tim O'Kelly), a sniper who has climbed the screen for a shooting spree. His targets include Jenny and Orlok.

Portland, High Street – The final scene of *Night of the Living Deb* (2015) takes place on the roof of the Westin Portland Harborview on High Street. Deb (Maria Thayer) and Ryan (Michael Cassidy) are trapped on the roof by the zombie hordes. Like any good romantic comedy, it ends with fireworks – just not in the usual way. See also **Andy's Old Port Pub, Commercial Street, Portland**.

Portland, Holiday Inn – In Rick Hautala's short story "Sources of the Nile" (*Masques #4*, 1991), a maniacal ommetaphiliac meets a victim in the parking lot of the Holiday Inn with tear-filled results.

Portland, India Street – Ryan (Michael Cassidy) has escaped his one-night stand (Maria Thayer) and has stopped in Coffee by Design for his morning brew in *Night of the Living Deb* (2015). Unfortunately, Ryan's favorite coffee shop loses its luster when he finds the barista (Ned Donovan) chewing on a previous customer. See also **Andy's Old Port Pub, Commercial Street, Portland**.

Portland, Mark's Topless Donut Shop – White Devil is having coffee with a friend at his favorite donut shop. He decides to buy a retired Korean War vet at the bar a drink at the exact same moment the World Trade Towers in NYC are attacked. As the customers look on in horror and shock, White Devil turns to each of them and accuses them of the sins they've kept buried. "Coffee with White Devil" by Peter Dudar debuted in his collection *Dolly and Other Stories* (2013).

Portland, Pine Groves Nursing and Convalescent Home – Mark has relocated to Portland to keep an eye on his elderly father. Mark's childhood was marred by abuse; now he's repaying his father with his careful selection of the old man's nursing home. "Live With it" by Holly Newstein appeared in *Wicked Tales* (2015).

Portland, Shore Drive – Newlywed Lara DeSalvo moves into her husband Vincent's home on Shore Drive only to be terrorized at night by ghostly visits and stalked by day by a shadowy figure. Her husband is also changing from a loving husband into a cold controlling stranger in Rick Hautala's *Shades of Night* (1995) and now Lara must solve buried secrets or join them.

Portland, Southern Maine Osteopathic Hospital – Judy Morrow is a nurse on the swing shift in the obstetrics wing at Osteo. Babies across the nation are starting to be born with no fingerprints and dead eyes. Doctor Thomas Jacobs is convinced the universe has run out of souls and these children are the result. And now, his wife is expecting in Rick Hautala's "Every Mothers' Son," originally published in *Maine Impressions*, March 1987.

Portland, Spring Street – Annik Miller inherits her great-aunt's house on Spring Street in Ann Brahms' novel *Run for Your Life* (1993). She uses the windfall to escape Boston and a stalker. When the stalker follows her to Portland, she flees to her great aunt's cabin on secluded **Wytopitlock Lake**.

Portland, Longfellow Square – Located at State Street and Congress, a half-mile down Congress from his childhood home, the square is home to Portland's monument to her favorite son, poet Henry Wadsworth Longfellow (1807-1882). The bronze statue is about 7-feet tall, atop a 10-foot pedestal. It depicts Longfellow sitting in a chair reviewing a manuscript. One of the popular "Fireside Poets," he wrote extensively about history, folklore and folk-legends, which gave him latitude for supernatural elements. His "The Skeleton in Armor" (*Knickerbocker Magazine*, January 1841) is narrated by a Viking ghost telling why he built the Newport

Tower in Rhode Island. It was considered sufficiently preternatural that Virgil Finlay included it in his poetry series in *Weird Tales* (June 1938). See also **Wadsworth-Longfellow House, Portland; Western Cemetery, Portland**.

Portland, Thompson's Point Road – Thompson Point is the new home of the International Cryptozoology Museum. Founded in Maine in 2003 by leading cryptozoologist and prolific author Loren Coleman, the collection includes life-size models of a Bigfoot, a coelacanth, and an unrivaled collection of mysterious hominid footprints, spoor, and hair samples. The collection is a serious, educational discussion of the existence of animals, unverified by science but evidenced by reports within the creature's local community, such as the Yeti, Lake Monsters, and Sea Serpents. You'll know you're near the museum when you see the 9-foot tall, 800 lb., wooden Bigfoot sculpture, created by chainsaw artist Snuffy Destefano.

Portland, University of Southern Maine – In the first novel based on White Wolf's "Wraith the Oblivion" RPG, Rick Hautala's *Beyond the Shroud* (1995) tells the tale of wraith David Robinson who is trying to cope with being newly dead even as he must deal with a talisman that could change the Shadowlands forever. The talisman is a knife owned by Jack the Ripper and the target is Robinson's former wife, a librarian at USM.

Portland, Wadsworth-Longfellow House – Henry Wadsworth Longfellow (1807-1882), grew up in the 1785 house on Congress Street that is now the oldest standing structure in Portland and the home of the Maine Historical Society. Longfellow spent his childhood here and returned to the Congress Street home regularly throughout his life. Longfellow, besides reinvigorating interest in the Norse discovery of America, frequently introduced the supernatural into his work. In "Haunted Houses," part of the collection *The Courtship of Miles Standish, and other Poems* (1838), Longfellow advises his readers that "All houses wherein men have lived and died/Are haunted houses." His 1855 epic poem "The Song of Hiawatha" weaves a tale based on the legends and lore of the Ojibwe Indian tribe, including supernatural adventure. He also touched upon the Salem Witch Trials in "Giles Corey of the Salem Farms," a section of his *New England Tragedies,* a verse drama history of Christianity in the style of a medieval mystery play. Even his wildly popular *Tales of a Wayside Inn* (1863) includes "The Mother's Ghost." See also **Longfellow Square, Portland**.

Portland, Western Cemetery – Western Cemetery is the final resting place of John Neal (1793-1876), an important voice in 19th-century literature both as a writer and critic. As editor of *The Yankee and Boston Literary Gazette*, Neal promoted the writings of Poe, Hawthorne, and Longfellow during the early stages of their careers. As an author, his most widely acclaimed tale was *Rachel Dyer* (1828), a gothic novel about the life of a Salem witch.

The unexpectedly empty family tomb of the Longfellow family.
Photo courtesy of Michelle Souliere.

Western Cemetery was also home to the granite tomb housing Stephen and Zilpha Longfellow, parents of the poet Longfellow. But, in the summer of 1986, city workers open the crypt to remove the old iron gate and brick up the door. Longfellow's parents, two brothers, an aunt, and an infant grandniece were supposed to be entombed there. Instead, the tomb was empty. There were no signs of vandalism and the padlock was still locked. It is assumed the remains were transferred to some other burial spot, but there is no record. The Longfellow descendants and the City remain perplexed. See also **Longfellow Square, Portland**.

Portland, Western Prom – Across from the historic Western Promenade public park, Western Prom is a street of elegant Victorian mansions, including number 155. This stately brick home was used as a filming location, both interior and exterior for *Night of the Living Deb* (2015). Deb (Maria Thayer) and Ryan (Michael Cassidy), fleeing the zombie apocalypse, reach the fortified house of Ryan's father Frank (Ray Wise). Frank seems to know more about the zombie outbreak than expected, and even worse, Ryan's ex-fiancée (Syd Wilder) has also sought refuge here. As far as Deb is concerned, being out among the walking dead is looking better and better. See also **Andy's Old Port Pub, Commercial Street, Portland**.

Potowonket – In August of 1913, a meteorite landed in the sea off the coast of Potowonket. When it is dredged ashore, a notebook was found embedded in the rock. Impervious to damage or chemical analysis, the notebook was filled with text written in classical Greek. "The Green Meadow," originally published in the Spring 1927 edition of W. Paul Cook's amateur journal, *The Vagrant*, was co-written by H. P. Lovecraft and Winifred V. Jackson as Elizabeth Neville Berkley and Lewis Theobald, Jr.

Pownal – In the near future of Stephen King's *The Long Walk* (1979), published as Richard Bachman, one hundred boys are selected to enter an annual contest where the winner will be awarded whatever he wants for the rest of his life. The game is simple – out-walk the other contestants while maintaining a steady pace without stopping. Three warnings and they shoot you. The narrator of the novel is Ray Garraty from the outskirts of Pownal. As the only Maine contestant, he is the crowd favorite for the first 350 miles of the trek that starts in the northeast corner of Maine and ends when there's only one contestant still alive. See also **Woolman's Free Trade Center Market, Freeport; Limestone; Route 2A, Hainesville; Stillwater River.**

Pownal, Birches Cemetery – Stephen King's *The Dead Zone* (1979) ends with Sarah Hazlett visiting Johnny Smith's grave. Whether Johnny's sacrifice will prevent the Armageddon he foresaw remains to be seen. See also **Cleaves Mills.**

Preacher's Corners – In Steven King's novella "Jerusalem's Lot," first anthologized in *Night Shift* (1978), the locals in the village of Preacher's Corners are justifiably a little nervous. Charles Boone has moved into Chapelwaite, the Boone family mansion overlooking the Atlantic. There he is slowly pulled into a world of insanity and the supernatural as he explores his family's cursed past in the house. See also **Jerusalem's Lot.**

Presumpscot River – Each night for the last three years, John Newcomb walks halfway across an old black iron railroad bridge outside of town, gazing down at the river and mourning his dead family. Lately, someone has been watching from the end of the bridge. Could it be Death himself? "Black Iron" by Rick Hautala first appeared in the anthology *In Delirium 2* (2007).

Rafford – A construction crew uncovers a massive rune stone next to a skeleton wrapped in silver chains in *Talons* (1993) by John Peel. An archaeologist and Kari, a local teen, uncover small silver figures and a Norse village model. The silver figure is stolen and Kari is having nightmares of a winged monster.

Does this have anything to do with the increase in the mortality rate in a local burglary ring?

Rangeley – The 175-acre Wilhelm Reich Museum is the former home, library, and laboratory of Austrian-born psychoanalyst Wilhelm Reich (1897-1957). Reich studied with Freud in the 1920s but drifted from mainstream science. It was here that his newfound studies culminated in the establishment of the Orgone Energy Observatory. Orgone energy was Reich's theorized hypothetical universal life force. Reich believed that a lack of internal orgone was the cause of many diseases. To combat these shortages, he designed "orgone accumulators," essentially large wooden boxes with a chair inside. Research screeched to a stop when the U.S. Food and Drug Administration arrested him for making false health claims and destroyed all orgone-related materials at the institute. Orgone accumulators were used by several prominent authors, most notably William S. Burroughs and J. D. Salinger. But orgone didn't seep into horror until the 80s band Devo started wearing their iconic red "energy domes" in concert, designed to recycle orgone energy escaping through the head. With or without their domes, Devo provided five songs for the soundtrack of *Slaughterhouse Rock* (1988) starring Toni Basil as the ghost of a heavy metal vocalist who tries to help a man whose brother has been possessed by a cannibal demon on Alcatraz. Devo also contributed songs to the films *Tank Girl* (1995) and *Dr. Jekyll and Ms. Hyde* (1995).

Repentance – Regis Hardy's dreams of being a pulp writer have all come true except for a collection of his works in book form. When a publisher offers to publish the collection, Hardy leaps at the chance. He flies to Maine to meet the publisher and the cover artist Simeon Dimsby. He soon learns the difference between writing weird fiction and experiencing the weird is a fine line. "Simeon Dimsby's Workshop" by Richard A. Lupoff first published in the NecronomiCon 2001 program book.

Riker's Valley – The 1995 movie version of the King short story "The Mangler" was directed by Tobe Hooper and starred Robert Englund. The setting was moved to Riker's Valley, a rural town that boldly and over-optimistically called itself the "Industrial Heart of Maine." See also **Chamberlain Center**.

Riverston – Fran Thomas is a burnt out LA journalist who returns to his hometown to savor small town life as a reporter for the local paper. He covers the death of the town drunk in neighboring Steel Harbor. The official verdict is heart failure, but the hermit who found the body says the body was attacked by a pack of supposedly extinct wolves in *Winter Wolves* (1989) by Earle Wescott. See also **Channel Islands; Steel Harbor**.

Rock Harbor – Using filming locations throughout Massachusetts and New Hampshire, the fictional upscale seaside town of Rock Harbor was created. Mark Evans (Elijah Wood) is sent to Maine to stay with relatives after his mother's death. It is there he meets evil incarnate in the form of his cousin Henry (Macaulay Culkin) in *The Good Son* (1993).

Rockland – Knox County Superior Court on Union Street, built in 1874, was briefly transported to Connecticut as a filming location for 1996 movie version of Stephen King's 1984 novel *Thinner*. In a pivotal scene, attorney Billy Halleck (Robert John Burke) is exonerated by Judge Rossington (John Horton) after killing a gypsy woman crossing the street. Her father Tadzu Lempke (Michael Constantine) is so angry he places a curse of the obese lawyer. If the judge looks familiar, it may be because the actor's previous film role was as the judge who sentenced Andy Dufresne (Tim Robbins) to life in the film version of Stephen King's *The Shawshank Redemption* (1994). See also **Elm Street, Camden**.

Rockport – The workers on the night shift at the fish cannery have a lot in common; they're all working there as part of their rehabilitation after fatal accidents in "Recovery" by Christopher Fahy, first published in Fahy's short story collection *Matinee at the Flame* (2006).

Rockport, Carleton Shipyard – Melanie Gierek walks through the night from her abandoned car in Camden in order to take work on the schooner *Louisa Lee*, a 19th-century sailing vessel. Now she finds herself trapped on a ship with a malevolent presence of its own and to save her life, she must seek answers in the ship's past in Erin Patrick's novel *Moontide* (2001). See also **Camden**.

Rockport, Seacrest – Seacrest, is a top secret Naval Intelligence research facility, disguised as a dilapidated estate on the coast, north of Rockport. Parapsychologist Dr. Sarah Stuart "volunteers" to bring her senior staff to Seacrest for a project. Andrei Illich Itzhevnikov is a high-ranking Soviet official who defected to the West. He's also quite dead from the defection's failure. Dr. Stuart and her team are going to attempt to raise the ghost of Itzhevnikov, or "It," so they can still debrief the defector. They are successful, which turns out to have been a very bad idea in the Raymond Hawkey novel *It* (1984).

Rockport Harbor – In the film *Casper* (1995), Kat Harvey (Christina Ricci) and her father (Bill Pullman), a ghost therapist, arrive in Friendship to exorcize the ghosts. The harbor in the distance is actually Rockport Harbor. See **Friendship**.

Rockwell – In October 1957, the USSR launched Sputnik, which did nothing to alleviate the creeping paranoia of the Red Menace. Nine-year-old Hogarth Hughes (voiced by Eli Marienthal) sees a falling star crash into the forest. Instead of a meteorite, Hogarth finds a giant robot (voiced by Vin Diesel). Now the government is investigating, and Hogarth must protect the childlike robot in the animated classic *The*

Iron Giant (1999). The movie was based on the children's book *The Iron Man* (1968) by British Poet Laureate Ted Hughes.

Rocky Rhodes – Dennis Clarke spins out on a snow covered road after swerving to avoid a woman in the road wearing a thin white dress, oblivious to the storm and cold. He takes her into the nearby town of Rocky Rhodes to seek help. The next day, his car is found in the middle of the road, full of blood and no sign of the Good Samaritan or the passenger. As *Woman in White* (2016) by Kristin Dearborn progresses, we learn Dennis wasn't the first or the last disappearance, and all of the missing persons were men.

Rocky Terrace – When Rose Hilary inherits the sprawling estate along the Maine coast, she also inherits the family curse. Now amid premonitions and specters, she must solve an ancient family disappearance and lift the curse. *The Twilight Web* (1968) was written by W. E. D. Ross. One of his other aliases was Marilyn Ross, author of 32 *Dark Shadows* novels set down the coast in Collinsport.

Roodsford – Robert Bloch introduces us to the backcountry village of Roodsford in "Satan's Servants." Lovecraft offered some revisionary notes, including moving Roodsford to Maine. First appearing in the Arkham House anthology *Something about Cats and Other Pieces* (1949), Celtic witches are planning to sacrifice children to Shub-niggurath and have apparently found a local source. See also **Wells**.
The search for sacrificial fodder continues in Bloch's *Weird Tales*, May 1951 story "Notebook Found in a Deserted House." Willie Osborne is a 12-year old orphan sent to live in the same hills he was warned about by his late parents. Now he battles to survive his cultist kinfolk with tree shoggoth minions who think Willie will do quite as nicely blood offerings go.

Saco River – In the 1670s, a sachem, angered by settlers, cursed the river to claim the lives of three white men each year. In

2012, the embodiment of that curse, a self-aware giant snakehead fish, lost control of itself and slaughtered all of Bernie Garfield's friends. Bernie was spared because of a loophole – he's black. The snakehead senses Bernie is coming back but doesn't know he's brought a hired gun, an eccentric hunter who calls himself The Black Rider. The quest for revenge escalates into a mission to save the world from something even worse in *Snakehead* (2015) by Eric Dimbleby.

Sagadahoc County – Artie has a dairy farm out in the boondocks. When he kills a kitten, he discovers that cats have nine lives and karma has a long memory in "Emmett" by Dahlov Ipcar, first anthologized in *The Nightmare and Her Foal* (1990).

Sagadahoc River – See **Lambardton**.

St. Agatha – A social call turns into a battle of survival when a scientist decides to expand his mind control experiments to humans in "Death Is a White Rabbit" by Frederic Brown, first published in *Strange Detective Mysteries*, January 1942.

St. Ann's – Rick Hautala's novel *Night Stone* (1986) tells of the Inman family who moves into their ancestral home at the foot of Hunter Hill. Soon, the family is embroiled in a battle against the supernatural side effects of having an astronomically aligned stone circle and a sacrificial table in your backyard, both of which are remnants of a Paleolithic Indian death cult. See also **York High School**.

St. Eustace Island – St. Eustace Island is a small island located off the coast of Collinsport. Upon the island are the ruins of an abandoned chapel, where the relapsed vampire Barnabas Collins (Jonathan Frid) brings the reincarnation of his beloved Josette (Kathryn Leigh Scott). Instead of a wedding, the lovelorn bloodsucker finds denouement in *House of Dark Shadows* (1970), the film version of the TV series. The filming location for the abandoned monastery was actually the

Lockwood-Mathews Mansion in Norwalk, Connecticut. See also **Collinsport**.

'Salem's Lot – See **Jerusalem's Lot**.

Sanctuary – See **Dutch Island**.

Sanford – Trisha McFarland lives in Sanford with her mother and brother. They moved to Maine after her parents' divorce in Stephen King's *The Girl Who Loved Tom Gordon* (1999). Her family seems to be getting along better, now that she's lost in the woods being threatened by an unseen menace. See **Motton**.

Saxham Island – In *Isle of the Whisperers* (1999) by Hugh B. Cave, Saxham Island is a summer resort, sparsely populated in the off-season. Looking for petroglyphs in the caves on the island, archeologist Martha Rowe accidentally breaks the seal on a rune that has kept demons at bay for millennia. Now, with most of the locals under demonic control, she must rally the survivors and find a way to again close the passage before they too are possessed.

Schooner Bay – Overlooking the harbor outside of the fishing village of Schooner Bay is Gull Cottage, built in the previous century by Captain Daniel Gregg. Captain Gregg still haunts the cottage which he begrudgingly shares with young widow Mrs. Muir and her family in the television series *The Ghost and Mrs. Muir* (1968-1970). The show was based on the 1947 movie version starring Rex Harrison, which was based on the 1945 novel of the same name written by Josephine Leslie under the pseudonym R. A. Dick. Both previous incarnations were set in England.

Secret Cove – Teri MacIver is a 14-year-old who kills her mother and stepfather in a house fire. After the "unfortunate accident," she is sent to live with her father and abusive stepmother in the secluded and wealthy community of Secret Cove. Her half-sister Melissa has her own secret – an invisible friend who helps her survive her mother's punishment. Teri decides to eliminate Melissa and enjoy the life she believes she's entitled to. Unfortunately for Teri, Melissa's invisible friend is actually a ghost with her own agenda in John Saul's *Second Child* (1990).

Setauket Point – See **Barsham Harbor**.

Shadow Creek – Eddie Townsend was a naval officer who fell in love with Jasmine, a stripper in the Philippines. He learns too late she wasn't even human, by which time he was complicit in the death of several pregnant women on his base. The only way to stop her was to kill her. Now Eddie is the town drunk in his fishing village hometown. Now things are happening in Shadow Creek that Eddie remembers. Now he fears he didn't actually kill Jasmine, and she's followed him from the Philippines in *Bleeding the Vein* (2012) by T. G. Arsenault.

Shaker Harbor – Justin is like a godson to his neighbor Winter, and he is the one that helps Winter build a new house for Winter's new bride. Vala is from Iceland and is not familiar with trees, but she is well versed in the lore of the Huldufólk and the rocks. When a ruthless millionaire is threatening the last of the local old growth forest, Vala's quirky ways may be useful to save the trees in "Winter's Wife" by Elizabeth Hand. The story first appeared in *Wizards* (2007).

Shawshank Maximum Security Prison – Banker Andy Dufresne is falsely convicted of murdering his wife and her lover. The story "Rita Hayworth and Shawshank Redemption" takes place between 1947and 1975 and is told by Red Redding, another lifer at the prison. The original Stephen King novella was published in *Different Seasons* (1982). The novella was adapted for the screen in 1994 as *The Shawshank Redemption* with Tim Robbins as Andy Dufresne and Morgan Freeman as

Red Redding. The Ohio State Reformatory stood in for the Maine prison.

Based on the former Maine State Prison in Thomaston, the prison is as much a staple of King's Maine as his towns of Castle Rock and Derry, appearing in such diverse works as the TV series *The Dead Zone*, the novel *IT* (1986), and the Richard Bachman novel *Blaze* (2007).

Shaymore – The "Arrowhead Project" is a secret project suspected of being under the control of U.S. Department of Scientific Intelligence, better known to Stephen King readers simply as "The Shop." The project was located in a research facility in Shaymore, just close enough to Bridgton that when the events in King's novella "The Mist" (*Dark Forces*, 1980) are unfolding, the mysterious Arrowhead Project is assumed to be the source. See also **Long Lake, Bridgton**.

Based on the Shop's track record, Bridgtonians may not be incorrect. The Shop was the agency tasked with capturing the pyrokinetic child Charlie McGee in *Firestarter* (1980) and were sent to investigate the aftermath of events in *The Tommyknockers* (1987). The Shop also underwrote the experiments that resulted in the 1991 miniseries *Golden Years*. None of these projects ended well.

Shaysville – First published in the Joseph Payne Brennan anthology of short stories *The Borders Just Beyond* (1986), "The Blizzard of Shaysville" tells the tale of Mr. Slaton, hired as a personal secretary to a wealthy merchant. Now he is in an isolated village in northwestern Maine riding to a mansion that is no longer there.

Sheep's Head Island – See **Lake Onwego**.

Silk Island – See **Kennequit**.

Skowhegan – Settler's Wall is located along the road to Skowhegan. A local curiosity, the ten-foot high wall is apparently a Downeast example of non-Euclidean geometry: the wall has only one side and trying to cross the wall brings you right back where you started. "Settler's Wall" was originally published as "The Long Wall" in *Stirring Science Stories,* March 1942 by Robert A. W. Lowndes under the pen name Wilfred Owen Morley.

Ben Jacobs has been saying that things in central Maine aren't like they used to be. But in the last 24 hours, the murders make it seem that things have hit the point of no return in "Flash Point" by Gardner Dozois, which first appeared in *Orbit #13,* 1974.

Smoke Island – In *The Shapechanger* (1989) by Elizabeth Ergas, Smoke Island is a small island off the coast of Puffin Landing and the former home of artist Lothar Voss. Voss's studio is there, and his estate has allowed two other artists to use the island for inspiration. Neither sabbatical ended well. It seems that Iye, an evil Algonquin shaman shapechanger, was imprisoned on the island in the distant past. Now artist Chip Windsor and his wife have arrived and Iye is slowly regaining the powers he lost millennia before.

Smuttynose Island — On March 6, 1873, Louis Wagner rowed to Smuttynose from Portsmouth, New Hampshire. His plan was rob the home of John Hontvet while Hontvet, his brother, and his brother-in-law were on the mainland. Having previously lived and worked for Hontvet, Wagner was well aware that the house was still occupied by Maren Hontvet, her sister Karen Christensen, and her sister-in-law Anethe Christensen. Wagner broke into the house, killed Anethe with an axe and strangled Karen, by which time Maren had escaped. With Maren as an eye witness, Wagner was soon caught, tried and hanged. The murders continue to fascinate and have been the subject of a variety of works, including the 24-verse "Ballad of Louis Wagner" by John Parrault, and the essay "A Memorable Murder" by poetess Celia Thaxter (*Atlantic Monthly,* May 1875). See also **Thomaston**.

Esau Eldridge was the controversial painter who worked and lived in a lighthouse on Smuttynose Island in Will Murray's short story "The Eldridge Collection," first published in *Disciples of Cthulhu II* (2003). The secret Cryptic Events Evaluation Section of the National Reconnaissance Office has been tracking his paintings for years. Now, it appears the cursed paintings have been collected in one place, for purposes unknown.

South Berwick, Portland Street – All the homes of author Sarah Orne Jewett (1849-1909) are located along Portland Street. Jewett, a New England regionalist writer noted for her realistic settings, also wrote a number of dark fantasy and supernatural themed short stories during her career, including witchcraft in "In Dark New England Days" (*Century Magazine,* October 1890), curses in "The Landscape Chamber" (*Atlantic Monthly,* November 1887) and magic in "The Green Bowl" (*New York Herald,* November 3, 1901). See also **Deephaven; Dunnett Landing; Mount Agamenticus.**

The Jewett-Eastman House at 37 Portland Street is now South Berwick Public Library but was formerly the childhood home of Jewett. The Sarah Orne Jewett House at 5 Portland Street is a museum open seasonally. It was in this home that Jewett did most of her writing. Located just off Portland Street on Agamenticus Road is the Portland Street Cemetery, Sarah Orne Jewett's final home - the Jewett family plot.

South Berwick, Witchtrot Hill – On April 30, 1692, former Salem, Massachusetts minister George Burroughs, now living in Wells, was accused of witchcraft. Since Burroughs was obviously evil, constables were sent to Wells to arrest and return him to Salem for trial. Adding to the arresting officers' nervousness, Maine was still prone to attacks in the French & Indian Wars. So the constables decided to avoid the heavily traveled coastal road and decided to travel a less frequented path through the woods. Halfway through the forest, a storm arose, terrifying the constables and spooking their horses.

Lightning struck a tree nearby, which would not help Burrough's defense, and the horses took off at a trot. Ever since that incident both the hill and the road have borne the name Witchtrot. See also **Post Road, Wells**.

South Freeport – After debilitating abuse by his father, Clayton Blaisdell, Jr. is made a ward of the state and sent to Hetton House in South Freeport, a state home for boys. When not being beaten by the sadistic administrator, the boys are farmed out to locals as hired help. Years later, after blowing his cover in the Gerard kidnapping, Blaze would flee back to the abandoned Hetton House try and hide the baby for a few more days *in Blaze* (2007) by Stephen King, writing as Richard Bachman. See also **Apex; Ocoma Heights; Brighton Avenue, Portland**.

South Portland, High Street – Following the death of Engineman First Class Jensen during a rescue, the Coast Guard cutter Adrian, berthed at the Coast Guard Base in South Portland, is haunted by the crew's speculation on how Jensen died. It is also haunted by something less contemplative and more spectral in *The Jonah Watch* (1981) by Jack Cady.

South Portland, Maine Mall – Mike Berger is terrified of appliances and his technophobia in full force when he's forced to go Christmas shopping. A panic attack leaves him regrouping in a chair that turns out to be a blood pressure testing machine. And the chair doesn't seem to like him much either in Rick Hautala's "Off the Cuff," originally published in *Fang*, April 1992.

A blizzard is approaching Portland, but it doesn't matter to Meg Clarke. She's volunteered to spend the night in her aunt's music store at the mall with a small crew of employees doing inventory. But once the doors are locked and the snow makes the roads impassable, ghostly faces and messages begin to appear in windows. Soon Meg and the others are trapped in the store by things that should not exist. Meg has kept a terrible secret to herself for a year. Tonight, that secret demands resolution. And survival may mean trying to stay alive out in the blizzard. *Chills* by Rick Hautala was published in 2013.

South Portland, Montressor Chemical Company – Claire McMullen hates her job at the chemical plant, isn't that crazy about her roommate, and just wants to settle down with a nice guy. "Mr. Right" turns out to be Samael – tall, rich, handsome, and a demon. Rick Hautala offers a horror writer's take on an urban paranormal romance in *The Demon's Wife* (2013).

South Portland, Old Settlers Cemetery – The cemetery is South Portland's oldest landmark, established in 1658. It is where 16-year old Abigail Cummings was buried after she died in a shipwreck off the coast. Abby has been dead for a century, but not at peace. She is awakened from her slumber by the song of the mockingbird, a summons to help recently departed spirits come to terms with their own death in what she calls the Dead Lands. Here, she sleeps in a netherworld version of her cemetery until called. *The Dead Lands: A Mockingbird Bay Mystery* (2014) was planned as the first in a series of young adult mysteries with a supernatural background. Instead, it was author Rick Hautala's final novel.

Southwest Harbor – Southwest Harbor is a town on the "quiet side" of Mount Desert Island. The quaint storefronts along Main Street were transformed into a fishing village for Stephen King's TV miniseries *Storm of the Century* (1999). See **Little Tall Island**.

Spreewald – Benny picks up a hitchhiker on the road in Spreewald. Instead of a ride, he gives her a tranquilizer dart in the throat. Benny brings the drugged girl to his special room, a homemade surgical suite. Benny likes to torture girls and watch them struggle and beg. Benny has made a grievous error this time and his "victim" is Valerie Redfern, who is going to demonstrate to (and on) Benny what it's like to be on the receiving end of his games. "Playmate Wanted" by Rob Smales first appeared in *Dark Moon Digest #5* (2011).

Taking a year off to hitchhike cross-country seemed like an adventure at the time. Now Tommy is in the backwoods of Maine and having second thoughts. A truck pulls up behind him and forces him off the shoulder into a drainage ditch. The passengers shine a spotlight, announces he's not the prey and drives off. Hidden in the deep grass on the side of the ditch is Sarah, hiding from her brothers and cousins. She's not a runaway – she's playing a game, a hide and seek type game. And in Spreewald, games during the full moon tend to have a toothsome ending. "Night Game" by Rob Smales appeared in *Demonic Visions: 50 Horror Tales #3* (2014).

David is on the cusp of adolescence and troubled by vivid dreams. But these are not puberty's wet dreams, these are more visceral. His father understands perfectly in "Spreewald Dreams" by Rob Smales. The story debuted in the anthology of stories by Post Mortem Press authors, *44 Lies by 22 Liars* (2016).

Spreewald, Palladium Theater – Valerie Redfern, her friend Hilary, and her mother go to see a movie. On the way back to the car, they are threatened by armed thugs. Trapped in an alley after a chase, it looks bad. But Valerie has a special set of skills, and she's not afraid to use them, especially the claws and fangs. "A Night at the Show" by Rob Smales first appeared in *Wicked Seasons* (2013).

Spreewald, Police Station – Carl Hickey and his grandson Kyle go to the police so Carl can confess to a crime. Carl claims he murdered the Spellman kid, a local boy who's missing. Carl also claims he is a werewolf and at the age of 70, has been having dreams of the moon and running with the pack. As he transforms in his cell, it is obvious Carl is a half-breed, not a full blood lycanthrope. The Police Chief is sympathetic. It's a leadership trait of an Alpha Male. "A Man Does What's Right" by Rob Smales first appeared in his collected works *Echoes of Darkness* (2016).

Squampottis Island – Early in his career, horror writer Brian McNaughton wrote cringe-worthy, mass market novels under a number of pen names. *Tide of Desire* was published in 1983 under one such pseudonym, Sheena Clayton. A struggling New York poetess, Antonia Shiel, receives an unexpected windfall – a grant from the Caleb Marsh Foundation to spend a year in a cabin on the island to work on her art. It turns out Caleb Marsh was the estranged brother of Obed Marsh of Innsmouth, Massachusetts. McNaughton, probably without the publisher's knowledge, created bodice-ripper that also functions as a sequel to H. P. Lovecraft's *The Shadow over Innsmouth* (1936).

Stage Island – See **Monument Island**.

Standish – Mark Hodgson climbed into a tree to rescue a kitten. He slipped and fell, getting his head lodged in the V of a branch. By the time rescuers arrived, he had strangled to death. This is the sort story reporter Jay "The Ghoul" Benson loved covering for his newspaper. When a Portland socialite falls out of her penthouse, Benson sneaks in to get a photo from her balcony. He's about to discover how easily his sort of headline can be written in "Burning Man Decapitated in Fatal Fall" by Rick Hautala. The story first appeared in *Shroud Magazine* #6 (Spring 2009).

Steel Harbor – *Riverston Register* reporter Fran Thomas is investigating reports of a wolf pack attacking the locals in Steel Harbor. Wolves have been extinct for decades in Maine, but that doesn't seem to be slowing down the body count in *Winter Wolves* (1989) by Earle Wescott. See also **Riverston**.

Stillwater River – In Stephen King's *The Long Walk* (1979), published as Richard Bachman, the dwindling population of walkers cross the Stillwater at Old Town. This is a long anticipated benchmark in the walk, not because of the river, but because it means the route switches from the torturous hills to the flat Maine Turnpike. See also **Pownal**.

The Stillwater Slasher, named after the river where he dumped his 18 victims in Rick Hautala's short story "Rubies and Pearls" (*Predators,* 1993), has a near-death experience and discovers prison is not the worst punishment he has waiting. See also **Warren**.

Stockton Harbor – From a lighthouse in Stockton Harbor and down the East Coast, people are suffering from amnesia. All were listening to the shortwave radio at the same frequency. Now it's up to the Fringe team to determine if it's a fluke or a harbinger of something far more serious in "6955 kHz" (3:06), a third season episode of *Fringe.*

Stockton Springs – When 10-year-old Tiffany Blair removes a finger bone of a Native shaman skeleton from an ancient Indian burial ground, it unleashes a curse upon Stockton Springs. Now a lupine elemental spirit is loose in the area, driving the residents to commit unspeakable acts of evil in Jessica Palmer's *Shadow Dance* (1994).

Storybrooke – The fantasy drama *Once Upon a Time* is set in the seaside town of Storybrooke, the townsfolk are actually fairy tale and fictional characters who were transported to the "real world" and robbed of their memories, courtesy of the evil queen. Since it runs on the ABC TV network, which is owned by Disney, the Disneyfied version of fairy tale characters are used. This also explains how Anna and Elsa from *Frozen* (2013) can appear with such characters as Rumpelstiltskin and Henry Jekyll.

Stratford – Kiera Davis is seeing things. Her visions involve an accident thirty years ago when her boyfriend was killed. Now, people associated with the accident are starting to die. Things continue to spiral out of control as dead boyfriends return and she meets her twin, created when trauma split her personality into two different people in *Unbroken* (2007) by Rick Hautala writing as A.J. Matthews.

Stroudwater River – Running Road Hill Bridge crosses the Stroudwater near the Westbrook town line. Late one snowy evening, two men face fate in a deadly game of cause and effect in Rick Hautala's "A Little Bit of Divine Justice" (*Voices from the Night,* 1994).

Summerfield – In *Dark Silence* (1992) by Rick Hautala, Edward Fraser tries to sell off land only to see his son fall under a curse placed centuries before by a witch who vowed vengeance on anyone trying to profit from her stolen property.

Tarker Mills – A werewolf has come to Tarker's Mills and each full moon brings another grisly death. Marty Coslaw is a wheelchair-ridden 10-year-old and the only one who has survived an encounter with the killer in Stephen King's *Cycle of the Werewolf* (1984). But only the family black sheep Uncle Al believes Marty is still in danger. The 1985 film version, filmed in North Carolina, was re-titled *Silver Bullet* and starred Corey Haim as Marty and Gary Busey as Uncle Red.

Tarryton – An elderly spinster buys the abandoned lighthouse on Lighthouse Point and converts it into her retirement home. She hears long vanished seals on the rocks and meets an unexpected visitor of mythic proportions in "One Old Man, with Seals" by Jane Yolen, first published in *Neptune Rising* (1982).

Tashmore Glen – In Stephen King's novella "Secret Window, Secret Garden," first published in *Four Past Midnight* (1990), writer Mort Rainey moves into his summer cottage along the north bay of Tashmore Lake (not to be confused with another King location, Tashmore Pond in Vermont). There, he is confronted by John Shooter, who claims Mort stole one of his stories and demands justice. The story was the basis of the 2004 film *Secret Window* with Johnny Depp as the tormented Rainey, although the lake was moved from Western Maine to upstate New York. See also **Kansas Street, Derry**.

Technor – Billy Halleck has tracked the gypsies up the Eastern Seaboard, finally catching up with them outside of Bar Harbor in Technor. When the Taduz Lemke refuses to lift the curse he has placed on Halleck in Stephen King's 1984 novel *Thinner* (written as Richard Bachman), Billy places a curse on the gypsies. At the caravan's next stop in Bankerton, they would discover the lawyer is not joking. See also **Elm Street, Camden**.

Temple – Freya is a reporter in a news van with her cameraman Jared. They're on assignment, reporting on the severity of the Nor'easter hitting the area. Driving on Route 101, they narrowly miss a deer and spin out on the road, hitting a strange bump in the snow. After moving the van back, they find the bump is a body, frozen to the road. Freya recognizes the man from the last gas station they stopped at. As they climb the crest of a hill, they see the man's car rolled on its side, and road covered in additional frozen human moguls in "Shrouds of Snow" by Philip C. Perron. The story appeared in *Dark Passages 2* (2016).

Thomaston – In 2002, the Maine State Prison was closed and the prisoners moved to a new facility in nearby Warren. They left behind the old prison burial ground where the unclaimed remains of prisoners were interred. The oldest marker in the fenced-in lot is Louis H. F. Wagner, who was hanged for the murders of Karen Christensen, and her sister-in-law Anethe Christensen. See also **Smuttynose Island**.

Thornton – The town of Thornton, nestled along the Saco River, is where Kip Howard's parents buy land on Kaulback Road for a new family home. While clearing brush, they discover an old cellar hole reputed to be that of a colonial witch. *Little Brothers* (1988) is the introduction of Rick Hautala's *Untcigahunk*, "Little Brothers" of Indian lore, creatures who emerge from underground every five years. Kip's mother was killed by the malevolent creatures and Kip has struggled to recall the events of that day. It's been five years and now the cycle of death is about to begin again.

In the anthology *Night Visions 9* (1991), Hautala established a mythological background by introducing three short stories written in the style of recorded Indian tales: "Little Brother," "Little Brother Speaks," and "Redman."

Thornton, Clay Farm – Old Man Clay has a barn with an ancient stone tunnel beneath it. His grandson Tyler and his buddy Chuckie are fascinated by the tunnel and an iron gate that keeps them out. In Rick Hautala's "Deal with the Devils," first published in *Night Visions 9* (1991), it's not what Clay is keeping out of the tunnel, but what he's keeping in.

Thornton, Cooking Pot Cove – Eric and Patty Strasser are camping along the Saco River at Cooking Pot Cove when they discover something that is not in the travel brochures – the *Untcigahunk*, fabled Indian folk creatures. Unfortunately, the legends are very true in Rick Hautala's *"The Birch Whistle,"* first published in *Night Visions 9* (1991).

Thornton, Dixon Oil Company – Ken Brewer's furnace cuts out at 4 AM during the first heavy snow of the season. That's bad. Even worse, the repairman isn't sure he has the part. But neither will be a real problem once they realize that the *Untcigahunk* have a tunnel into the cellar. "Oilman" by Rick Hautala debuted in his collection *Occasional Demons* (2009).

Thornton, Kaulback Road – Hautala would expand and embellish the *Untcigahunk* backstory in *Eulogies: A Horror World Yearbook 2005*. He creates a historical record with the

"The Witch House," the story of the original house on Kaulback Road.

Thornton, Pingree Park – The 1961 home run derby at Pingree Park is interrupted by the fire klaxon. Twelve-year-old Billy Crowell and his friends rush to protect the town from an approaching forest fire. Billy is separated from the group and lost deep in the forest, where he discovers that the fire is not what is terrifying the wildlife. Something else is loose in the woods - the *Untcigahunk*. Rick Hautala's novella *Indian Summer* (2012) was the author's last Little Brothers story.

Thornton, Route 25 – The State is finally straightening out Route 25 where it wraps around Watchick Hill on the south side of Thornton. Stan Walters explores the caves the construction opened on the hill. Instead of rocks for his collection, he finds a large cocoon with some sort of strange humanoid figure in it. "Chrysalis," first published in *Night Visions 9* (1991), continues Rick Hautala's saga of the tiny but vicious killing machines that are the *Untcigahunk*.
Meanwhile, on 25 North of Thornton, a prison work crew escapee and an archaeology team studying petroglyphs are on a collision course along the Saco River. Unfortunately for everyone involved, the *Untcigahunk* do not take prisoners. "Love on the Rocks" was first published in *Night Visions 9* (1991) and reprinted in *Wicked Tales* (2015).

Three Rivers – In the tranquil town of Three Rivers just outside of Augusta, Matt and Brenda Ireland have no peace. His ex-wife keeps attempting to break in and now they are being victimized by an ex-convict who shared a cell with a criminal that Matt sent to prison in the A. J. Matthews (Rick Hautala) novel *Looking Glass* (2004). See also **Warren**.

Tower Hill – A new semester starts in an isolated college town as *Tower Hill* (2008) by Sarah Pinborough begins. And with the new semester comes the new town priest and a new teacher.

Neither are who they claim to be. They are in search of ancient artifacts. Now the artifacts are changing into them something less than human, and are also exerting control over the townsfolk. Two incoming freshmen recognize something supernatural is happening, but how do you fight what you don't understand?

TR-90 – TR is a term used by the State of Maine to designate small, sparsely populated, unincorporated townships. On Stephen King's map of Maine, Township Region 90 includes **Dark Score Lake** and the town of **Motton**.

Tranquility – Tess Gerritsen's novel *Bloodstream* (1998) tells of recently widowed Dr. Claire Elliot, who thinks that moving to small town Maine will be a life better suited to raise her son. That decision is reconsidered about the same time a teenager randomly shoots a teacher in the middle of class. Soon, the town's teens are all committing violent crimes, just the way a teenage crime spree happened in town 50 years before.

Tuboise – Hugh and Angie returned from a trip to their home in the tiny village, but something isn't quite right. People seem to suddenly vanish, others silently scream in windows, and all the townsfolk are offering cryptic warnings. Now Angie has disappeared and Hugh realizes that nobody is who they appear to be in "Ghosts with Teeth" by Peter Crowther. The novella appeared in *A Book of Horrors* (2011).

Tucksport – See **Buck Cemetery, Bucksport**.

Unity – *Frankenstein: The Legacy* (2001) by Christopher Schildt finds FBI agent Susan Weaver in search of the diary of Victor Frankenstein, presumed lost in the fire that killed one of Frankenstein's followers, Daniel Levy, thirty years before. Things don't quite add up in the files, and the trail has led her to an isolated cabin in the wintry Maine woods.

University of Maine – See **University of Maine, Orono**.

Van Daam Landing – A man with a mysterious blood disease travels to a remote island where his ancestors lived, hoping to find a cure for his illness. It turns out the Van Daams were driven from Holland and chose the island to keep their bloodline pure. Now, centuries of inbreeding have driven the family underground, hideously malformed, hermaphroditic and carnivorous. When the local graveyard is disturbed, the primary food supply of the creatures gets shut off. Now, there is going to be a family reunion of sorts in the film *Bleeders* (1997).

Warren – The Maine State Prison was erected in Thomaston in 1824 and relocated to Warren in 2002. It is where, in the A.J. Matthews (Rick Hautala) novel *Looking Glass* (2004), Jeromy Bowker is serving a life sentence. So how can he also be somewhere else, wreaking havoc in the lives of Matt and Brenda Ireland? See also **Three Rivers**.
Also in the prison is The Stillwater Slasher, named after the river where he dumped his 18 victims in Rick Hautala's short story "Rubies and Pearls" (*Predators*, 1993). See also **Stillwater River**.

Waterside – An archaeologist (Hill Harper) uncovers an Egyptian chamber in Maine. When he places an ankh in a slot on the door, the chamber sends an electromagnetic pulse across the Atlantic to Stonehenge. The sarsen stones begin to shift and send off another discharge that incinerates tourists on its way to other ancient sites. Jacob Glaser (Misha Collins), a scientist turned host of a fringe science radio program, watches as other ancient sites collapse and become active volcanoes. He knows what is happening – ancient astronauts left behind a device that is now starting to terraform the planet. But can he shut it off in time? *Stonehenge Apocalypse* (2010), not surprisingly, is a movie made for the SyFy Channel.

Waterville – Sarah Lahikainen's grandmother lives in a nursing home in Waterville. As she slowly slips into senility, she talks about the family ghost and how she cared for it for so long. As Sarah visits her grandmother, she begins to suspect that her imaginary friend Tully might be a tulpa, a demonic manifestation of her anger and fears in Rick Hautala's *Cold Whisper* (1991). See also **University of Maine, Orono; State Route 26, Westbrook.**

Waterville, St. Pete's Hospital – Dean Winchester (Jensen Ackles) and the angel Castiel (Misha Collins) are searching for the Archangel Raphael (Demore Barnes) as the battle to prevent the Apocalypse continues. A policeman in Waterville who witnessed Raphael battling demons tells them that the answer is at the hospital. There they find the husk of the archangel's former host. Suddenly there are even more questions in "Free to Be You and Me" (5:03) episode of *Supernatural*.

Wayne – In the opening scenes of *Behind the Mask: The Rise of Leslie Vernon* (2006), the opening narration discusses previous serial killers and their haunts. Director Scott Glosserman recalled his summers in Wayne when scouting filming locations and an abandoned camp on an island in Lake Androscoggin became the filming location of the frozen ruins of Camp Crystal Lake of *Friday the 13th* movie series fame.

Wellfield – Johnny Petrie inherits the Conroy estate in Wellford. The windfall is unexpected as the late owner, Benjamin Conroy, is a total stranger. It turns out Johnny was adopted and he is the last of the Conroys. It also turns out that his birth father was a failed necromancer and 18 years ago, killed the entire family except for Johnny. Now Johnny tries to discover his past while surviving a haunted house with its own agenda in *Dead Souls* (2007) by Michael Laimo. The book was re-released in 2012 with additional text and a new ending, to coincide with the release of a film version for the Chiller Network with Jesse James as Johnny Petrie.

Wells – Roodsford, Robert Bloch's village of bloodthirsty Celtic cultists, have a plan to pierce the veil by sacrificing children to Shubniggurath. Their supply of children for the plan will be the unsuspecting village of Wells in Bloch's "Satan's Servants," first appearing in the anthology *Something about Cats and Other Pieces* (1949). See also **Roodsford**.

Wells, Post Road – The Historical Society of Wells & Ogunquit maintains the historic meetinghouse. In 1692, the minister was the widely respected George Burroughs. Burroughs had made the grievous error of serving as a minister in Salem, Massachusetts for several years before deciding in 1683 that Indian attacks in Maine were preferable to dealing with the feuding congregation in Salem. Twelve years later, his service to Salem was rewarded by being accused of witchcraft, arrested, and brought back to Salem to be hanged on August 19. The only good to come of it was the audience suddenly realized that if a Puritan minister could be executed based only on "spectral evidence," so could anyone. That realization was the beginning of the end of the hysteria. See also **Witchtrot Hill, South Berwick**.

Wells Harbor – Thirteen-year-old Rynn Jacobs (Jodie Foster) lives in a house with her reclusive father. A precocious child who spends so much time alone attracts the gossip mongers and perverts of the small town. One of the latter is Frank Hallet (Martin Sheen), the adult son of landlady Cora Hallet (Alexis Smith), one of the former. Yet the crude sexual advances and vicious prying do not disturb the girl, nor her absentee father. But as she explains to her friend Mario (Scott Jacoby), she prefers if people stay out of the basement in *The Little Girl Who Lives Down the Lane* (1976).

West Belfry – Can trees haunt their former landscape? According to Joe Hill in his short story "Dead-Wood," one of the most famous ghost trees was the West Belfry fir. Chopped down in

1842, it continued to haunt the building that replaced it – the walls even bled sap. The story was first collected in *20th Century Ghosts* (2005).

West Buxton – A year after he helped end the reign of terror of serial killer Moses McCrory, the demon known as Hellboy returns to West Buxton to salute a fallen comrade. In a deserted bar, Hellboy recounts the tale of a reanimated killer and the hunt to stop a killer already dead in "Scared Crows," written by Rick Hautala with Jim Connolly, originally published in *Hellboy: The Anthology* (2000).

Westbrook – Jeff Cameron is a real estate agent trying to survive a soft market, a divorce, and a child in college. One late night he gets a call from an old friend. There's going to be a reunion on Sheep's Head Island for the campers of Tent 12, hosted by another friend and real estate developer Evan Pike who has bought the property to develop. Soon, Jeff will have another thing to survive, and not just metaphorically, in *The Wildman* (2008) by Rick Hautala. See also **Camp Tapiola**, **Arden**.

Westbrook, State Route 26 – On an isolated stretch of State Route 26 outside of Westbrook, Marie Lahikainen is brutally murdered while her daughter Sarah watches in horror hidden in the roadside trees. After the murder, she is taken to live with her father Devin, in Hilton. Even though she leaves her school friends in Westbrook, she brings her invisible friend with her in Rick Hautala's *Cold Whisper* (1991). See also **Waterville**.

Westbrook, Saint Hyacinth Cemetery – Band leader, vocalist, and singer Rudy Vallee (1901-1986) is buried in Westbrook. As a musician and vocalist, his material is too mainstream for a horror soundtrack, but his performance of "You're Driving Me Crazy" was a perfect for John Water's first feature length film *Mondo Trasho* (1969). As an actor, Vallee usually played himself or a musician, with notable exceptions such as on a three-episode *Batman* story arc (3:11-13) where Batman (Adam West), Robin (Burt Ward), and Batgirl (Yvonne Craig) travel to Londinium to do battle with Lord Marmaduke Ffogg (Vallee) One of his final roles was as a shopkeeper in *Sunburst* (1975), released to video as *Slashed Dreams* to cash in on the newfound fame of a costar named Robert Englund.

White Cliffs – Just beyond the town of White Cliffs, overlooking Pleasant Bay, is the ancestral home of the Roff family. In the made-for- TV drama *Buried Secrets* (1996), Annalisse Vellum (Tiffani-Amber Thiessen) is visited by the ghost of a young girl who wants her mother's murder solved.

White Falls – Life in a small town is disrupted by the growing power of an amulet that has waited for centuries to unleash its evil. Now a psychotic madman and the hooker he kidnapped must save the world from the legions of the dead in *Bloodstone* (2006) by Nate Kenyon.

Kenyon returns to White Falls in "Keeping Watch." As children, Dave and Alley discover a lake in the woods. Several years later, a friend slips off a rock and hurts herself. By the time Dave reached her, something else had gotten there first – something large and carnivorous that lives in a fissure in the rocks. Years later, a child has disappeared, and Dave knows it is the thing he fears most – the beast has reawakened. The story appeared in *Monstrous* (2008).

White Harbor – In *Coffins* (2002) by Rodman Philbrick, Dr. Davis Bentwood is summoned to the home of his friend Jebediah Coffin to battle a family curse that is dispatching the Coffin family in a variety of bloody and unpleasant manners. With the Civil War looming, it soon appears that Jebediah's abolitionist work as a stop along the underground railway may not entirely be altruistic.

Willow – According to Stephen King in "Rainy Season" first published in *Midnight Grafitti* (1993), it rains every seven years the tiny town of Willow. Unfortunately for the tourists, it rains carnivorous toads.

Wood's Hole – The town of Wood's Hole was envisioned to grow when the trains came through. The trains never came and the town was abandoned. Now the trains do stop, but only for subterranean vampires in *Trailer Trash* (2007) by Scott T. Goudsward.

Wytopitlock Lake – Annik Miller inherits her great-aunt's estate in Ann Brahms' novel *Run for Your Life* (1993). She uses the windfall to escape Boston and a stalker. When the stalker follows her to Maine she flees to her great aunt's cabin on the secluded lake. Suddenly her stalker is the least of her problems as a serial killer has also taken a fancy to Annik. See also **Spring Street, Portland**.

Yarmouth – Darcy and Bob Anderson have a good marriage, two kids, and a side business selling coins online. Twenty-seven years of marriage and Darcy just found out Bob has a hobby besides numismatics – serial killing. "A Good Marriage" is a novella by Stephen King, published in his collection *Full Dark, No Stars* (2010).

York Beach, Short Sands – Short Sands is a pocket beach on the coast of Cape Neddick and the real life counterpart of the village in *The Boy Who Drew Monsters* (2014) by Keith Donohue. In 2013, rough seas washed the sand away from the beach at Short Sands, exposing the remnants of a 160-year old shipwreck. This unnamed vessel also became part of the inspiration the novel, becoming the *Porthleven*, which wrecked in 1849. Holly Keenan is convinced much of the trouble afflicting her family is the ghosts of the crew never recovered. Her husband Tim is convinced a white beast roams the beach, and their ten-year-old son Jip, autistic and agoraphobic, is obsessed with drawing the monsters he sees. Is there a ghostly presence or is the power of Jip's pictures blurring the line between reality and fantasy?

York High School – In Rick Hautala's novel *Night Stone* (1986), Don Inman takes a teaching position at YHS, moving his family from Connecticut. It will not prove to be a good decision. See also **St. Ann's**.

Zachry – With a population of 67, Zachry is not noted for much other than the speed trap on Main Street. As James Ketchum discovers, there are some rules that are best not to break, especially in Zachry. Richard Matheson's short story "The Children of Noah" was first published in *Alfred Hitchcock's Mystery Magazine*, March 1957.
A year after her brother Jimmy Ketchum disappeared, Peggy and Bruce Lindley are tracing her brother's route in search of him. She knows he disappeared on the road to Chipping from Brewster and the only town between them is Zachry. Unfortunately for the Lindleys, she may be right in "Zachry revisited" by William F. Nolan. The story appeared in the Richard Matheson tribute anthology *He Is Legend* (2009).

Ziegler's Notch – The regulars in a local bar have discovered something weird is happening in the forest at night. The woodland creatures, both prey and predator, are gathering around a bonfire, performing some sort of ritual. The ritual grows more complex each night and the locals begin to suspect something far more drastic is about to happen. "Firedance" by Jack Ketchum first appeared in *Imagination Fully Dilated* (1998).

NEW HAMPSHIRE

New Hampshire's beloved icon Old Man of the Mountain was
destroyed in a 2003 rockslide.

America's Stonehenge – See **North Salem**.

Amherst – Longtime Amherst resident Dr. Robert Decareau (1926-2009) worked as a research and development scientist at Raytheon where he was instrumental in the creation of the microwave oven as a tool in home cooking, going so far as to write early microwave cookbooks. Suspicions of the safety of the microwave oven remained and has not been helped by horror movies, ranging from Lynn Peltzer (Frances Lee McCain) answer to dealing with kitchen vandals in *Gremlins* (1984) or the "death by spaghetti" of Evan Lewis (David Paetkau), triggered by a microwave in *Final Destination 2* (2003). Adding insult to injury, Dr. Decareau had previously worked on improving food storage techniques such as freeze-drying, a technique popularized in the 1973 film *Soylent Green*.

Amherst, Village Green – In the near future, a woman encounters the newest form of prejudice – religious bigots protesting the existence of clones. Instead of a quiet visit to a park, she finds herself in an increasingly antagonistic crowd. As a clone, she may or may not have a soul, but this religious lynch mob certainly doesn't deserve to have them either in "Dolly, Do I Have a Soul?" by Philip C. Peron. The story first appeared in *Anthology: Year Three: Distant Dying Ember* (2015).

Andover – The "autobiography" of Dr. Theophilus Cardan Zell begins in Andover. Theo is an orphan who flees to his grandfather's mansion in Amherst, where his mystical interests are nurtured. As the book continues, the good doctor travels the world in pursuit of occult wisdom. By the time Dr. Zell returns to New Hampshire, he has dabbled in a variety of forbidden fields such as astrology, ghosts, hypnosis, mind-reading, divination, personality exchange, and of course, cross-dressing. *Dr. Zell and the Princess Charlotte. An Autobiographical Relation of Adventures in the Life of a Distinguished Modern Necromancer, Seer and Theosophist* (1892) by Warren Richardson is usually considered fiction but may have originally been meant as a recruitment tool for a turn-of-the-century cult.

Andover, Potter Place – The section of Andover still known as Potter Place is the former location of the 175-acre farm of Richard Potter (1783-1835), America's first successful stage magician, hypnotist, and ventriloquist. The son of an English baronet and an African servant woman, he was born in Massachusetts but apprenticed as a cabin boy. In England, he became the assistant of a Scottish magician and ventriloquist named John Rannie. The two toured Europe before arriving in America with a traveling circus. When Rannie retired Potter went solo, becoming nationally acclaimed for his prestidigitation. By the time he was 50 years old, he had cut back on magic to focus on ventriloquism. Potter and his wife/stage assistant Sally are buried in a small lot in the corner of their former estate, located on Depot Street, across the tracks from the Potter Place Railroad Station, home of the local historical society. The State maintains a historical marker on the south side of Route 111.

Anniston – Dan Torrance and Abra Stone finally meet in person at the local library after psychic communications. Dan tells her about the Shining and Abra tells Dan about the lady in the top hat. She tells Dan about Bradley Trevor, who was killed and drained of his shining by the True Knot. Dan realizes he must track down these vicious psychic vampires and their top-hat wearing leader, to prevent them from feeding off Abra. He heads to Iowa to locate the boy's body. After retrieving Trevor's baseball glove, Dan now has a conduit to one of the villains in *Doctor Sleep* (2013) by Stephen King. See also **Frazier**.

Appalachian Trail – See **Ethan Pond Trail, Bartlett; North Conway**.

Arcadia Beach – Loosely based on Salisbury Beach, Massachusetts in the 1980s, Arcadia Beach is a seaside resort town past its prime with a small seasonal amusement park and tourist motels of various designs and architectures. Twelve-year-old Jack Sawyer is staying off-season at the Moorish-motif Alhambra Inn and Gardens with his mother, a faded movie star dying of cancer. He learns he has a gift to pass between this world and another called "The Territories." He embarks on a quest to locate the talisman that will save his mother and quite possibly the entire world in *The Talisman* (1984) by Stephen King and Peter Straub. The hotel is a direct nod to Washington Irving, one of Straub's influences. Irving's collection of tales from Moorish Spain was *The Alhambra (1832)*. Although Jack Sawyer would return in the 2001 sequel *The Black House,* the action had left New England for Wisconsin.

In King's *Tommyknockers* (1987), Jim Gardener wakes up on the beach after a binge and finds himself near the Arcadia Funworld Amusement Park. He meets a boy named Jack, who directs him to a payphone in the lobby of the nearby Alhambra Hotel.

Ashborough – Dr. Michael Cayle moves his family out of Manhattan to the security of small town living. Cayle soon discovers small towns have their own risks as he learns of disturbing local legends of the "Isolates," a race of deformed primitive cannibals. Now he wonders if the town still believes the legends, which include stories of blood sacrifice offerings as appeasement. *Deep in the Darkness* (2004) by Michael Laimo is an expanded version of the author's short story "In the Darkness, Golden Eyes" first appearing in *Epitaph* #3, 1997.

In 2014, the novel was made into a film. Sean Patrick Thomas starred as Dr. Cayle, with Moodus, Connecticut standing in as the filming location for small town New Hampshire.

Ashland – Green Grove Cemetery is the final resting place of Wardon Allen Curtis (1867-1940). Curtis was a journalist and a weird fiction author. He cut his teeth writing adventure stories for syndicated youth sections in newspapers nationally, and that distinctive balance of fantastic and adventure never quite left his works. Among his works is an early example of crypto-fiction, "The Monster of Lake LaMetrie" (Pearson's Magazine, September 1899), where a lake is a portal to a prehistoric hollow earth. The brain of a teen is transplanted into the skull of an elasmosaurus, which never ends well. He also dabbled in ghosts, the most notable example of which is "The Fate of the 'Senegambian Queen'" (*The Black Cat*, November 1900), in which pirates attempt to plunder the *Flying Dutchman*, which also never ends well.

Ashville – It's the 1980s, and Robby Asaro's great passion is his job – making pizza in the Funcave video arcade. A freak accident pulls him into the pizza conveyor with fatal results. Twenty years later, Robby's spirit remains within the electronics, watching over the arcade. When Robby protects one of his favorite patrons, Tiffany Park, from a bully, he absorbs the bully and his hate. Now a war is waging in Funcave and the gamers trapped inside are collateral damage in Adam Cesare's novella *Zero Lives Remaining* (2016).

Bartlett, Ethan Pond Trail – Ethan Pond Trail is a 14-mile section of the Appalachian Trail. Each year, private investigator Marvin Burke goes to the spot on the trail where he scattered his late wife's ashes. He tells her he has feelings for his client, a woman looking for the son she gave for adoption as a child. Unfortunately, for Burke, he found him. James Sutton has abandonment issues and a collection of body parts. Losing his newfound mother to a suitor might drive James further over the edge in *Abandoned* (2016) by Dan Foley.

Bartlett, Notchland Inn – Tess Devlin runs into her ex-husband on a Boston street but he pretends not to recognize her. She calls his cell to yell at him, only to discover that he's at the Notchland Inn in Bartlett. Unbeknownst to Tess, she has just joined a group of people who have had a chance meeting with a doppelgänger in Christopher Golden's *Dead Ringers* (2015). Things get complicated when the longer the duplicate exists, the more the originals lose their identities and their physical substance.

Bedford – Bedford is home to Segway Inc. of New Hampshire, USA, the manufacturer of the two-wheeled, self-balancing Segway. In *Twilight* (2008), Edward Cullen (Robert Pattinson) has admitted to Bella Swan (Kristen Stewart) he is indeed a vampire. He picks her up and races to the mountain top to show her what he looks like in the direct sun. His speed and strength are such that it almost appears he is flying. In *Vampires Suck* (2010), the spoof recreates the scene, with Edward Sullen (Matt Lanter) carrying Becca Crane (Jenn Proske). Only in this version, when the vampire clears the brush, his effortless gait is because he is astride a Segway.

Bentley Centre – The Banks House in Bentley Centre is the town's only tavern and inn. The primary business is catering to visitors passing through Franconia Notch to see the spectacular Flume Gorge. Annie Trumbull Slosson's tale "A Transient" tells what happens when a high-strung guest encounters the poltergeist of a child who died young but has continued to grow up at a regular pace. The story first appeared in *Harper's Magazine*, December 1898. See also **Franconia Notch State Park**.

Benton – The village is home to a campfire tale told to new members of Dartmouth College's Outing Club; Dartmouth College owns most of the mountain as a wilderness area. Dr. Thomas Benton returned home from medical school in Germany and quickly became a well-respected local physician. Smallpox killed his family in 1816 and he gave up medicine. He became a hermit and moved to a shack on neighboring Mount Moosilauke. Healthy farm animals began dying unexpectedly, a small cut behind their left ears. By the start of the Civil War, Benton's generation had died off, but witnesses continued to report an old man in a black cape wandering the woods. It was recalled that his professor in Germany also dabbled in alchemy in search of eternal life. And with sightings continuing into modern times, it appears Dr. Benton may have continued his mentor's research.

Sam Winchester (Jared Padalecki) and Dean Winchester (Jensen Ackles) are in Pennsylvania, investigating a possible zombie case. Instead, they discover Doc Benton (Billy Drago), still seeking the key to eternal life. His technique is stealing body parts to replace his own as needed. It is apparently successful since the Winchesters' father first killed him decades ago. *Supernatural* episode "Time Is on My Side" (3:15) find Sam about to be used for spare parts while Dean deals with demons. Just another day with the Winchesters.

Berlin – Alexa suspects her husband John is having an affair, based on his regular trips to Berlin to see an "old childhood friend." She follows him to Berlin where she discovers John's friend is less a paramour and more a lupine. Now jealousy is the least of her problems in "Pandora's Box" by Roxanne Dent. The story first appeared in *Epitaphs* (2011).

Dent returns to Berlin for "Bug Boy," first appearing in *Bugs: Tales That Slither, Creep, and Crawl* (2014). Carl is a brilliant child, but odd. His lack of social skills and love of insects makes him the perfect target for bullying - until one bully dies of a spider bite. Carl also has an odd hobby that involves creating oversized "super roaches," and seeing what happens when he grafts human parts to them. His latest creation, Naomi VI, has issues over who is the master of the house.

Berlin, Main Street – Louis Joseph Côté (1884-1934) was born in the family home in Berlin. His parents insisted he train to be a doctor, but while attending school, he performed in a school play and preferred the limelight. He arrived in Hollywood as Lew Cody and became a leading man in both silent films and early talkies. His career consisted primarily of romantic comedies and melodramas, including *The Grinning Skull* (1916), a drama where he plays a local philanthropist that loses his fortune, then his friends. Set against the San Francisco earthquake, audiences were astounded by the special effects of the city shaking apart. Coincidentally, this early precursor of the "disaster film" genre was released the same year Irwin "Master of Disaster" Allen was born.

Berlin Community Hospital – Stephen King's *The Shining (1977)* originally included a prologue that contained a brief scene from Jack Torrence's childhood where his drunken father terrorizes him. Jack's father is employed as an orderly at the local history. Removed prior to the book's publication, it first appeared in print as "Before the Play" in *Whispers,* August 1982.

Bethel – Chip Linton, his wife Emily, and their twin daughters relocate to the little hamlet near the Canadian border to make a fresh start. Chip, an airline pilot, had to ditch his regional jet in Lake Champlain resulting in 39 deaths. When Chip finds a door in the basement coal bin, sealed shut with 39 bolts, he begins to think it is no coincidence. Emily begins to think the neighbors are witches, and Chip believes his passengers are ghosts as the family struggles to determine who or what is haunting them in *The Night Strangers* (2011) by Chris Bohjalian.

Blackstone – A small coastal town has big plans – tear down the long abandoned old Blackstone Asylum looming over the town and replace it with the Blackstone Center, a complex of shops and restaurants. As the plans move forward, the town is rocked by supernatural deaths and public ruin. It seems that evil once locked away within the asylum walls has been freed to resume terrorizing the town. From January 1997 to June 1997, John Saul released chapbooks of a serial novel: "An Eye for An Eye: The Doll;" "Twist of Fate: The Locket;" "Ashes to Ashes: The Dragon's Flame;" "In the Shadow of Evil: The

Handkerchief;" "Day of Reckoning: The Stereoscope;" and "Asylum." Each chapter features an anonymous gift sent to a local resident, a gift which first belonged to an inmate at the abandoned asylum that leads to very bad things happening. The six parts were combined and released as *The Blackstone Chronicles* in 1997.

Bog Farm – In October of 1890, local authorities were alerted to trouble at Bog Farm, Dr. Thomas Windrow's therapy farm for treating mental disorders. When they arrived, they found the young teen Windrow sisters, Lucy and Sally, the only survivors of a gruesome murder scene. A legend grew up around the sisters, accusing them of cannibalism and murder. Newspaper accounts, books, even a theatrical recreation of events added to the clamor - except no one knew what happened except the sisters, who aren't talking. Twenty years later, the sisters remain recluses in Bog House. But a novice reporter has gotten the opportunity that could make or break his career – he's been invited to interview them in *Dinner with the Cannibal Sisters*, a novelette by Douglas Clegg, released in 2015.

Boscawen – On Contoocook Island along the Merrimack River is a statue of Hannah Duston. Less famous than fellow axe murderess Lizzie Borden, Duston was more successful because she became a heroine instead of a being arrested as a mass murderer. Duston had been captured by an Abenaki war party during the King William's War in 1697. After 15 days of hard travel, and being exchanged to other Indian parties, Hannah and two companions were camped out on the island with a small party of Indians bringing the captives north to Canada. Hannah killed 10 sleeping Indians: six children, two women, and two elderly men. She scuttled all but one canoe, scalped the ten corpses as proof of her heroism and headed back to Haverhill, MA. The Province of Massachusetts Bay awarded her £25, although the bounty on Indian scalps had been repealed. Hannah Duston became a cause célèbre for killing and mutilating the Indians. This statue erected in 1874 is the site of her escape from Indians. It shows Hannah Duston holding a hatchet in one hand and ten Indian scalps in the other. Hannah's gory image has been popularized in tchotchkes ranging from a commemorative Jim Beam decanter to a bobble-head doll.

Bosset's Way – In the woods beyond Laconia is the tiny hamlet where Henry Wilmarth hanged himself after a discovery not meant for mankind. So begins *The Haunter of the Threshold* (2010), Edward Lee's loosely based and pornographic sequel to Lovecraft's "Haunter of the Dark." Hazel Greene, her friends Sonia Heald and Frank Barlow set out to understand a mysterious box. Complicating things, Hazel's myriad of fetishes and rape fantasies begin to become indistinguishable from the horrors unleashed.

Bradford, Lake Massasacum – George Allan England (1877-1936) was a prolific pulp writer, best known for his dystopic science fiction stories. The lakefront cottage he called Camp Sans Souci was his home and his workspace. His occasional horror story was cosmic, such as "The Thing From –'Outside'" where explorers in Canada slowly go mad trying to escape from an invisible entity. The story was first published in the April 1923 issue of *Science and Invention*.

Bradford, Tashmore Pond – Bradford is on the New Hampshire side of Tashmore Pond. Once it is frozen over, Andy McGee snowshoes across from the Vermont shore to resupply the cabin where Andy and Charlie McGee hide while on the run in Stephen King's *Firestarter* (1980).

Brantford – *Jumanji* is the story of Allan Parrish, who has been trapped in a magical jungle game for 26 years. His only escape is to find someone to finish the game he has started. The 1981 children's book by Chris Van Allsburg was made into a 1995 film starring Robin Williams as the adult Allan Parish, who must now finish the game before the jungle creatures released with him destroy the town. See also **West Street, Keene; Mount Caesar Cemetery Swanzey**.

Camford – Sixteen-year-old Dan Crawford is attending a college preparatory summer program at New Hampshire College in Camford. When he arrives at the program, Dan learns that his dorm for the summer used to be a sanatorium. And not just any asylum but the dumping grounds of the criminally insane deemed incurable. Dan and his new friends explore the building and discover the asylum still hold secrets of its horrific past that refuse to stay buried in *Asylum* (2013) by Madeleine Roux.

Carversville – The Cousineau mansion was once the most notorious haunted house in New England. When it was finally demolished, a collector in Katmandu acquired the fireplace for his private collection. Unfortunately, Nepal is already a land where demons and gods wander the land. Now a new evil spirit walks the land in "The Night of White Bhairab," a novelette by Lucius Shepard that first appeared in *The Magazine of Fantasy & Science Fiction*, October 1984.

Chester – The July 25, 1831 issue of *The New England Review* included a poem from John Greenleaf Whittier titled "The Demon's Cave." While briefly working in a local shoe shop Whittier learned of "The Devil's Den," a haunted cave on Rattlesnake Hill overlooking Lake Massabesic. Whittier's poem chronicled the local legend and how the path leading to the cave always had a well-traveled path, created by the traffic of evil spirits in and out of the cave.

Chesterfield – The Timothy N. Robertson Burying-Ground is a small cemetery with burials dating back to 1775. The most prominent marker is the Robertson family monument where actor Royal Beal (1899-1969) is buried. Among the roles in his diverse career is Salem witch trials judge John Hathorne, summoned by Satan to preside at a trial for the soul of a New Hampshire farmer in a 1960 episode of *Sunday Showcase*. This incarnation of Stephen Vincent Benét's short story "The Devil and Daniel Webster" (1:22) also featured Edward G. Robinson as Daniel Webster. See also **Cross Corners**.

Chocorua – Along Route 16, opposite the far end of Chocorua Lake, William James (1842-1910) died at his beloved summer home. The older brother of Henry James, author of the archetypal ghost story "The Turn of the Screw," William James was a psychologist and Harvard professor. He also had connections to the supernatural, but at the cost of some of his academic status.

After the death of his young son, James became fascinated by the possibility of communication with the dead. As president of Boston's Society for Psychical Research, he spent years championing a medium, Leonora Piper, whose séances were egregious frauds; her spirit contacts included a French physician who spoke no French and didn't know medical terminology. James was buried in the family plot in Cambridge Cemetery, Massachusetts.

Cloverly – Pelerin's house is haunted and the weight of the problem is literally killing him. His friends Nadelman and Gage must fight an unseen force trying to smother the living. "The Challenge" by John W. Vandercook first appeared in *Ellery Queen's Mystery Magazine,* July 1952.

Coldbridge – Zelda, a new student at Colbin College, is unaware she is being stalked by a cross-dressing serial killer with a razor. George Denkin, wearing woman's clothes and a wig, is killing coeds and scalping them. Unknown to him, he himself is being stalked by two youngsters who think he's a vampire in *Incident at Potter's Bridge* (1991) by Joe Monninger. A paperback edition was released in 1993, renamed *Razor's Song*.

Colebrook –The intersection of Main and Bridge Streets is the former site of Vic's Service Station. On April 13, 1984, NH State Troopers noticed a gold Pontiac at the gas pump. The car matched a recent APB for Christopher Wilder, a serial killer known as "The Beauty Queen Killer." Wilder posed as a professional photographer to lure women, torturing and killing on a cross-country spree. With police closing in, he was headed to Canada. He didn't make it out of Colebrook. In a scuffle with police for his gun, he shot himself in the heart.

The made-for-TV movie, *Easy Prey* (1986), soon followed. Gerald McRaney was cast as Wilder and Shawnee Smith as a teen victim who was allowed to live and to lure new victims.

Comity – *X-Files* episode "Syzygy" (3:13) finds Mulder and Scully (David Duchovny and Gillian Anderson) in New Hampshire investigating claims of Satanic cult activity at a local high school. Very bad things keep happening and the only two things the tragedies have in common are a pair of cheerleaders who share a birthday (Wendy Benson and Lisa Robin Kelly) and the claims of Madame Zirinka (Denalda Williams) who blames a rare planetary alignment.

Concord – Veterinarian Joseph Randal is delighted when the Hansons move into his house – haunting an empty house can be lonely. After a few months, he begins to manifest himself to the Hanson daughter Kimberly, who reminds him of his own dead daughter. When the rest of the family realizes the house is haunted, they plan to move. So Joe does what any lonely ghost would do – make some company. "The Confession of a Confirmed Has-Been" by John McIlveen appeared in *Childhood Nightmares: Under the Bed* (2012).

Concord, Front Street – The offices and warehouse of S&L Finance take the place of the counting house of Marley & Scrooge in the Americanized version of the most famous ghost of them all - *A Christmas Carol* (1843) by Charles Dickens. *An American Christmas Carol* (1979) moves the story from

Victorian London to Depression-era Concord. Benjamin Slade (Henry Winkler) and his clerk Thatcher (R.H. Thomson) make their rounds on Christmas Eve to repossess items from debtors. That evening Slade unloads the truck and fires Thatcher just in time to begin the ghostly visitations made immortal by Dickens.

Concord, North Main Street – John Bell Bouton (1830-1902) was born on the northern end of Main Street near what is now called Bouton Street (in honor of his father). A novelist, travel writer, biographer, and newspaper editor, Bouton's body of work includes *The Enchanted - An Authentic Account of the Strange Origin of the New Psychical Club* (1891). The book follows the adventures of two men who decide ghosts are merely projections of mental energy. They learn to master this projection and begin traveling through time to significant places in literature, essentially becoming ghosts themselves.

Concord, Old North Cemetery – Old North was city's the first burial ground established in 1730. Franklin Pierce, 14th President of the US, is buried in Old North. His presidency was not considered successful by his peers, but New Hampshire has embraced their only native son to have lived in the White House by preserving his homes, naming colleges after him and erecting a statue at the State House. It was Pierce who discovered his old friend Nathaniel Hawthorne had died in his sleep while returning from the White Mountains. See also **Plymouth**.

A field adjacent to the cemetery holds the unmarked graves of the Friends Burial Ground. Among the Quakers in this graveyard is Levi Hutchins (1761-1855). Hutchins was already one of the premier clockmakers in New England when in 1787, his Yankee work ethic was distressed by sleeping past 4 AM. So, he invented the first American alarm. Although several European versions predated Hutchins' invention, the distinctly American obsession with work embraced the invention (albeit groggily). Its omnipresence is evidence in films as well, from the endless awakening of Bill Murray in *Groundhog Day* (1993) to the terror of 3:15 AM in *Amityville Horror* (2005).

Concord, Pleasant Street – The Concord Hospital is a designated as a quarantine center for people in New England infected with *Draco incendia trychophyton*, simply known as "The Scale" to a terrified public. The deadly and highly contagious disease is decimating the world in *The Fireman* (2016) by Joe Hill. Unknown to the public, the hospital is little more than an internment camp where the infected are held until they combust. See also **Little Harbor Road, Portsmouth**.

Conway – Orphaned as a teen, Mary Ann Jenness struck up a friendship with the one person more alone than herself – Norvle, the ghost of a young boy from Conway in "A Speakin' Ghost" (*Harper's Magazine*, December 1890) by Annie Trumbull Slosson.

Cooper Falls – Divorced teacher Bob Wentworth has moved to the small, isolated town of Cooper Falls. He soon learns that the full moon always brings death. A black magic spell has cursed a local with lycanthropy. Bob is convinced he is right, but the town fathers seem more concerned with hushing up the murders than catching the monster. Now he must face the creature alone, in *Moon Death* (1981), Rick Hautala's first novel.

Coös County – At a lonely farm in New Hampshire's northernmost region, a traveler seeks shelter for the night. There he meets the widow of farmer Toffile Lajway. She tells of the restless skeleton sealed in the attic, trapped there after the bones exhumed themselves from the cellar. She should know - she buried the body. Robert Frost's "The Witch of Coös" first appeared in the January 1922 issue of *Poetry*. See also **Robert Frost Farm, Derry**.

Cornish, Lang Road – J. D. Salinger (1919-2010) lived in Cornish for most of his life, choosing to write, but not publish in a remote house hidden along Lang Road. Considered a recluse by the publishing and journalism worlds, Cornish considered him a neighbor and fiercely protected his privacy. Although his short stories involving the difficulties living in the postwar world of superficial conformity and trite suburban banality border on horror, Salinger himself considered only one of his stories to be a bona fide horror tale – the unpublished "Mrs. Hincher."

An apparently infertile woman, Paula Hincher, suddenly tells her husband Frank that she is pregnant and will be bedridden for the duration of the pregnancy. For nine months, Mrs. Hincher locks herself in her bedroom. When Frank finally breaks into the room, he discovers his wife in a fetal position in the crib. Salinger completed the story in late 1941. He retooled the story, changed the name to "Paula" and sold it to *Stag Magazine* in 1942. The magazine never published the story and subsequently lost the finished version of the manuscript. In 2013, an incomplete draft cobbled together from fragments of both "Mrs. Hincher" and "Paula" was leaked online, a pirate transcription from the supposedly secure archive of Salinger's papers.

Stephen King would base the character of reclusive writer John Rothstein on Salinger in his detective novel *Finders Keepers* (2015). Morris Bellamy kills Rothstein and empties his safe. Bellamy is no mere burglar – he takes the cash, but he really wants the collection of notebooks that contain all of Rothstein's unpublished works. Bellamy hides the money and the notebooks before being locked away for another crime. Thirty-five years later, Bellamy is released only to discover his buried treasure has been found by someone else.

Cornish, Saint-Gaudens National Historic Site – New Hampshire's only national park preserves the home, gardens, and studios of Augustus Saint-Gaudens (1848–1907), one of America's foremost sculptors. His works include the bronze statue known as "The Puritan," located at a quadrangle in Springfield, Massachusetts. Memorializing Deacon Samuel Chapin, one of Springfield's earliest settlers, the work is better known to horror fans as the badly weathered and patina-coated statue haunting the dreams of Peter Proud (Michael Sarrazin) in the film version of *The Reincarnation of Peter Proud* (1975). See also **Plainfield**.

Coventry – Coventry was the original name of Benton, changed in 1840. See **Benton**.

Crawford Notch – The Notch is a steep and narrow gorge carved by the Saco River, creating a major pass through the White Mountains. The Notch is now a State Park and a popular hiking destination noted for several scenic waterfalls. See also **Frankenstein Cliff**.

"The Ambitious Guest" is a short story by Nathaniel Hawthorne, first published in *The New-England Magazine* in June 1835. A guest visits a cabin at the foot of a mountain prone to avalanches. He is planning his fame and fortune; his hosts are more intent on listening for rockslides. The basis of the story is the Willey tragedy at Crawford Notch in 1826, where the family similarly built a cave-like shelter near the house and fled to it. Instead of safety, they were killed by the avalanche which had been redirected by a ledge above the house, sparing it but destroying the shelter. Mount Willey, on the west side of the notch, is named in their memory.

Hawthorne, like his unnamed guest who dreamed of fame but who died in obscurity, also died in overnight lodgings in the White Mountains, but with fewer boulders and more acclaim. See also **Plymouth**.

Cross Corners – The Jabez Stone farm is located in this rural farming town, where Daniel Webster battles for the soul of his fellow New Englanders in "The Devil and Daniel Webster" by Stephen Vincent Benét. The story was first published in The *Saturday Evening Post,* October 24, 1936, and later adapted by

Benét for the stage and again as an opera. The story also was made into a 1941 film co-written by Benét and starring Walter Huston as Mr. Scratch. This film was also released as *All That Money Can Buy*. See also **Chesterfield**.

Darkness Falls – After writing a string of best-selling horror novels, Tyler Beckman has hit rock bottom. Giving up the booze, drugs, and sex, he returns to his childhood home, two decades after his family was slaughtered, to try and find his lost muse. Determined to confront his past, Tyler rents the home of his family's killer. Inspired again, he begins the novel that will put him back on top. But his return has reawakened demons, and not all of them are the personal type Tyler knows so well in *Darkness Falls* (2011) by Allan Leverone.

Dartmouth College – Dartmouth's School of Medicine, founded in 1797, is the fourth oldest in the nation. In its early days, Dartmouth would purchase the corpses of hanged criminals for the medical students to dissect as part of the curriculum. In 1874, the medical students got a special treat – Dartmouth had purchased the corpse of Franklin Evans, hanged for the rape, murder, and mutilation of his grand-niece. Known as the "Northwood Murderer," Evans was suspected to be responsible for at least five other similar heinous crimes across New England. His skeleton was then put on display in the medical school's Stoughton Museum of Pathological Anatomy. When the original medical building was demolished in 1963, the Stoughton Collection was dispersed across the campus. In the ensuing 50 years, the skeletal remains of the pedophilic serial killer have been misplaced, meaning someone is eventually in for a surprise.

Derry – Like most Massachusetts residents along the state border, Frank heads to New Hampshire to shop. Of course, Frank and his team are not concerned about sales tax – the zombie apocalypse took care of that. They arrive at a big-box store to grab food and ammunition but are trapped inside by a gang of murderous scavengers. Frank devises an exit strategy that involves blowing up a propane tank station outside the store with one of their shiny, newly acquired rifles. Had any scavengers survived, they may have learned that after the apocalypse, man can be scarier than zombies in *Fountain of the Dead* (2016) by Scott T. Goudsward.

Derry, Oak Street – Charles and Merritt met on the Internet and it wasn't long before Merritt invited him to stay at her apartment. Charles turns out to be a lazy, unemployed, artistic type and the relationship soon sours. But what is the metal box Charles keeps locked and why does Merritt hear something tapping? "The Box of Love and Hatred" by Gregory L. Norris was first published in the anthology *Nobody* (2006).

Derry, East Broadway – A video geek (Dan Merriman) uncovers an impossibly old videotape recording of a mad scientist testing a trans-dimensional transporter. With his friends in tow, he proceeds to the Derry Public Library on East Broadway to learn more of the scientist and his evil experiments. His first mistake is deciding to track down the old lab. His second mistake is restoring the transporter to working condition, in Brett Piper's film *Psyclops* (2002).

Derry, Miltimore Road – Among the earliest of Robert Frost's poems dealing with death, ghosts and the supernatural is "Ghost House," where the narrator is haunted by the cellar hole of his former home. First anthologized in *A Boy's Will* (1915), the poem was inspired by an old cellar hole and chimney on Miltimore Road, the boundary of the Frost Farm pasture. In 1867, the old Merriam place burned down, leaving the crumbling landmark that would inspire Frost.

Derry, Robert Frost Farm – In 1965, the State of New Hampshire purchased the 12.6-acre farm containing the two-story white clapboard farmhouse of poet Robert Frost and his family from 1900-1911, creating the Robert Frost Farm State Historic Site.

Unsuccessful as a farmer and barely surviving on a teacher's salary at nearby Pinkerton Academy, it was here he developed the regional colloquialisms and inflection of his poetry that would lead to his acclaim. In 1911, Frost sold the farm and used the money to underwrite his family's move to England where he began to be recognized as a major voice in American poetry. See also **Coös County; Miltimore Road, Derry; Ridge Road, Franconia; Grafton**.

When the undead apocalypse strikes, it not lumbering zombies, but nearly indestructible animated skeletons. Mel knows she needs to go somewhere remote and defendable. She knows her death is inevitable, so she chooses the farm of her favorite poet. Of course, then her Frost-loving ex shows up too. Mel said she wouldn't get back together with him if he were the last man on Earth. Now it looks like he might be. "A Bone to Pick" by Kristi Petersen Schoonover was originally published online in 2012 as well as in a limited edition chapbook.

Devonport – Ruth Hollis pines for her beloved friend Rosamund Ware, who has left town to live with her brother overseas. Then, unexpectedly, Rosamund arrives at Ruth's house, asking her to come with her to visit the Ware home. Alice Brown's "There and Here" (*Harper's Monthly*, October 1897) explores the fine line between the realm of the living and the memories of the dead. See also **Hawes Cemetery, Hampton Falls**.

Dover – Vic McQueen is on the run from the law as Joe Hill's novel *NOS4A2* (2013) continues. She uses the Shorter Way Bridge to come back from Iowa to rendezvous at her estranged father's house in the woods of Dover. Vic is returning to her father to get what she needs to destroy Christmas Land and put an end to Charlie Manx – a bag full of fuel-soaked explosives and detonators. See also **Terry's Primo Subs, Hampton Beach; Lake Road, Lake Winnipesaukee**.

Draconia – Two hundred years ago the townspeople of New Hope made a desperate bargain with an infernal stranger to save the town from certain doom. The town was saved but a gate appeared in the cemetery where the stranger exacted his terrible price. Today, New Hope is called Draconia and the legend of the gate is considered tourist fodder. Alison Crandell knows the old tale and sees parallels when real estate developer Adrian Blaise arrives in town in Elizabeth Ergas' *Devil's Gate* (1991).

Dublin, Town Cemetery – With interments dating back to 1751, Town Cemetery contains the graves of Dublin's saints, sinners, and soldiers. Among those buried here is Robb Hansell Sagendorph (1900-1970), founder, publisher, president, and guiding force behind the magazine *Yankee*, the magazine that maintains the unwavering New England spirit to the reading public since 1935. In 1939, Sagendorph bought the rights to the *Old Farmer's Almanac* and returned it to its original 1792 quaint but quirky format that had made old issues sought after by collectors such as H. P. Lovecraft.

The company also began publishing books in the 1960s, first releasing themed collections of previously published articles from *Yankee*, and then expanding into edited anthologies. The former widened interest in Yankee ghosts, witches, haunted lighthouses and other horror topics; the latter exposed regional short story authors to a wider market.

Dunbarton Center, Stark Cemetery – In 1946, Robert Lowell (1917-1977) published his second book of poems, the Pulitzer Prize-winning *Lord Weary's Castle*, blending Christian typology with a fascination with death in such works as "At the Indian Killer's Grave," "Colloquy in Black Rock" and "The Quaker Graveyard in Nantucket." Lowell is buried in the Winslow Family plot in Stark Cemetery.

Durham – Stephen King's *The Dead Zone* (1979) has the Chatsworths living in a mansion in the college town of

Durham. Johnny Smith is tutoring Chuck Chatsworth when he predicts a fire at a restaurant in Somersworth. See also **Ridgeway**.

Durham, Runaround Pond – During a collision in a hockey game, 6-year-old Johnny Smith receives a head injury in Stephen King's *The Dead Zone* (1979). It would not be the worst head injury Johnny will endure. See also **Ridgeway**.

Durham High School – In 1977, 81 people were killed in a fire at a restaurant in Somersworth. The majority of the victims were seniors at the high school per Stephen King's *The Dead Zone* (1979). See also **Ridgeway**.

Durham, University of New Hampshire – See **University of New Hampshire**.

East Derry, Forest Hill Cemetery – In the cemetery is a memorial to Derry's hometown hero, astronaut Rear Admiral Alan Shepard Jr. (1923-1998). Shepard, born in East Derry, was one of the original seven Mercury program astronauts. In May 1961, Shepard became the first American in space. He also later commanded the Apollo 14 flight (1971). Shepard died at his home in California and his ashes scattered at sea. His cenotaph in Derry aside, his true legacy as the first American in space was in ushering in the age of low-budget astronaut horror movies, such as *The Crawling Hand* (1963) and *Frankenstein Meets the Spacemonster* (1965).
The short film *Granite Voices* (2002) is the story of two teenage mediums that unwillingly allow restless spirits to air their final message. The film was shot almost exclusively in the cemetery.

East Dunham – Set in the immediate aftermath of *Motherless Child* (2012), Glen Hirshberg's novel *Good Girls* (2016) moves the setting from the Deep South to East Dunham, home to a satellite campus of the University of New Hampshire. Rebecca is a UNH-D student who cares for Jess's grandson. An orphan, Rebecca finds in Jess a familial bond, something she has never known. Jess is in hiding from the Whistler, the monster who turned Jess's daughter Natalie into a vampire. The Whistler has arrived in East Dunham looking for Jess, and Rebecca becomes an unwitting a pawn in a bloody battle against the insane vampire.

East Lebanon – In November 1848, Phineas Gage returned to convalesce with his parents at his childhood home on the farm of his mother's family. Gage (1823-1860) had been working on railway construction projects, tamping explosives into drilled holes when a spark ignited the explosives and drove the metal tamping rod into Gage's head. It entered on the left side of his face, passing behind his left eye, and out at the top of the head. The rod's path destroyed most of his left frontal lobe and for the injury completely modified his personality and behavior, but not his memories. Gage would become a medical marvel and his survival revised 19th-century medical views on the mind and brain. He died in 1860 and was buried in San Francisco. His doctor in Boston heard of his death and convinced his mother to have him exhumed and the skull shipped east for additional study. His headless remains stayed in California while his skull and the iron bar that went through it are on display at Harvard's medical museum in Boston.

Eastman –– Kate Harrison, framed for the murder of her husband and sister, flees authorities to exonerate herself. She discovers her brother-in-law is a latter-day Knight of Malta trying to retrieve a powerful magic talisman stolen from the Vatican by the mafia in *Eyes of the Virgin* (2002) by Thomas F. Monteleone.

Eaton Falls – A century ago, a Christmas Eve massacre left half the townsfolk dead. The cause of the madness was never determined. But now, it appears history is about to repeat itself in *Eaton Falls* (2014) by Franklin E. Wales.

Edwardtown – Sally Benedict is a big city reporter who has returned to her small hometown to give birth. Now graves are being desecrated and strange events begin to unfold and they all seem to involve Sally's ancestors. Soon Sally begins to suspect that there may be a bigger threat looming for her unborn child in *Infinity's Child* (1997) by Harry Stein.

Ellenton – Two hoodlums are robbing tourists and making it look like vampires attacked them. Now Professor Jerome Howell is coming to investigate. However, somebody else is also on the trail, somebody much scarier than mere thugs, per Hugh B. Cave's "The Second Time Around," first published in *The Mammoth Book of Dracula* (1997).

Errol – After a ski vacation in Dixville Notch, NH, a small aircraft leaves the Errol airport in spite of weather warnings. The plane's planned destination is Boston. The actual destination is into the side of a mountain in *Quietus* (2002) by Vivian Schilling.

Exeter – Editor Robert Luczak leaves his home in southern New Hampshire for Calcutta when a missing Bengali poet re-appears with new works. The poet has written an epic poem cycle about Kali, the goddess of death. Now Luczak finds him surrounded by a cult of Kali with a plot to unleash this demon-goddess upon the earth in the novel *Song of Kali* (1985) by Dan Simmons.

Exeter, Phillips Exeter Academy – Joe Hill's short story "20th Century Ghosts" (originally published in *High Plains Literary Review*, Volume XVII, No.1-3, 2002) finds Alec Sheldon as the owner-operator of the Rosebud Theater, where as a child in 1945, he first encountered Imogene Gilchrist. Imogene is young, beautiful, and an expert on movies. She's also dead, but still an avid movie fan. Alec fears what will happen when he dies and the Rosebud shuts down. And apparently, so does Imogene, which is why Alec's childhood friend, film director

Stephen Greenberg has summoned him to the set of his new movie on the Exeter Academy grounds.

Exeter, Water Street – On September 3, 1965, at 2:24 AM, 18-year old Norman Muscarello entered into the Exeter Police Station on Water Street. He had been hitchhiking home along Route 150 in neighboring Kensington when he saw a group of five bright red lights in a line, pulsating in sequence. Police officer Eugene Bertrand, Jr. drove back to the location with Muscarello. When something big rose above the trees with flashing lights, Bertrand radioed for back-up. Exeter policeman David Hunt became the third witness. There had been several UFO sightings reported in the weeks leading up to that night, and several more afterward, but Muscarello's encounter, backed by two police officers, would prove to be the one that triggered a media storm and an ongoing debate over who saw what.

Journalist John G. Fuller was among those who came to investigate. His book *Incident at Exeter* (1966) became a bestseller, as did his next UFO book about the Betty and Barney Hill abduction, which took place later that month. Both UFO cases are passingly referenced by Stephen King in *From a Buick 8* (2002), King referring to Exeter as "flying saucer sightings around the power lines." Corona discharge from the power lines was offered as one possible explanation at the time. See also **Lincoln**.

Farmington – Lenny and Carl are heading home after a hard night of drinking at the 3 Sisters Bar & Grill. On the way back, they start seeing road signs have been changed and the insults and accusations on the signs seem to be aimed at them. Lenny may know the source, but it will be difficult to prove. "Signs" by John McIlveen first appeared in McIlveen's collection *Inflictions* (2015).

Francestown – Sylvester H. Roper (1823-1896) was born on his father's Francestown farm. Sylvester had neither the heart nor the head for farming and wanted to be a machinist. He left home and headed to Boston at an early age, moving from one shop to another. By 1867, Roper was a well-known Boston engineer and inventor. He incorporated a coal-fired steam engine onto a bicycle frame, creating the earliest known motorcycle. Therefore, he must take the credit (or blame) for such motorcycle-oriented horror films as *Night School* (1981), *Chopper Chicks in Zombietown* (1989), and *Ghost Rider* (2007). Roper later died in a crash while demonstrating his motorized velocipede at a bicycle velodrome, giving him the dubious distinction of also being the first motorcycle accident fatality.

Franconia – Annie Trumbull Slosson's "Dissatisfied Soul" was first published in *Atlantic Monthly*, July 1904. The soul in question is Franconia's Maria Bliven, a restless sort of woman who travels between the homes of her relatives, staying at one place just briefly. Even after death, she can't stay in one place and decides to come back to earth.

Franconia, Ridge Road – Robert Frost and family returned from living in England and moved into the farmhouse they would call home from 1915 to 1920 and then use as a summer home for another 19 years. Two books of his poetry had been published in England and the 1915 American release of the two, *A Boy's Will* and *North of Boston*, established him as the preeminent poet of his time. Included in these first two volumes are such dark poems as "Ghost House," "Home Burial," and "The Fear." Today, "The Frost Place" is owned by the city and serves as a Frost Museum & Poetry Center. See also **Robert Frost Farm, Derry**.

Franconia Notch State Park – Located in the heart of the White Mountain National Forest, Franconia Notch was the home of the beloved icon Old Man of the Mountain until a rockslide in 2003 claimed the famous profile. Before the profile's untimely demise, it had been immortalized in prose and poetry by such noted names as Henry Wadsworth Longfellow, Mary Baker

Eddy, Daniel Webster and Nathaniel Hawthorne. See also **Hellbent Mountain**.

Still extant is the Flume Gorge. Discovered in 1808, the Flume is a natural gorge extending 800 feet along the base of Mount Liberty. The granite walls rise to heights of 70 to 90 feet and narrow in from 20 to 12 feet apart. The notch has always been a popular tourist destination. See also **Bentley Centre**.

Frankenstein Cliff – The cliff, the chasm, and the railroad trestle that crosses the gulf are all named for landscape artist Godfrey Nicolas Frankenstein (1820-1873), a member of a family of gifted German immigrant artists. Frankenstein was noted for his oils of the White Mountains and Niagara Falls. The location was named after the artist by Boston dentist Dr. Samuel Bemis (1793–1881), who owned much of Crawford Notch at that time and was also one of the earliest photographers of the White Mountains. The Frankenstein Trestle as originally built as part of the Maine Central Railroad to connect Portland to the Great Lakes. It is still in use, carrying excursion trains through Crawford Notch.

Godfrey Frankenstein's surname was originally Tracht. His father changed their name to Frankenstein upon immigrating to Ohio, apparently as a reminder of the ruins of Frankenstein Castle, near their old homestead in Darmstadt, Germany. These castle ruins are the same ones that Mary Shelley visited on a boat trip down the Rhine River in 1814, learning of the castle's former owner, Johann Dippel, a physician who developed his own interpretation of theology with a strong alchemical influence. Two years later, she wrote the first draft of the story of a physician playing god *Frankenstein; or, The Modern Prometheus* (1818).

Frazier – *Doctor Sleep* (2013), Stephen King's sequel to *The Shining* (1977) finds Dan Torrance arriving in New Hampshire. Frazier is the final stop for Dan, figuratively and possibly literally. On a downward spiral of booze and drugs, he has hit rock bottom. Here in Frazier, he begins to rebuild his life with a new job and attending AA. Complicating matters is when his shining makes contact with that of twelve-year-old Abra Stone, whose nascent shining abilities surpass Dan's at his strongest. But Abra's telepathic strength has also attracted the attention of the "True Knot," a group of near-immortal psychic vampires who feed on children with the shining. See also **Anniston**.

Frazier, Teenytown – Dan Torrance becomes an orderly at a local hospice where he gets the nickname Doctor Sleep for his ability to aid dying patients to pass over. Before that job, he worked for the town doing yard work on the town commons, home to a scale model of Frazier and a miniature railroad that carries tourists around the park. The far end of the rail line is "Cloud Gap," a picnic area and scenic vista. As events unfold in Stephen King's *Doctor Sleep* (2013), the True Knot sends a team to Frazier to snatch Abra Stone. The attempt is thwarted when they walk into an ambush at Cloud Gap, courtesy of Abra's ability to channel her thoughts through Dan in a form of psychic ventriloquism. The war has begun.

Friar – In 1940, the entire population of Friar stopped what they were doing, walked out of town and up an ancient mountain trail. Bodies found along the path did not indicate where the surviving citizens went, and the legend is that they disappeared without a trace. As *Yellowbrickroad* (2010) opens, a team will follow the path and attempt to solve the mystery. This will turn out to be a very bad idea. See also **Lancaster; Pittsburg**.

Gaiten – Gaiten Academy is on State Route 102 (Academy Avenue) in Stephen King's *Cell*, both the 2006 novel and 2016 film versions. Clay Riddell has survived the Pulse, a mysterious signal that turned everyone using a cell phone into zombies. The actual Route 102 runs from Nashua to Raymond; the spot where the fictional Gaiten Academy would be located is where the real town of Derry is located. Derry, of course, is also the name of King's favorite fictional town in Maine. Coincidence? See also **Kent Pond**.

Gardiner – Edwin Arlington Robinson (1869-1935) is buried in a family plot in Oak grove Cemetery. An acclaimed poet, Robinson is, unfortunately only remembered today for a few short poems from his prolific body of work. Of note to the morbidly inclined, "Luke Havergal" is a poem about a man whose lover has committed suicide and calls him from the grave to also kill himself, because Hell really isn't that bad; "Richard Cory" describes a wealthy and well-respected man whose amiableness is a façade he chooses not to maintain. Both poems first appeared in Robinson's collection *The Children of the Night* (1897).

Gideon – Ig Perrish wakes up after a bender to find bumps on his head. The bumps grow into horns and now everyone he talks to tells him their darkest secrets. Like how they all believe he killed his girlfriend Merrin and what awful things should happen to him because of it. The longer he has the horns, the more Ig learns to focus their power over people. Now he will find Merrin's killer himself, no matter how much hell he has to raise in *Horns* (2010) by Joe Hill. The 2013 movie version starred Daniel Radcliffe as Ig.

Gilmanton – The 1825 house located at 500 Province Road has the dubious honor of being the birthplace of America's first documented serial killer, Herman W. Mudgett (1861-1896). In 1893, Mudgett was in Chicago operating a hotel for World's Fair visitors under the alias of Dr. Henry Howard Holmes. There, he killed anywhere from 27 to 230 people in a custom-built "Murder Castle," complete with crematorium and lime pit. Robert Bloch's *American Gothic* (1974) and Erik Larson's 2003 bestseller *Devil in the White City* are based on the story of Dr. Holmes.

The birthplace of America's first documented serial killer, Herman W. Mudgett aka H. H. Holmes. Photo courtesy of J.W. Ocker.

The "Murder Castle" episode of *Lights Out*, an early radio series specializing in horror, aired on August 3, 1943. Arch Oboler, who pushed the envelope on radio horror was inspired by H. H. Holmes. Joseph Kearns starred as Henry Stewart, a gentleman, who hires a young woman as his personal secretary. The turnover rate in the position is impressive and permanent.

Supernatural episode "No Exit" (2:6) finds the Winchester brothers (Jared Padalecki and Jensen Ackles) in Philadelphia, where the ghost of Holmes continues to practice his favorite vice in the apartment building next to the former prison where he was hanged.

H. H. Holmes saw a resurgence in popularity when serial killer Culverton Smith (Toby Jones) admits his inspiration was H. H. Holmes the BBC series *Sherlock*. Unfortunately for Smith, another Holmes, Sherlock (Benedict Cumberbatch), is on the case in "The Lying Detective" (4:02).

Glenhaven – Mr. Murdoch inherits a small fortune and moves to New Hampshire to fulfill his life-long dream of living in a haunted house. After lovingly restoring a colonial farm, he is dismayed to discover he has everything he ever wanted except a ghostly boarder in "Mr. Murdoch's Ghost" by Richard Frede, first published in *The Magazine of Fantasy & Science Fiction*, May 1977.

Goffstown, Church Street – Buck is waylaid by two masked men who threaten him and his family unless he does what they say. He is to go to a pawn shop on Church Street and buy something called the "Prexy Box." If it's not for sale, he is to acquire it by any means possible. The pawnbroker, on the other hand, has a few security measures that are beyond the norm in "The Pawn Shop" by Tony Tremblay, writing as T.T. Zuma. The story first appeared in *Wicked Tales* (2015).

Goffstown, Piscataquog River – Two retirees meet fishing from the bridge. The friendship is cut short when a hitman kills the wrong one. The intended victim initiates his fallback plan in "The Old Man" by Tony Tremblay, writing as T.T. Zuma. The story of malleable identities first appeared in *Anthology: Year One* (2012).

Grafton – An elderly widow needs to become a ward of the town, an expensive legal obligation that colonial towns took great pains to avoid. So, as the courts decide which town will be forced to care for the indigent, she reflects on her transition from sensual young bride to feared old crone. She readily admits she is a witch but her power seems to be mostly perception. Robert Frost's "The Pauper Witch of Grafton" first appeared in *The Nation*, April 13, 1921. Later compilations of Frost's work collect "The Pauper Witch of Grafton" and "The Witch of Coös" together as "Two Witches," treating them as a single work. See also **Coös County**.

Granite Falls – John Saul's *Nightshade* (2000) chronicles the transition of Matthew Moore from all-American teen to a haunted delinquent. It starts when Grandmother Emily moves in, along with her obsession with her other daughter, the dearly departed Cynthia. Now the family is plagued by demons, and they may not all be supernatural.

Great Bay –Things are bad in Great Bay, and they are about to get much worse with the arrival of Hiram Grange, a perverted, drug and alcohol addicted, occult investigator with an unhealthy obsession with Jodie Foster – and those are his good points. And he is the final, bleary-eyed line of defense against Hell literally breaking loose in Great Bay. All he has to do is sober up long enough to battle an undead, sledgehammer toting, church lady and her army of demonically possessed lawn gnomes. *Hiram Grange and the Village of the Damned* (2009) by Jake Burrows is the first novella in the "Scandalous Misadventures of Hiram Grange" series.

Greymant, Fosque Motors – Ray Latham is a newly hired used car salesman at Fosque Motors. He discovers an overgrown side lot full of old cars, known to the employees as the "Night Lot." Working late one night, Ray sees a mysterious black vehicle easing in and out of the parking lot. His curiosity whetted, Ray waits for the car to study it. Unfortunately for Ray, he figures it out in "Dead Car Smell." The story appeared in *The Fierce and Unforgiving Muse* (2012) by Gregory L. Norris.

Greymant, Height Street – Chris has fled Texas to escape her violent ex-girlfriend, Lisa. The landlord assumed she was a he and refuses to rent Chris the apartment. A quick visit from the law and the housing authority and Chris has her new apartment. The new problem is that something was left behind by the previous tenants, hidden in the basement in a blood stain. "The Cycle" by Gregory L. Norris appeared in *The Fierce and Unforgiving Muse* (2012).

Greenfield – Nine-year-old Anna Wheaton is critically injured in a sledding accident and discovers she is a "jumper," a person

167

who can shift to alternative worlds where the dead co-mingle with the living. There she discovers armies of restless souls preparing to wage the ultimate battle led by the Shadow Monster, a composite of dead souls that pursues the jumpers to absorb them in *Jumpers* (1997) by R. Patrick Gates.

Grover's Corner – Thornton Wilder's 1938 Pulitzer Prize-winning play *Our Town* is a drama about everyday life in turn of the century Grover's Corners. The third act is devoted to the dead discussing whether or not to revisit their lives. Playwright Wilder himself has since joined the discussion and is buried in Connecticut.

Actor and writer Frank Craven helped adapt the screenplay, including his original Broadway role as the Stage Manager, for the 1940 film version of *Our Town* starring William Holden and Martha Scott. It was followed by countless versions on television, particularly in the 1950s, when live drama was a staple of the medium.

Halcyon – After Carter Cage is exposed as the serial killer "The Mutilator," his wife packs up her young children, Ethan and Mary, and flees to New Hampshire. Years later, the teenage Ethan is battling sudden bursts of rage and drug use as he struggles to come to grip with his father's legacy. But the Mutilator has escaped from prison and he's heading to Halycon, leaving a trail of bodies in *The Cage Legacy* (2012) by Nicholas Conley.

Hampstead – Robert and Eliza own a drafty old farm house outside of Hampstead. A winter storm has cut the power and Robert heads into town to buy a generator. Eliza simply cannot warm up, in spite of sitting near the wood stove. They invite some other powerless friends over for dinner but Eliza seems worse. When the frozen body of the handyman is found outside, Robert begins to think something worse than a winter storm is occurring. Robert had found an old tin in the cellar with a hidden treasure the week before, and he's beginning to wonder if it might somehow be related. *Ice Storm* (2016) is a novelette by John W. Dennehy.

Hampstead, East Road – Myrta Alice Little (1888–1967) was a lifelong resident of Hampstead. She played hostess to H. P. Lovecraft on several occasions hoping to spark a romance, to which Lovecraft appears to have been oblivious. On his first visit, Lovecraft read a new story to the family. Myrta suggested a change which Lovecraft implemented. The modified story was called "The Outsider," which would not appear in print for another five years (in *Weird Tales*, April 1926). See also **Stratham**.

Hampton – A town with a rich supernatural history, Hampton was repeatedly used by John Greenleaf Whittier in such ballads as "The Changeling," "The New Wife and The Old" (1843) and "The Wreck of Rivermouth" (1864). See also **Moulton Mansion, Hampton; Pine Grove Cemetery, Hampton; Tuck Museum, Hampton; Elmfield, Hampton Falls; Hampton River; Melvin Village; Sheppard Beach**.

Hampton, Moulton Mansion – The former home of General Jonathan Moulton (1726-1787) is actually the second Moulton Mansion in Hampton. The first burned in 1769, allegedly by Satan in retaliation for being outsmarted by Moulton. The mansion was known locally as a haunted house at the time of Whittier's visits to Hampton, with reports of ghosts and attempted exorcisms dating back to Moulton's death.
Fifty years after Moulton's death, Whittier published "The New Wife and the Old" (1843), a liberal reinterpretation of local lore. In the poem, Moulton's second wife awakens on her wedding night to discover the ghost of Moulton's first wife, who had died less than a year before. The deceased wife had come to reclaim her wedding ring, given to the current wife by General Moulton. See also **Hampton**.
Scott T. Goudsward revisits the Whittier poem in "The Autumn Years," first appearing in *Snowbound with Zombies* (2015). In

this version, the first wife is still seeking her wedding rings. She's a little more substantial than a ghost in this retelling, but just as dead.

Hampton, Pine Grove Cemetery – General Jonathan Moulton (1726-1787) was buried on his property. There is no longer any sign of the grave or a headstone and the General's final resting place is presumed to have been destroyed when a railroad track was built across the property. A cenotaph was placed in Pine Grove to General Moulton, the "New Hampshire Faust." Moulton was the wealthiest man in Hampton. His success came so easily and quickly that the locals suspected he had sold his soul to the devil. As the tale is told, Moulton sold his soul in return for Satan filling the General's boot with gold once a year. The deal was negated when the devil found Moulton had cut a hole in the boot and the gold was pouring through a hole in the floor and filling the basement. Satan burned down the house in retaliation and the gold vanished. The story appears in a number of folklore texts which led to even greater notoriety when Whittier borrowed from the General's legend. See also **Hampton**.

Hampton, Tuck Museum – The home of the Hampton Historical Society is near the shanty where Eunice "Goody" Cole (1590-1680) lived out her final years. After being condemned as a witch in 1656, Goody Cole was jailed three separate times, spending most of her last twenty years in a Boston jail. Whittier gave her national notoriety in his poems "The Changeling" (1865) where Cole is blamed for a baby exchanged for a demon and "The Wreck of the Rivermouth" (1864) has Goody Cole summoning the squall that caused the shipwreck. See also **Hampton River**.

A cenotaph to Hampton's accused witch Goody Eunice Cole.

Cole's Hampton citizenship was restored in 1938 and a waterworn rock on the Tuck Museum property serves as a cenotaph to her unmarked grave. Goody Cole's rock is located near another infamous grave marker, the relocated stone of Leif Ericsson's brother Thorvald, who, at least in local lore, was buried on Hampton's coast.

Hampton Beach – Thirty years of alcoholism has left the narrator with nothing. His wife has drowned herself off the Hampton Beach jetty and finally sober at last, he tries to locate his lost daughter. Now he will discover there are many types of scars that don't heal in "Infliction" by John McIlveen, first published in *Borderlands 5* (2003).

Hampton Beach, Lafayette Road – Soldier is a changeling, stolen as an infant to be raised as a servant to the ghouls that dwell in the tunnels beneath Rhode Island. Possessing special gifts, she is the rare Child of the Cuckoo allowed to roam the surface world. She works for the Bailiff, a mysterious figure with arcane gifts. Soldier and her driver Sheldon must follow precise directions mapped out for them by the Bailiff as the route to their current mission. In this case, they head north from Rhode Island on I-95 to the New Hampshire border, then doubling back at Hampton Beach to proceed south on Route 1, Lafayette Road. The mission will not end well, which is rare for a seasoned killer like Soldier. *Daughter of the Hounds* (2007) by Caitlín R. Kiernan is the third book in a trilogy that began in 2001 with *Threshold*.

Hampton Beach, Terry's Primo Subs – Vic McQueen leaves the family house while her parents are fighting about a lost bracelet. She crosses the derelict Shorter Way Bridge in Haverhill, MA and suddenly finds herself in Hampton Beach. Somehow she has been transported 15 miles beyond the bridge to the sub shop where the bracelet was last seen. Vic has discovered she has a gift of "finding" things presumed lost by crossing the bridge. In Joe Hill's novel *NOS4A2* (2013), Vic will discover this gift may also be a curse. See also **Dover**.

Hampton Falls – In 2020, Jewelle Gomez's former slave turned vampire Gilda has become a reclusive romance writer in a world teetering on the brink of Malthusian collapse. Now, her anonymity has been shattered by a television report on her alter ego and the undead heroine must decide how to reinvent herself again in *The Gilda Stories* (1991).

Just outside of Hampton falls, a small farm is isolated by the weather in "Snowbound with Zombies." Now, the McAvoys are getting a crash course in psychopomps when a stranger comes to call. David Bernard's story first appeared in *Snowbound with Zombies* (2015).

Hampton Falls, Elmfield – Elmfield was the ancestral home of Sarah Gove, a longtime friend of Whittier. The poet frequently spent his summers at Elmfield and died there September 7, 1892. The colonial mansion was purchased, dismantled and moved to Connecticut in the mid-1990s.

Hampton Falls, Exeter Road – Architect, historian and author Ralph Adams Cram (1863-1942) was born on Exeter Road. Cram was a leader of the Gothic Revival architecture movement and his towering buildings remain landmarks in Boston and on colleges across the nation. Cram also wrote fiction; a collection of his stories, *Black Spirits and White* (1895) includes "The Dead Valley." A ghost story set in Sweden, H. P. Lovecraft considered "The Dead Valley" to be "memorably potent" in his famous essay, "Supernatural Horror in Literature."

Hampton Falls, Hawes Cemetery – Noted New England regionalist author Alice Brown (1856-1948) is buried in Hampton Falls near the family farm where she was born. Her supernatural contributions include tales aboard ships such as "The Flying Teuton" (*Harper's Magazine*, August 1917) and ghostly encounters in World War I battlefields such as "The Empire of Death" first anthologized in *The Flying Teuton: And Other Stories* (1918). See also **Devonport; Sudleigh**.

Hampton River – The Hampton River empties into the Atlantic at an inhospitable rock shoal known locally as the "Rivermouth Rocks." John Greenleaf Whittier's "The Wreck of Rivermouth" first published in *Atlantic Monthly*, April 1864 expands on the true story of a local shipwreck from 1657 by adding local witch Goody Cole. See also **Tuck Museum, Hampton**.

Hamtucket – Charles L. Grant, writing as Lionel Fenn, spoofs H. P. Lovecraft in *668: The Neighbor of the Beast* (1992), book 5 in the "Kent Montana" series. Actor Kent Montana agrees to spend the night in an abandoned mansion to meet the terms of his inheritance. However, the house is actually the sanctum of cultists looking for a sacrifice for a ritual from the pages of the dreaded *Bingonomicron*.

Hancock – Homicide detective Frank O'Hara lives in Hancock in *A Room for the Dead* (1994) by Noel Hynd. Dealing with snow, alcoholism and impending retirement, O'Hara must also investigate brutal murders that appear to have been committed by serial killer Gary Ledbetter. Ledbetter, however, was executed five years earlier.

Hanover – Dr. David Mallory is at a loss when a routine childbirth results in a formerly healthy mother becoming a corpse drained of blood. The inexplicable exsanguination sends Dr. Mallory to medical records where he finds that ten similar births have occurred in the last decade. More disturbing, each of the attending obstetricians was murdered within a year of the birth, in *The Twelfth Child* (1990) by Raymond Van Over.
Dr. David Monroe is guilt-ridden when a healthy young woman dies giving birth. As he investigates the cause, he begins to believe the cause of death was not a medical condition but related to a satanic cult preparing the way for the Anti-Christ in *Purgatory's Gate* (2007) by Raymond Van Over.

Hanover, Dartmouth College – See **Dartmouth College**.

Harlowe – Harlowe is a sleepy little farming town until auctioneer Perly Dunsmore arrives. Dunsmore's influence grows and slowly corrupts the townspeople, threatening first their way of life, and then their very existence in *The Auctioneer* (1975) by Joan Samson.

Haunted Woods – New York socialites Lamont Cranston (Bret Morrison in his debut in the role) and Margot Lane (Marjorie Anderson) arrive at the rural New Hampshire home of Margot's Aunt Susan only to find her missing. As if the house being next to Haunted Woods wasn't a clue, the nearest neighbor is Professor Alexander Sergoff, a mad scientist with a god-complex and a secret lab. Now Margot has been captured as a food source and the Shadow is trapped in a room filled with blood-thirsty experiments. "The Gibbering Thing" episode of *The Shadow* radio series was first broadcast in September 1943.

Haver-Towne – Billionaire Stewart Fanshawe's therapist suggests he leave New York for somewhere more secluded to help him overcome his obsessive voyeurism. The recovering peeping tom ends up in Haver-Towne, the self-proclaimed "Salem of New Hampshire." But old evil still survives here, centuries after the torture and burning of hundreds of witches. There's something evil in the water, and Fanshawe's perverted past gives him a front row seat to Hell on Earth in *Witch Water* (2011) by Edward Lee.

Haversford – A poor, widowed cooper has a nightmare about the destruction of his town and the slaughter of the villagers. His problem is the dream was so vivid it almost felt like a premonition in "The Devil's Constitutional." The story appeared the collection of Scott Thomas's work *Urn & Willow* (2012).

Hawthorne – Ever since Gillian Foster received a strange letter in the mail, she's seen shadowy figures lurking around her. Fearing for her daughter's safety, she flees Hawthorne. Twenty years later, she has been diagnosed as schizophrenic and committed to Hawthorne Psychiatric Facility. Her daughter has received a similar letter and is being tormented by the same unseen force. Has she contracted her mother's mental illness or is the something out there with an agenda against the Foster women? *Debt to be Paid* (2015) is the debut novella of Patrick Lacey.

Hebron – In 1915, while living in New York, Aleister Crowley ghost-wrote two books on astrology for renowned astrologer Evangeline Adams. Between 1913 and 1918, Adams owned the Jonathan K. Pike House (built c.1803) on Church Lane in Hebron. Adams built a one and ½ story study on the property. This new building is where Crowley, self-proclaimed "wickedest man in the world," stayed during the summer of 1916 on an extended "magical retirement." Various stories from this trip to Newfound Lake, which he refers to by its original name of Lake Pasquaney, include encounters with ball lightning, frog crucifixions, and what is referred to as the "star sponge vision." His novel *Moonchild* (1929) was a roman à clef of his personal life and hallucinations, in which rival societies of black and white magicians battle over attempts to incarnate a supernatural being. *Golden Twigs* (1988) is a collection of short stories written by Crowley during this retreat.

Hellbent Mountain – In John Bellairs' *The Curse of the Blue Figurine*, the profile of The Hag on Hellbent Mountain substitutes for The Old Man of the Mountain. Originally published in 1983, Bellairs ends his Johnny Dixon adventure with the Hag's collapse. Twenty years later, the Old Man collapsed as well. See also **Franconia Notch State Park**.

Henniker, Old Center Cemetery – The graveyard behind the old town hall has a famous occupant – Mary (nee Wilson) Wallace (1720-1814). A ship of Ulster Scot immigrants was captured off Boston by pirates. The pirate captain heard an infant cry, discovered James Wilson and his wife Elizabeth, who had just given birth. The captain promised to spare the lives of the captives if the baby was named for his mother. And that is how "Ocean Born Mary" received her nickname. In 1798, the 78-year old widowed Mary moved from the family's home in

Londonderry to Henniker and lived with her son, William. Her grave is marked and she never lived with her son Robert, much to the chagrin of the ghost hunters who continue to "identify" her spirit at the wrong house. See also **Robert Wallace Homestead, Henniker**.

Henniker, Robert Wallace Homestead – The house on Bear Road still bears the marker that announces it is the "*Homestead of Robert Wallace, also known as Ocean Born Mary House, 1784.*" The problem is that "Ocean Born" Mary Wallace (1720-1814) never lived there. She lived over a mile away, with her other son, William, when she was 71. The William Wallace House burned down a century ago. The Robert Wallace House was purchased by hoaxster Louis Roy of Wisconsin in 1917, who began promoting it as the Ocean Born Mary House until his death in 1965. Roy charged admission to tour the home, claimed it contained buried treasure, Mary's furniture, Mary's ghost, and her unmarked grave. See also **Old Cemetery, Henniker**.

Hillsborough – The summer folks have slowly been changing the way of life in the backcountry. And as more farms sell off land to build summer cottages and local markets are turned into antique shops, tensions begin to mount among those determined to prevent further changes. "The Summer Rebellion" first appeared in *The Collected Stories of Hortense Calisher* (1975).

Hobb's End – Director John Carpenter's *In the Mouth of Madness* (1995) pays homage to both H. P. Lovecraft and Stephen King. A private detective played by Sam Neill is hired to investigate the disappearance of horror writer Sutter Cane. Cane has been missing for months along with his latest manuscript and the publisher would like both back in New York as soon as possible. The investigation leads to the town of Hobb's End – a supposedly fictional creation of Sutter Cane.

Holts Corners – Sister Anne Feeney runs Hope Cottage, a collection of hard luck girls at St. Anthony's School for Homeless Girls in the White Mountains. The Cardinal pulls her from the school for a special mission – investigate claims of a virgin birth that may be the advent of the apocalypse in *Virgin* (1980) by James Patterson.

Hooksett – The former Mercy Hall of defunct Mount Saint Mary College in Hooksett is now a luxury apartment complex. The exterior retains its air of academic elegance with a hint of foreboding, making it perfect for scenes in the films of Matt Farley and Charles Roxburgh.

In *Freaky Farley* (2007), the building's façade is shot with a focus on the tower that gives the structure a vibe similar to a Kirkbride building, appropriate, since it standing in for Farley Wilder's (Matt Farley) new home, the Menomenee Home for the Criminally Insane. See also **Morgantown**.

The exterior became the outside the Farnum Finishing School for Girls of New England where Allie Stone (Sharon Scalzo) has just been unceremoniously expelled. Fortunately, the legendary tutor Neil Stuart (Matt Farley) has returned to River Town in *Don't Let the Riverbeast Get You!* (2012). See also **River Town**.

Hooksett, Main Street – Main Street crosses the Merrimack River at the narrows as two trestle railroad bridges. On the south shore of the river, just off Main, there is an unofficial beach where locals have set up a rope swing. This swimming spot is a regular hangout of the Manchvegas Outlaw Society (Matt Farley, Marie Dellicker, Tom Scalzo), where they contemplate their grand plans. Of course, between newspaper routes, band practice, hunting serial killers, and tracking gospercaps, there isn't much time for swimming anymore in *Monsters, Marriage & Murder in Manchvegas* (2009). See also **Manchvegas**.

Isles of Hampton – The Isles of Hampton are Brendan DuBois' thinly disguised version of the Isles of Shoals in "The Tourist

Who Wasn't There," first published in *Lighthouse Hauntings* (2002). Cranmore Island is the largest of these Islands and serves as the point of departure for tours of Ivory Island and its famous lighthouse. Nora Donnelly works for the State Parks and between her lecherous boss, idiot tourists, and inexplicable ghost lights, it looks like it's going to be a long summer. See also **Isles of Shoals; Ivory Island**.

Isles of Shoals – The Isles of Shoals are a group of small islands with a rich history of folklore and tragedy. The Massachusetts Bay Colony governed the islands until New Hampshire's contested border was finalized. The boundary was drawn so that all the islands north of Star Island remained part of the Maine Province, still governed by Massachusetts. Six miles off the coast of New Hampshire, where they are visible from the shore, both tourists and writers tend to assume all the Isles are part of New Hampshire but only Star, White, Seavey, and Lunging Islands are within the borders of New Hampshire. See also **Isles of Hampton; South Cemetery, Portsmouth**.

Ivory Island – Nora Donnelly gives tours of the scenic Ivory Island Lighthouse as part of her duties for the NH State Park Department. After seeing lights on the uninhabited island, she learns the legend that the island is haunted, but only when the lighthouse itself is threatened in "The Tourist Who Wasn't There" by Brendan DuBois, first published in *Lighthouse Hauntings* (2002). See also **Isles of Hampton**.

Jackson – Will Reed (Treat Williams) is a widow trying to deal with his increasingly difficult teen son Seth (Jonathan Jackson). Seth blames Will for the loss of his mother in a house fire when he was a child. When a murder rocks the town, Will begins to suspect it was Seth. *Skeletons in the Closet* (2001) was filmed exclusively in the Mount Washington Valley, in particular in Jackson, where local restaurants, shops, and the Honeymoon Covered Bridge are easily spotted. See also

Wentworth Inn, Jackson; Memorial Hospital, North Conway.

Jackson, Mirror Lake – Scenic Jackson Lake becomes a scene of terror as a filming location in *The Good Son* (1993). Quinn Culkin plays the sister of budding sociopath Henry Evans (her real-life brother Macaulay). When she falls through the ice while skating near their home in Maine, no one believes Cousin Mark (Elijah Wood) when he claims it was neither an accident nor an isolated incident. See also **McIntyre Road, Newington**.

Jackson, Town Hall – In Stephen King's *The Dead Zone* (1979), Johnny Smith attempts to assassinate Presidential candidate Greg Stillson at a campaign stop in this building. See also **Ridgeway**.

Jackson, Wentworth Inn – A throwback to the golden age of White Mountain resorts, the Wentworth is also a destination for social events. In *Skeletons in the Closet* (2001), it is the location of the high school's senior prom. Will Reed (Treat Williams) comes to the Inn. His son Seth (Jonathan Jackson) is drunk and has pushed his girlfriend (Schuyler Fisk). In the kitchen of the Inn, the yelling match suddenly stops when Seth blurts out something that makes Will realize his son's issues may be far more complicated than he suspected. See also **Jackson**.

Jaffrey Center – In the Old Burying Ground, a simple headstone marks the final resting place of author and poetess Willa Cather (1873-1947). Among her numerous works are such classic Victorian ghost tales as "The Affair at Grover Station" (first published in *The Library*, June 16 1900), "The Fear That Walks by Noonday" first appearing in *Sombrero* (1895) and the gruesome children's Christmas tale "The Strategy of Were-Wolf Dog" (*Home Monthly*, December 1896).

Jericho – The novella "Investigating Jericho" by Chelsea Quinn Yarbro was first published in *The Magazine of Fantasy & Science Fiction*, April 1992. IRS agent Morton Symes is sent to northern New Hampshire to investigate why none of the residents have paid their taxes in two years. In the deserted logging town, he learns that there are worse things than tax evaders.

Jericho Falls – A van crashes in the White Mountains, killing the driver and releasing a deadly virus that infects the town of Jericho Falls. Now Sheriff Jack Slater must stop the spread of the virus before the townsfolk kill each other off or worse, the government destroys the town in *Jericho Falls* (1986) by Christopher Hyde.

Keenan – Tom Russell (James Van Der Beek) is paroled from prison and returns home to a ghost town. Ten years earlier, all of the world's children under the age of nine fell into a catatonic state simultaneously. The economy crashed as parents were forced to pay for the care of their unresponsive offspring. Suddenly the all the children wake up, with a collective consciousness, growing smarter by the moment with one singular thought – kill the adults. *The Plague* (2006) was produced by Clive Barker.

Keene, Pearl Street – Pearl Street was the final residence of actor Bramwell Fletcher (1904-1988). Remembered by horror fans for his brief appearance in *The Mummy* (1932) as the archaeologist driven mad by Boris Karloff's resurrected Imhotep, Fletcher's horror credits ranged from Little Billee in *Svengali* (1931) to *The Undying Monster* (1942). And he was briefly married to Helen Chandler, Mina Seward to Bela Lugosi's Count in *Dracula* (1931). In 1943, Fletcher returned to his New York City theatrical roots to concentrate on Broadway. Since television studios were in New York, he also dabbled in that new medium, most notably as the evil Frollo in a two-part episode of "The Hunchback of Notre Dame"

(6:8/9) on *Robert Montgomery Presents*. When TV moved to Hollywood, Fletcher retired and moved to New Hampshire.

Keene, West Street – The exterior scenes of *Jumanji* (1995) were primarily filmed in Keene. After Allan Parrish disappeared, his father was so distraught that he let the family shoe factory fold, destroying the town's economy with it. Prop and set crews worked to make Keene look like a prosperous town and then like a mill town on hard times. The recognizable landmarks include the stampede-surviving Central Square bandstand and a large mural painted on a brick wall at the intersection of West Street, advertising Parrish Shoes. See also **Brantford**.

Keene Railroad Station – Henry Akeley sends Professor Wilmarth of Miskatonic University a piece of black stone from a monolith, proof that something is amiss in the woods of Vermont. However, the package is stolen from a Boston and Maine baggage car at Keene. Now Wilmarth will venture into Vermont to investigate himself in "The Whisperer in Darkness" by H. P. Lovecraft (*Weird Tales*, August 1931).

Keene State College – Charles H. Hapgood was a professor at Keene State when in 1966 he published *Maps of the Ancient Sea Kings*. Hapgood's theory was that ancient maps such as the 1513 "Piri Reis map" were copies of far more ancient maps, the originals of which were drawn before the Ice Age by an ancient civilization, which is why the maps accurately show the Antarctic coastline as it exists beneath the ice cap. Colin Wilson would introduce Hapgood's theories to a different audience in his sequel to Lovecraft's "At the Mountains of Madness." In "The Tomb of the Old Ones," first published in *The Antarktos Cycle* (1999), Hapgood becomes a correspondent of Daniel Willoughby, noted expert on Antarctica. See **University of New Hampshire**.

Along the side of the Putnam Science Center is a stone marker commemorating one man's war against gravity. Roger W.

Babson (1875–1967) made millions in the stock market by applying Newtonian Physics principles to financial decisions. He also considered gravity to be his personal enemy. He became obsessed with gravity at the age of 18 when his younger sister Edith drowned. When his grandson drowned in 1947, it became a personal vendetta for the rest of his life. He created the Gravity Research Foundation to conquer the force he held responsible for the deaths of his kin. In the 1960s, in return for financial donations, Babson was allowed to erect monuments on college campuses along the East Coast, placed to remind students of the benefits soon to be forthcoming when gravity was harnessed. See also **Meetinghouse Road, New Boston**.

Professor Katherine Phillips (1913–2008) taught acting, film, and screenwriting classes at Keene for over 20 years before retiring in 2006. As actress Kay Linaker, she appeared in more than 50 films during the 1930s and 1940s before switching to screenwriting in the 50s. Professor Phillips has a small but important role in horror movie history: under her married name Kate Phillips, she co-wrote the original script for the 1958 version of *The Blob*.

Kensington – See **Water Street, Exeter**.

Kent Pond – Graphic artist Clay Riddell (John Cusack) lives in Boston. His estranged wife and son live on Kent Pond. In the film version of Stephen King's *Cell* (2016), Kent Pond is moved from Maine to New Hampshire. Clay cannot determine the fate of his son, so he begins a treacherous journey by foot from the burning ruins of Boston back to Kent Pond. See also **Gaiten**.

Kingston – Greenwood Cemetery holds the graves of Betty and Barney Hill. The Hills claimed to have been abducted by a UFO in 1961, only recovering the memory of the event several years later through hypnosis. See also **Lincoln**.

Laconia, Thrill Village – Hitchhiker Alan Parker gets a ride from George Staub. Alan soon discovers George is already dead and is taunting him with facts only Alan knows, such his trip to Thrill Village, a small amusement park where as a 12-year old, he balked when about to board the thrill ride known as "The Bullet." "Riding the Bullet" is a novella by Stephen King that was originally published as an e-book. It was later collected in *Everything's Eventual* (2002).

Lake Massabesic – See **Chester**.

Lake Nubanusit – New Yorker Seth Moran is taking his family to Lake Nubanusit deep in the Monadnock region. A wrong turn puts them at the mercy of a cult of white supremacists led by a psychotic general who never returned from 'Nam. Their captors threaten to rape his wife and daughter if Seth does not take a gun into Boston and randomly kill a black family in *Horror Story* (1979) by Oliver McNab.

Lake Pasquaney – See **Hebron**.

Lake Waukewan – A man vacationing in the Lakes Region discovers the 19th-century diary of a woman who is caught up with the Millerite movement, a group of fanatics expecting the end of the world on April 3, 1843. When it didn't happen, Miller's followers, who had given away all their earthly possessions, were a little angry. And as evidenced in Glen Hirshberg's story "Like a Lily in a Flood," such anger can survive across the generations. The story first appeared in *Cemetery Dance* #50 (Oct 2004).

Lake Winnipesaukee, Lake Road – Part of Vic McQueen's rehab regimen is making amends. She rents a cottage at the Lake and brings her son Wayne with her. Her plans were to clean the carriage house and turn it into an artists' studio. Those plans changed with the return of the malevolent Charlie Manx. As she is forced to flee the police by finding the Shorter Way

Bridge, she realizes that the bridge is closer than expected in *NOS4A2* (2013) by Joe Hill. See also **Dover**.

Lake Winnipesaukee, Minge Cove – An old farm adjacent to a campground has a history of disappearances. Pete claims it's a dimensional portal, and the other kids aren't sure whether to believe him or not. Years later, Bobby is a nightmare-wracked adult, unable to recall what happened that summer when his six friends disappeared in "Endless Hunger" by Karen Dent. The story appeared in *Call of Lovecraft* (2012).

Lancaster – Lancaster sits along the Connecticut River, nestled between the White Mountain National Forest and the Great North Woods. The isolated downtown makes it the perfect stand-in for the town of Friar, which has slowly repopulated itself after a mass exodus in 1940. The 1930 Rialto Theater is particularly recognizable as a landmark that may be more than a place to buy popcorn in *Yellowbrickroad* (2010). See also **Friar**.

A state historic marker notes the location where Betty and Barney Hill were abducted by aliens.

Lincoln – While driving in the White Mountains in 1961, Betty and Barney Hill spotted a UFO. They stopped the car to observe the craft in the vicinity of Indian Head, a knoll on Mount Pemigewasset. This was the start of one of the most well-known alien abduction cases in history. The 1975 film version, *The UFO Incident* with James Earl and Estelle Parsons as the Hills, was handled more as a horror film than the docudrama it was supposed to be. See also **Kingston**.

Lost Valley – Wilson, a traveling salesman, visits Lost Valley on his yearly route. He arrives just as the entire village is heading out into the woods for a Walpurgis Sabbat. "Night Train to Lost Valley" by August Derleth was first published in *Weird Tales*, January 1948 under his pseudonym.

Lyston – The elderly Winchs are shunned in post-Revolution Lyston – two of their sons were Tories. The simmering resentment erupts in false accusations and retribution. Now Zaccheus is dead and Eunice's revenge is haunting in "A Nice Warm Bed." The story appeared the collection of Scott Thomas's work *Urn & Willow* (2012).

Madison – On September 2, 1962, Edward Estlin Cummings (1894-1962) suffered a stroke at Joy Farm, his beloved summer home near Silver Lake. He died early the next morning at Memorial Hospital in North Conway. As author e. e. cummings, he skirted the edges of the horror genre with works like the whimsical Halloween poem [hist whist] or his references to classical myths as allegories for modern messages, such as "All in Green Went My Love Riding," using the story of Artemis and Actaeon. Both poems were first collected in *Tulips and Chimneys*, 1923.

Malton – Geoffrey Thorne returns to his childhood home, bringing his stalled writing career and a newly diagnosed brain tumor. He reunites with his childhood friends, bonding over failed jobs, failed marriages, and the secret they share -

the accidental death of a schoolmate they caused as children. Now their numbers dwindle as a mysterious killer stalks them in *The Jokers Club* (2011) by Gregory Bastianelli.

Manchester – The start of the presidential primaries means that the candidates flock to New Hampshire. Johnny Smith tries to meet the candidates and use his psychic skills to determine their true merit. Smith meets Jimmy Carter at a Manchester appearance and foretells he will become President of the United States in Stephen King's *The Dead Zone* (1979). See also **Ridgeway**.

First anthologized in *Christmas Trees and Monkeys* (2002), Daniel G. Keohane's short story "The Monkey on the Towers" finds a giant ape swinging between radio towers in Manchester. Is he a figment of a mass delusion, a symbol of chaos in the lives of the locals, or just a really big monkey?

Manchester, Beech Street – Manchester Hebrew Cemetery is the final resting place of Ralph Baer (1922-2014), the inventor known as "The Father of Video Games." In 1966, the German immigrant was a defense industry engineer who conceived the idea of an electronic device that would allow people to play games on their television. In 1971, Baer patented the device that would become the Magnavox Odyssey, the first commercial home gaming system. As the technology improved, so did the complexity of the games. The popularity of these later games, of course, led to film adaptions of video games such as *Resident Evil* (2002), *House of the Dead* (2003), and *Alone in the Dark* (2005).

Manchester, Brickhill Manufacturing Company – Ben Richards is being hunted by the government's murderous hitmen. The longer he survives, the more funds go to his family and the higher the ratings. An ally in Boston has arranged for Ben to mail the videos he must post. Ben sends them to Boston, using fake mailing labels from a Manchester company, where his ally mails them locally to confuse the trail. It seems to be helping – Ben has set a new record for surviving in *The Running Man* (1982) by Stephen King, writing as Richard Bachman. See also **Winthrop Street, Manchester**.

Manchester, Canal Street – The Manchester Transportation Center on Canal is where Greyhound buses stop. Prior to its construction, the Greyhound Terminal was on Elm Street. In neither case does the terrain or description match the denouement in Alice Sebold's *The Lovely Bones* (2002). The 2009 film version is true to the book about the demise of the serial killer as his victim Susie watched from beyond.

Manchester, Elm Street – Local gustatory landmark Queen City Cupcakes serves as the hangout of Neil Stuart (Matt Farley) and his stalwart band of tutors (Bryan Fortin and Millhouse G.). Neil has just returned to town and the homecoming has not been joyous. His ex-fiancée is now engaged to a jerk, the sheriff wants him to leave, and the town still mocks his claims of seeing a riverbeast. Even his fellow tutors and cupcakes can't help Neil when the aquatic terror rises again in *Don't Let the Riverbeast Get You!* (2012). See also **River Town**.

Manchester, Life Services Institute – In a mill turned research facility on the outskirts of town, the Life Services Institute is close to a breakthrough in life-extending genetics research. Now all they need is the genetic code of a particular infant in *Infinity's Child* (1997) by Harry Stein. See also **Edwardtown**.

Manchester, Rock Rimmon Park – Rock Rimmon is the largest park in the city at almost 140 acres centered on forested granite cliffs. Denise the Town Witch (Steff Deschenes) and the mysterious Ninja accompany Farley Wilder (Matt Farley) into the rugged woods to battle the carnivorous trogs that threaten the town. Considering Farley's superhuman rage, the backup may not be necessary in *Freaky Farley* (2007). See also **River Town**.

Director Charles Roxburgh would return to Rock Rimmon Park for his next film *Monsters, Marriage & Murder in Manchvegas* (2009). Manchvegas ingénue Melinda Corbin (Sharon Scalzo) is missing. Her frantic father (Kevin McGee) believes her bad boy suitor Vince (Kyle Kochan) is responsible. Police chief Delvecchio (James McHugh) dismisses the idea, so Corbin enlists the aid of the Manchvegas Outlaw Society and plucky local reporter (Elizabeth Peterson) to find her. Unfortunately, Melinda has been captured by the murderous sasquatch-like gospercaps of the Manchvegas Woods. See also **Manchvegas**.

Manchester, Winthrop Street – It's 2025 in the totalitarian dystopia that used to be America. With the nation's economy in ruins, Ben Richards can't find work. His daughter is ill and Ben can't afford medication. In desperation, he volunteers to participate in the government-operated Games Network show *The Running Man*. Now hunted by the network's killers, he flees from New York to Boston to Manchester. The longer he stays alive, the more money his family receives. In Manchester, he masquerades as a priest while dodging the hunters. *The Running Man* (1982) is by Stephen King, writing as Richard Bachman. See also **Brickhill Manufacturing Company, Manchester**.

Manchvegas – *Monsters, Marriage and Murder in Manchvegas* (2009) is the story of the Manchvegas Outlaw Society. Marshall (Matt Farley), Jenny (Marie Dellicker) and All-Star Pete (Tom Scalzo) are three young adults living their life as if they were still tweens. And that's fine in a small town like Manchvegas, where 20-something-year-olds running errands in a little red wagon, pretending to be a rock band, and delivering newspapers is perfectly fine. In fact, if it wasn't for the reports of murderous hominids in the woods and the serial killer targeting newlywed brides, life would be perfect. Now if Marshall would just ask Jenny out – everyone knows he likes her. See also **Main Street, Hooksett; Rock Rimmon Park, Manchester**.

Marlborough – W. Paul Cook (1881-1948) is buried in a family plot in Pine Grove Cemetery. A close friend of H. P. Lovecraft, he was the author of *In Memoriam, Howard Phillip Lovecraft: Recollections, Appreciations, Estimates* (1941), still considered one the most touching tributes to Lovecraft. An officer and official publisher of the Amateur Press Association, he had previously started up several amateur press magazines. The first and only edition of one of his magazines, *The Recluse* (1927), was the first appearance of Lovecraft's landmark essay, "Supernatural Horror in Literature."

Melete – Imogen and her sister Marin escape their controlling mother by attending the prestigious artist retreat on the banks of New Hampshire's Mourning River. Imogen is a writer, putting to paper the fairy tales she has used as a coping mechanism since a child. Marin is a dancer, whose art is her sole driving purpose. Fairy tales often require sacrifices for happy endings, but will Marin allow her the opportunity in the urban fantasy *Roses and Rot* (2016) by Kat Howard.

Melham – In "The Eye of Hlu-Hlu" by Donald Burleson, Charles Lloyd Hutchinson inherits his grandfather's estate including his research files into global mythologies involving an ancient demon called Cthulhu. He soon discovers his grandfather bought the house because of a stone circle in the woods behind the property, a portal to something evil beyond comprehension. The story was first published in *The Morgan and Rice Gazette* #38, 1993.

Melvin Village – The lawn of the Melvin Village Community Church includes a weathered bronze Native American in silhouette with a drawn bow. The arrow, both the Indian's and one beneath him point the direction to "The Grave of the Giant." In 1817, skeletal remains nearly seven feet in height were found buried in the sand along Moultonborough Bay. It would be a forgotten local curiosity until John Greenleaf

Whittier learned the story on one of his visits. His poem "The Grave by the Lake" (*Atlantic Monthly*, May 1865) enjoyed a surge of national attention, resulting in the sign that points to both the grave and the past days of Whittier's superstar influence in literature. See also **Hampton**.

Meredith – Comic strip illustrator Bob Montana moved to Meredith in 1946 and continued creating and drawing the "Archie" comic strip from his farm on Meredith Neck. After his death in 1975, the comics continued by other artists, evolving with the times. The most recent mutation is the darker, grittier "Archie Horror Imprint." *Afterlife with Archie* is Archie and his diminishing number of friends battling to survive in a zombie apocalypse. *The Chilling Adventures of Sabrina* has the teen witch embracing her supernatural side, battling with and against demons, Cthulhian cultists, and similar sorcerous malcontents.

Merrimack – While grocery shopping, Tina Osterlund is approached by a creep. Not your run-of-the-mill creep, but a religious fanatic looking to help her find the true path. Tina rejects him and upon taking her groceries to her car, discovers the creep brought his "order" with him. And apparently, salvation comes at a very high price. "Fields of Salvation" by Philip C. Perron first appeared in *Chiral Mad 2* (2013).

Merrimack, Daniel Webster Highway – The DW in Merrimack is home to one of the five Anheuser-Busch breweries that offer tours of the facilities. The 1-million-square-foot plant, built in 1969, is set on 294 acres. The brewery is the New England home to the Budweiser brand, so when you see camp counselors head out for a night on the town in *Friday the 13th part 2* (1981), those Buds are from this plant; those scenes were shot at a bar in New Preston, Connecticut. If a brewery tour, Clydesdale horses, and beer samples aren't sufficient to change your vacation plans, don't forget the 1999-2002 advertising campaign based on the phrase "Whassup?" that became so pervasive that it was a parody target in *Scary Movie* (2000).

Merrimack, Souhegan River – Long before colonists arrived, Wazoli and Nolka wandered the woods. The couple decides to head to where the Souhegan joins the Merrimack River only to discover carnage on the shores. Nolka fears it is Tsi-Noo, the demonic devourer of souls. Wazoli has his bow and wants to investigate. The choice may be a poor one in "The Place of Strong Current" by Philip C. Perron. The story first appeared in in *Bugs: Tales That Slither, Creep, and Crawl* (2014).

Merrimack County – Becky Woomer (Paula Lindberg) was a moderator in a chat room dedicated to "number stations," computer-generated voices reading streams of random numbers on the radio in a variety of languages. No one knows what they mean, but they've been broadcasting for years. Becky, however, no longer cares – she's one of the people who contracted amnesia after the last broadcast and now can't even remember her own name. "6955 kHz" (3:06) was a third season episode of *Fringe*.

Milburn – Scott Mast returns to his hometown for his father's funeral. A frustrated author who now writes greeting cards, he discovers a partial manuscript of a horror novel, *The Black Wing*, started by his father. The story ties a local ghost story to his family's history through a mysterious house in the woods. When Mast discovers the house exists, he begins to wonder if the manuscript is fictional. If not, Scott may be in for a short and messy end to his return home in *No Doors, No Windows* (2009) by Joe Schreiber.

Milford – The Whatneys move in next door to a blue collar warehouse worker. He senses something is not normal about his new neighbors. An involuntary trip to an abandoned factory in the woods proves he is horribly correct in "Mercy of Madness" by Gregory L. Norris. The story appeared in *Call of Lovecraft* (2012).

Milford, Drummond Hill – Author Fiona Sumerlin receives a faceless doll in the mail. The package says the sender is Emmanuel Devil, which is the name of a character from her popular novel series. The doll does not remain featureless for long - as Fiona goes to dispose of the doll, a vicious mouthful of teeth appear and chomp down on her hand. Now she is in a pitched battle to the death with the doll. Only later does she discover some of her own hair woven into the doll's hair - someone from her past has made a devil doll of her in "Grinn" by Gregory L. Norris. The story appeared in his collection *The Fierce and Unforgiving Muse* (2012).

Milford, Elm Street Cemetery – Caroline H. Cutter's headstone (1805-1838) is proof that some grudges outlive the parties. Her stone includes a 145-word diatribe claiming she was murdered by the Baptist church (and names names) in neighboring Nashua. Her husband, Dr. Calvin Cutter had underwritten the building of a new church building and when the minister and deacons defaulted on their shares, Cutter lost everything. When they demanded reparation, the church refused them a public hearing and excommunicated the Cutters. Caroline did not take the humiliation well and Dr. Cutter blamed the church for her premature death. In addition to the litany of complaints on the headstone, Dr. Cutter toured the country for at least a decade, lecturing on the evils of the church, adding adultery, embezzlement, and other crimes to the list of sins by the church.

Milford, Hemlock Road – Faddy McCallister is a widower living in a mobile home with his two daughters. After a neighbor, Karl Bellingham, gives his eldest a ride home, Faddy finds the man insinuating his way into their lives. With his monster truck and an array of scars and tattoos, Faddy dubs Karl "The Evil One." When his eldest is killed in an auto accident, Faddy is convinced Karl caused it. Then he finds footprints in the snow leading to his youngest daughter's window. Faddy takes protecting his daughter into his own hands. A late night visit to Karl's trailer reveals him for what he really is. Faddy's nickname for Karl was eerily accurate in "The Evil One" by Gregory L. Norris. The story appeared in the collection of his work, *The Fierce and Unforgiving Muse* (2012).

Milford, Ibister Farm Road – A teen girl's neighbor dies amidst mysterious rumors. As the seasons pass the house falls into disrepair. Her boyfriend Tommy is fascinated by the empty house. And fascination turns to an obsession with tragic results. "Indian Summer" by Philip C. Perron appeared in the anthology *Pentagonal Sextet* (2016).

Milford Haven – FBI Special Agents Mulder and Scully travel to tiny Milford Haven in *X-Files* episode "Die Hand Die Verletzt" (2:14). They head to the isolated town to investigate the murder of a Crowley High School student, a killing that has all the markings of a satanic cult ritual.

Morgantown – Meek Farley Wilder (Matt Farley) deals with his domineering father (Kevin McGee) by becoming a peeping tom. He begins to emerge from his shell one day when he meets Scarlett (Sharon Scalzo). But Farley's father will not give up control, so Farley engages in some therapeutic patricide, triggering a killing spree. Now safely locked away, the town seeks his homicidal rage to defeat monstrous trogs terrorizing the woods. Fortunately for the town, Farley already doesn't like trogs in *Freaky Farley* (2007). See also **Hooksett; Rock Rimmon Park, Manchester.**

Grave of Claude "The Invisible Man" Raines in Moultonboro.
Photo courtesy of J.W. Ocker.

Moultonborough – Actor Claude Rains is buried in Red Hill Cemetery. The British stage actor's American film debut was *The Invisible Man* (1933). Although his career would include some of Hollywood's most notable film such *Casablanca* (1942) and *Lawrence of Arabia* (1962), to horror fans, he will forever be remembered as Lon Chaney's father in *The Wolfman* (1941), and the disfigured musician in *The Phantom of the Opera* (1943). See also **Little Pond Road, Sandwich**.

Mount Chocorua – Forest rangers Whitman (Tim R. Morgan) and Stillman (Mike Magri) are investigating a series of disappearances that seem to be centered around a lodge on Chocorua, but the owner (Charles Majka) seems unconcerned. An ancient Indian legend about a demon may be the key if Ranger Whitman can survive long enough to stop the carnage in *Winterbeast* (1991). See also **Newbury**.

Mount Monadnock – In September 2009, a self-described performance artist walked around Mount Monadnock wearing a cheap Bigfoot costume and then ditched the fur suit and did video interviews with hikers who sighted "Bigfoot." When he returned to shoot more footage, he was told that he needed a filming permit and insurance. He sued the state for violating his free speech, and in 2012, the state Supreme Court agreed, only because the peak is so popular among hikers, it qualifies as a public forum. It remains the only case on record of the courts siding with Bigfoot.

Mount Moosilauke – See **Benton**.

Mount Pemigewasset – See **Lincoln**.

Mount Washington – Mount Washington is the highest peak in the Northeastern United States at 6,288 feet. Avalanches are common in the winter and hurricane-force wind gusts are observed from the summit on average of 110 days per year. Over 135 people have died on Mount Washington, most of whom were hikers, so true masochists can choose to walk the Crawford Path, the oldest mountain hiking trail in the United States, laid out in 1819 and still in use. For the less outdoorsy types, the eight-mile Mount Washington Auto Road climbs to the summit from the east with an average gradient of 11.6%. The Mount Washington Cog Railway ascends the western slope. The narrow gauge track is 3 miles long and is the second steepest rack and pinion railway in the world with an average grade of over 25% and a maximum grade of 37%. See also **Thompson and Meserve's Purchase**.

Mount Willey – See **Crawford Notch**.

Mystery Hill – See **North Salem**.

Nashua – Richard Kinnell's ex-wife runs an animal shelter out of her trailer in Nashua in "The Road Virus Heads North," by Stephen King, first appearing in *999* (1999). Kinnell heads there for a quick visit after buying a painting at a garage sale that seems to be changing to reflect carnage on the road, with each change a little closer to Richard.

New Boston – In 1989, amateur press journal *Crypt of Cthulhu* (v.8 No 6, Roodmas 1989) was host to an epic round-robin by some of the top Lovecraftian writers of the time. The topic was the further adventures of H. P. Lovecraft's "Herbert West – Re-Animator," first published as a six-part serial in *Home Brew*, February-July 1922. Part four was "What Came Up from the Cellar" by Donald R. Burleson. West's assistant discovers West is experimenting in reanimating bodily fluids in rural New Hampshire. It's enough to make you sick, but vomiting is not currently recommended. The round-robin was reprinted in *Legacy of the Reanimator* (2015).

New Boston, Meetinghouse Road – At the intersection of Meetinghouse Road and High Street is a stone marker to millionaire Roger W. Babson (1875– 1967) and his Gravity Research Foundation. Babson considered gravity to be his personal enemy and set up the foundation in New Boston in 1948. The foundation still exists, awarding annual prizes for papers on gravity. But the only association with Babson remaining in New Boston is the marker.

In the 1960s, in return for financial donations, Babson was allowed to erect monuments on college campuses up and down the East Coast, placed to remind students of the benefits soon to be forthcoming when gravity was harnessed. See also **Keene State College**.

New Castle, Walton Tavern – For three months in 1682, rocks tossed by unseen hands battered the tavern of George and Alice Walton. The attacks seemed centered around George Walton who was hit with flying stones in his fields and even while traveling by boat to the mainland. One witness to the poltergeist or witchcraft was the secretary of the British Colony of New Hampshire, who later published his accounts of the events as *Lithobolia, or the Stone-Throwing Devil, of Great Island* (1698).

New Castle, Wentworth by the Sea – The Wentworth by the Sea was the crown jewel of the New Hampshire shoreline, an elegant Victorian summer resort. By the time it was used as a filming location for *In Dreams* (1999), it had been abandoned for 20 years and was on the verge of demolition. So, the hotel was perfect as the setting of the decrepit hotel of Claire Cooper's dream (Annette Bening). These dreams somehow link her to serial killer Vivian Thompson (Robert Downey Jr.), who killed Claire's daughter. Thompson is hunting another child, and only Claire can stop him – assuming she can convince someone she is sane.

In Sarah Smith's short story "The Red Storm Comes," the Wentworth is the site of a peace conference that hopes to slow Europe's race toward World War I. Susan meets an attending dignitary named Count Zohary. The Count seduces Susan with promises of power and the ability to see the future. She is unaware that the power only comes with at the cost of her soul. The short story was first published in the anthology *Shudder Again* (1993).

New Oxford – David Banner (Bill Bixby) helps a young woman (Carol Baxter) move back into her childhood home. Plagued by guilt over the death of her twin sister years before, it now appears her dead sister has returned and is carrying a grudge against the surviving sibling. David Banner doesn't believe in ghosts, but his big green alter ego (Lou Ferrigno) may come in handy against a poltergeist in "Haunted" (2:14), an episode of the TV series *The Incredible Hulk*.

Newbury —Thanks to the magic of filmmaking, the Wild Goose Lodge was moved from the Lakes Region into the White Mountains. Shelburne Falls, MA served as the village and Wild Goose Lodge played itself, only now atop Mount Chocorua. Filming of *Winterbeast* (1991) took place over a number of years. The lodge was closed and abandoned when the scenes were filmed. By the time the film was released, the property had been acquired by the state and integrated into Mount Sunapee State Park. See also **Mount Chocorua**.

Newfound Lake – See **Hebron**.

Newington, McIntyre Road – Using filming locations throughout Massachusetts and New Hampshire, the fictional but realistic wealthy Maine seaside town of Rock Harbor was created. Mark Evans (Elijah Wood) is sent to Maine to stay with relatives after his mother's death. It is there he meets evil incarnate in the form of his cousin Henry (Macaulay Culkin) in *The Good Son* (1993). Henry's latest malevolent trick is to toss a dummy off an overpass onto a highway just to watch the cars crash. An overpass on McIntyre Road was the filming location of the crash scene that affirms Mark's suspicions of his cousin's evil nature. See also **Mirror Lake, Jackson**.

Newington, Crossings at Fox Run – In Stephen King's *The Dead Zone* (1979), Johnny Smith meets presidential candidate Sargent Shriver at the Newington Mall. In the 1990s, the interior shopping area was demolished and a row of storefronts was built between the anchor stores. The plaza is now known as The Crossings at Fox Run. See also **Ridgeway**.

Newmarket, Mall at Fox Run – Brothers Alex and Cullen are hiking in the White Mountains when they witness three major explosions in the distance. They realize it is the nuclear destruction of Portsmouth, Boston, and Providence. They hole up in a cave as long as they can before setting off to search for surviving family only to have Alex killed by radioactive cannibals at the mall. Cullen soon discovers surviving may be worse in "Desolation" by John McIlveen. The story first appeared in McIlveen's collection *Inflictions* (2015).

Newport – Ralph Gentry was a school department bureaucrat, safely obscure in SAU #43 covering Newport, Croydon, and Sunapee. Back in 1982, his father was dying of cancer as chronicled by Stephen King's short story "Ayana," first published in *The Paris Review*, Fall 2007. Now that Ralph is dead, his brother feels free to tell of the miracle in 1982 and a little girl named Ayana.

Newport, East Mountain – Sarah Josepha Buell (1788-1879) was born on the family farm on East Mountain. Under her married name, Sarah J. Hale, she is credited as the driving force behind Thanksgiving being designated a national holiday; it had previously only been celebrated on various dates in the New England states. As the "godmother of Thanksgiving," Hale is therefore also responsible for such Thanksgiving horror films as *Blood Freak* (1972), *Home Sweet Home* (1981), *ThanXgiving* (2006), and *Thankskilling* (2009).

Hale is also the author of the poem "Mary Had a Little Lamb," first appearing in 1830 and quickly becoming a popular nursery rhyme. Naturally, when the first volume of an anthology featuring mash-ups of zombies and fairy tales was published, Hale's poem would be included. "Mary Had a Little Limb" by Wendy Dabrowski appeared in *Once upon an Apocalypse* (2014).

North Conway – Trisha McFarland gets lost along the Appalachian Trail in Stephen King's *The Girl Who Loved Tom Gordon* (1999). The original plan was to walk a 6-mile stretch of the trail to North Conway.

The Fornoy family owns a summer cottage outside of North Conway. It is here that brothers Howard and Robert Fornoy await the apocalypse caused by Robert's attempt to save the world from itself by filling a volcano with a calmative and wait for it to erupt. Stephen King's "The End of the Whole Mess" first appeared in *Omni Magazine*, October 1986.

"The End of the Whole Mess" was included as an episode of Turner Network Television's 2006 series *Nightmares &*

Dreamscapes: From the Stories of Stephen King, with Ron Livingston and Henry Thomas playing the apocalypse-inducing brothers.

North Conway, Memorial Hospital – *Skeletons in the Closet* (2001) used the Memorial in a number of scenes throughout the film, including a pivotal scene where Will Reed (Treat Williams) must bring his girlfriend Tina (Linda Hamilton) to the ER. Will is convinced his son Seth (Jonathan Jackson) is responsible, but even Tina is convinced Will is being paranoid. The question is rapidly becoming which is crazy – father or son? See also **Jackson**.

North Hampton, East Side Cemetery – East Side is the burial location of poet and author Ogden Nash (1902-1971). Nash's copious works include the short story "The Three D," a tale of cursed gravestones originally published as "Victoria" in *Harper's Bazaar*, April 1948 and the poem "A Tale of the Thirteenth Floor," a tale of a door that only opens on Walpurgis Night that first appeared in *The Magazine of Fantasy & Science Fiction*, July 1955.

North Salem – Atop Mystery Hill is America's Stonehenge, a collection of stone structures and standing stones seemingly centered on a 4 ½-ton grooved sacrificial table. H. P. Lovecraft visited the site prior to writing "The Dunwich Horror" (*Weird Tales,* April 1929) and the stone altar and legends of the skull-strewn hilltop in Dunwich may have originated from that visit.

*The 4 ½ ton "sacrificial table" at America's Stonehenge,
atop Mystery Hill.*

Karl Edward Wagner's makes note of the sacrificial table as well,
using a postcard sold at the site's lodge for a visual
comparison to one found in upstate New York in "Sticks," first
published in *Whispers*, March 1974.

Joseph Payne Brennan's short story "The Seventh Incantation"
was first anthologized in *Scream at Midnight* (1963). The story
finds Emmet Telquist heading out to a sacrificial slab
surrounded by a circle of stones to summon Nyogtha. Telquist
soon learns summoning demons is best left to professionals.

Brennan and co-author Donald M. Grant mention Mystery Hill by
name extensively in their account of the first World Fantasy
Convention in 1975. *Act of Providence* (1979) finds Brennan and
detective Lucius Leffing descending into uncharted caverns
beneath Providence, Rhode Island in search of a stolen
Lovecraft document and a kidnapped scholar. What they find
is a lost civilization with sacrificial tables covered with Punic
carvings similar to text on tablets found at Mystery Hill. The
tables are used by subhuman creatures to worship and feed
their god, a Cthulhian horror that Lovecraft himself could
appreciate.

Northridge – Faxon has arrived at the Northridge train station to start a new job only to discover they have forgotten to send a sleigh. Stuck at an unheated train station in the dead of winter, there he meets the sickly Frank Rainer, coming to meet friends on the next train. Frank invites Faxon to stay the night at his uncle's home. The uncle is financier John Lavington and Faxon is asked to witness Frank's will. Now Faxon has started seeing a doppelgänger of Lavington in Edith Wharton's "The Triumph of Night," first published in *Scribner's Magazine*, August 1914.

Nottingham – Greg and Winnie move from Chicago into the old Hoitt place. Their retirement project will be restoring the Revolutionary-era farmhouse back to its original glory. During their numerous dinner parties, Greg regales guests with stories about the ghosts who haunt their home. Then Winnie actually starts seeing ghosts and with increasing unease, begins to see she is no better than a ghost, for hers is a hollow existence, having lived hers through her husband and daughter. *The Moon Lamp* (1976) by Mark Smith asks whether a house can still be haunted by the past when the modern world holds the past in such superficial disregard.

Odiorne Point – Back when Mary Ann Jenness was still a teen, her family lived on Odiorne Point in Portsmouth. Her father and three brothers drown off the point and her mother dies of grief soon after. Alone in the world, she struck up a friendship with the one person more alone than herself – Norvle, the ghost of a young boy from Conway, NH in "A Speakin' Ghost" (*Harper's Magazine*, December 1890) by Annie Trumbull Slosson.

Old Man of the Mountain – See **Franconia Notch State Park**.

Oxham – Midwife Mary Witham keeps seeing Lydia Hardy. However, Lydia killed herself after her child was born stillborn. Now Mary must deal with an expectant mother and a post-partum specter in "The Ghost and the Midwife." The story by Scott Thomas appeared in *Quill & Candle* (2010).

Pelham – A hippie starts a commune at the edge of the woods, much to the resentment of the locals. A series of murders has each side blaming the other until the tracks of a Bigfoot are discovered. Now both sides are united against a common enemy in *Sasqua* (1975). Filmed around Lowell, Massachusetts, the house used for the commune suddenly became unavailable mid-shoot, requiring a quick relocation to an abandoned farmhouse in Pelham.

Pelham was also the filming location for Brett Piper's *Drainiac!* (2000). Julie (Georgia Hatzis) is dealing badly with her mother's recent death. Now her abusive father has bought an abandoned house out on Miskatonic Road and expects her to clean it up for resale. Unfortunately for Julie and her friends, the house is not just squalid; it is also possessed by a water demon trapped in the pipes.

Peltonville Center – In 1897, the town drunk Copernicus Droop stumbles across a giant metallic mosquito in Burnham's Swamp. It is a time machine from 2582 and the time traveler invites the inebriate to take a ride with him. Unfortunately, the man from the future catches pneumonia and dies, leaving the time traveling Panchronicon in the hands of Droop. Naturally, Droop decides to head back to 1876 and become wealthy by pre-inventing things like the gramophone, the Vitascope, and a type of cough syrup he really likes. What could possibly go wrong, other than overshooting the target and ending up in Tudor England? *The Panchronicon* (1904) was written by Harold Steele MacKaye.

Pembroke, Academy Road – A 15-foot-tall marker marks the location where 17-year-old Josie Langmaid was assaulted and decapitated while walking to school. In the 1990s, the Three Rivers School was built across the street from the marker, offering the students not only a touching eulogy for the late student but details on her death and the discovery of the body. It also includes unsettlingly specific directions to where the body and head were located when found. See also **Buck Street Cemetery, Suncook**.

Peterson – Melissa and her husband are out of state, so they ask Melissa's recently widowed sister Sarah to move in as a caretaker. The homestead is deep in former Abenaki territory. Melissa believes that the spirits of the Natives are embedded in the glacial boulders in her garden, so she paints the boulders to resemble local wildlife and folklore creatures. When a freak accident claims the lives of two locals, Sarah begins to suspect that the massive stones are somehow involved in "Mekoomweso's Revenants" by Esther M. Leiper-Estabrooks. The story appeared in *Not Your Average Monster: A Bestiary of Horrors* (2015).

Pittsburg – In the corner of New Hampshire where the state meets Canada and Maine, the vast and rugged terrain of Pittsburg was the location picked to film scenes of *Yellowbrickroad* (2010). The team of filmmakers is following the path into the woods that the residents of Friar took 70 years before. And like seven decades before, madness and death walk the trail with them. See also **Friar**.

Plainfield – Playwright Percy MacKaye, (1875-1956) was part of the "Cornish Colony," a group of diverse artists, writers, and architects that settled around the home of Augustus Saint-Gaudens. The colony disbanded after Saint-Gaudens death in 1907, but MacKaye was so enamored of the area he purchased a summer home to continue the tradition, where he would die in 1956. MacKaye took Nathaniel Hawthorne's story "Feathertop: A Moralized Legend" (*The International Magazine*, February and March 1852) and adapted it into the 1911 Broadway play "The Scarecrow." MacKaye's version proved more popular than Hawthorne's and has seen more adaptations than the original story of a scarecrow brought to life by the magic of a spiteful witch in Salem. *Puritan Passions* was a 1923 silent film version, starring Glenn Hunter and Mary Astor. The play also won an Emmy in 1972 for the Gene Wilder version, performed on public television's *Hollywood Television Theatre*. See also **Saint-Gaudens National Historic Site, Cornish**.

Plaistow, Main Street – From 1922 to 1926, amateur press publisher Charles W. "Tryout" Smith convalesced in a secluded farmhouse near the intersection of Main Street and Westville Road. He continued to publish monthly issues of *The Tryout*. In a letter to H. P. Lovecraft, Smith offered the concept of a new story that Lovecraft would transform into the short story "In the Vault." The story about an undertaker trapped in a crypt debuted in the November 1925 issue of *The Tryout* and was dedicated to C. W. Smith. See also **Maplewood Cemetery, Plaistow**.

Plaistow, Maplewood Cemetery – H. P. Lovecraft's amateur journalism associates included Edgar Davis (1908– 1949) of Merrimac, Massachusetts. Davis accompanied Lovecraft on his first visit to Newburyport, the inspiration of Lovecraft's blighted town of Innsmouth. The Davis family is buried on the New Hampshire side of this cemetery, which straddles the state line with Haverhill.

Edgar's sister Ada (1904-1991) is also buried in the family plot. She may also have a connection to Lovecraft's "In the Vault." In the story, the name of the old village doctor is Davis. Lovecraft wrote the story in September 1925 – the same time that Ada was starting classes at Boston University Medical School. Dr. A. Frances Davis opened her practice in the family house in Merrimac, MA, where it remained until 1966 when she retired and turned to missionary work. See also **Main Street, Plaistow**.

Plaistow, Westville Depot – On June 8, 1921, H. P. Lovecraft stepped off the B&M train at Westville Depot on his first of many visits to the Merrimack Valley. His hostess for this trip was Miss Myrta Alice Little, a fellow amateur journalist. Also on this trip was a visit to Haverhill, Massachusetts to meet a long time correspondent, Amateur Press Association's legendary publisher, Charles W. "Tryout" Smith. See also **Hampstead; Maplewood Cemetery, Plaistow; Main Street, Plaistow**.

Plymouth – Plymouth is the gateway to the White Mountains, and the Pemigewasset House was the ultimate expression of that claim. Both northbound and southbound trains from the White Mountains stopped at the depot attached to the hotel which could accommodate 300 guests. The hotel was destroyed by fire in the 1950s and the area redeveloped extensively; the site of the Pemigewasset House is unmarked and unremembered, but generally believed to have been located on Main Street just south of Highland Street.

One such visitor in the spring of 1864 was author Nathaniel Hawthorne. Hawthorne's health was failing, so his old college friend, former president Franklin Pierce traveled with him to the White Mountains, hoping the mountain air could help restore the author. On the return trip, they stopped at the Pemigewasset House for the evening. The next morning, Pierce discovered Hawthorne had died overnight. See also **Old North Cemetery, Concord; Crawford Notch**.

Port Arbello – In John Saul's *Suffer the Children* (1977), something evil is happening to the children of Port Arbello. As they disappear, thoughts turn to the town's history and a century old curse that haunts the town. And is the amazing resemblance between young Elizabeth Conger and a long dead ancestor somehow related?

Elizabeth Conger will marry and move to **Blackstone** where she longingly reminisces of her childhood home on Conger Point in John Saul's *The Blackstone Chronicles* (1997).

Portsmouth – In August 1923, H. P. Lovecraft made his first visit to Portsmouth. Having been driven through town in 1921, he had been so intrigued by the Georgian architecture that he immediately planned to return and explore the city. Lovecraft was beyond entranced with the town. He professed that Portsmouth's antiquity surpassed that of his beloved Salem, Massachusetts and challenged Marblehead as his favorite destination for antiquarian sightseeing. See also **Congress Street, Portsmouth; Wentworth-Coolidge Mansion, Portsmouth; Stratham**.

In the Joyce Carol Oates short story "Night-Side," first anthologized *Night-Side* (1977), an 1887 society of psychical investigators compare their current case to one of their more spectacular frauds, the dwarf Eustace, a charlatan spiritualist in Portsmouth with a flair for the dramatic.

Melinda attends an exclusive underground rave, held in an abandoned warehouse on the edge of Portsmouth. Her invitation ushers her into a world of casual sex and ample drugs. Melinda's not adverse to a quick hook-up, but she's looking for someone special. And for his sake, she'd better not find him in "A Pulse of Ultraviolet" by Philip C. Perron. The story first appeared in *Pentagonal Sextet* (2016).

Portsmouth, Borthwick Avenue – Harper Grayson was a school nurse when the Dragonscale epidemic started in *The Fireman* (2016) by Joe Hill. Now she's a volunteer at Portsmouth Hospital, dressed in a hazmat suit and directs the flow of the injured, both infected and not infected. It is at the hospital where she first encounters The Fireman and Nick Storey, soon to be pivotal characters in her life. See also **Little Harbor Road, Portsmouth**.

Portsmouth, Congress Street – Portsmouth was a favorite city for Lovecraft and he visited numerous times to explore "the city of the Georgian age" where he felt transported back to colonial times. On these visits, as was his custom, he would stay at the local YMCA, then located at 143 Congress. On his 1927 trip, the YMCA was closed, so he walked across the street to 104 Congress and stayed at Kearsarge House Hotel. Both buildings have been restored but neither has maintained its original function. See also **Portsmouth**.

Portsmouth, Goshen College – Roger Corman turned the Henry James short story "The Ghostly Rental" into his 1999 film *The Haunting of Hell House*. Instead of a Harvard divinity student, the hero is now James Farrow (Andrew Bowen), an art student at Goshen College, who is haunted by the ghost of his lover, whom he abandoned to die after a botched abortion. He finds a kindred spirit in Professor John Ambrose (Michael York), who is also haunted by his past mistakes.

Portsmouth, Harmony Grove Cemetery – Anethe Christensen (1847-1873) and Karen Anne Christensen (1833-1873) are buried in Harmony Grove. Louis Wagner rowed out to Smuttynose Island from Portsmouth to rob the home of John Hontvet whom he knew was on the mainland. Wagner broke into the house, killed Anethe with an axe and strangled Karen, by which time Honvet's wife Maren had escaped. He was quickly captured, and since Smuttynose is part of Maine, was tried and executed in that State. The murders continue to fascinate the public and have been the subject of, among other things, crime books, ballads, and novels such as Anita Shreve's mystery novel *The Weight of Water* (1998). The thriller was made into a 2000 film of the same name. See also **South Street Cemetery, Portsmouth**.

Portsmouth, Little Harbor Road – Camp Wyndham, on Little Harbor Road, was a Christian summer camp before the Dragonscale pandemic. Now it is a sanctuary, guarded by lookouts and snipers, for infected refugees hiding from police and the vigilante "Cremation Squad." The entire camp attends church daily, to sing and go into "The Bright," a state of consciousness where they are mentally linked. More importantly, "The Bright" releases a chemical which stops them from combusting in *The Fireman* (2016) by Joe Hill. See also **Pleasant Street, Concord; Borthwick Avenue, Portsmouth; South Street Cemetery, Portsmouth**.

Portsmouth, Proprietors Burying Ground – Brevet Brigadier General Justin Dimick (1800-1871) is interred in Proprietors Burying Ground, now part of the group of cemeteries known collectively as South Street Cemetery. During the Civil War, the seasoned veteran was considered too old for active service and appointed the commander of Fort Warren Military Prison in Boston Harbor. The newlywed wife of a captured confederate soldier dressed as a man and packing a pistol and a pick, smuggled herself into the fort to free her husband and help the confederates seize the fort. The prisoners were caught digging a tunnel, and, surrounded by Union soldiers, the bride fired at Dimick. Instead of killing the commander, the gun exploded and killed her husband. Dimick then hanged the grieving widow as a spy, giving birth to the ghostly legend of the "Lady in Black" who is said to still haunt the fort. See also **South Street Cemetery, Portsmouth**.

Portsmouth, South Street Cemetery – Technically there is no South Street Cemetery. It is the name given to the collection of five local cemeteries that are collectively so large that the property includes a pond in the middle.

The Fireman has led a group of survivors to the cemetery after the destruction of their safe haven. Nick Storey has been stockpiling supplies diverted from the camp in the caretaker's shed. The new plan is to regroup, tend their wounds, and wait for the fires to die down a bit before setting off to a new sanctuary on Martha Quinn Island off the coast of Maine in *The Fireman* (2016) by Joe Hill. See also **Little Harbor Road, Portsmouth**.

Portsmouth, State Street – State Street was the final residence of Floyd "Gary" Newton (1935-2000), founder and artistic director of The Players' Ring Theatre in Portsmouth. As actor

Gary Newton, he was the ghoulish Simon of *Simon's Sanctorum*. From 1970 to 1974, Newton's greasepaint ghoul ruled the Boston airwaves on Saturday nights on WHDH Channel 5 (now WCVB). Newton was the first actor to play a horror host in Boston but was not the first televised host. Simon was preceded by the alien Feep at rival Channel 7.

Portsmouth, Wentworth-Coolidge Mansion – The 1750 Wentworth-Coolidge Mansion on Little Harbor Road is a Georgian style house built as the home, offices and working farm of Benning Wentworth, named New Hampshire's first Royal Governor by King George II in 1741. One of the few royal gubernatorial residences to survive almost unchanged, even ardent Anglophile Lovecraft thought the sprawling, 40-room house may have been excessive, referring to in his letters a "rambling." See also **Portsmouth**.

In *Innsmouth* (2015), the short film directed by Izzy Lee, Detective Olmsted (Diana Porter) is in Arkham investigating a murder. The body has an unidentifiable bite wound and a mysterious egg sac on her back. Sediment in the wound leads back to Devil's Reef off the coast of Innsmouth. Olmstead heads to Innsmouth and confronts the leader of a cult, Alice Marsh (Tristan Risk.) Marsh claims to be the daughter of Innsmouth's colonial founder Captain Obed Marsh. The detective is caught up in the cult's depraved ceremonies and sexual fetishes, only to discover what really lies under their skin. The Wentworth-Coolidge Mansion served as the exterior of Marsh ancestral home.

Portsmouth Harbor – Old Sailor Jack died in the Seaman's Home in Portsmouth, but he refused to be buried in the ground. Portsmouth Harbor was the first attempt to bury Jack at sea in "The Ballad of Jack Ringbolt" first published in *Selections from the Writings of James Kennard, Jr.* (1846).

Elias Perkins was a hard-bitten Yankee sailor, with 20-years of experience sailing the Caribbean. He was the first officer aboard the *Hope* when it was captured by the ruthless pirate

Fawcett. Now the seaman has a choice, die an honest sailor or join Fawcett's crew in "Seven Turns in a Hangman's Rope." The story by Henry S. Whitehead first appeared in *Adventure*, July 15, 1932.

A cursed pirate ship washes ashore, decades after terrorizing the seacoast. The locals reuse the timbers to build a bridge, only to discover that free lumber comes at a heavy cost. "The Shipwreck Bridge" by Hannah Gonsman, first appeared in the John Greenleaf Whittier-themed anthology *Snowbound with Zombies* (2015).

Ridgeway – Stephen King's *The Dead Zone* (1979) has Greg Stillson elected mayor of Ridgeway (1973-75), his first elected office in a series that could end with the presidency of the US. As an early warning of Stillson's true nature, he is involved in several real estate developments in Ridgeway of questionable legality. See also **Durham; Jackson Town Hall; Manchester; Crossings at Fox Run, Newington; Somersworth; Trimbull; University of New Hampshire**.

River Town – Local tutor Neil Stuart (Matt Farley) fled town, a laughingstock after claiming to have seen the fabled riverbeast. Now he has returned to exonerate himself and win back his ex-fiancée by destroying the menace in the Merrimack River with the assistance of his fellow tutors, his plucky tutee (Sharon Scalzo), and a former professional athlete (Kevin McGee). Charles Roxburgh's *Don't Let the Riverbeast Get You!* (2012) is equal parts satire and homage to earlier indie horror filmmakers such as William Castle and Del Tenney. See also **Hooksett; Elm Street, Manchester**.

Romney Mountain – Phillip and Margaret are on vacation at a B&B in the foothills of the mountain where they meet Laszlo, the elderly caretaker of the Hagendorn estate on the mountain crest. He offers them a tour of the private estate in T. E. D. Klein's "Well-Connected" (*Weird Tales*, Spring 1988).

Unfortunately, Laszlo neglects to mention that the mansion burned down years ago.

Rosewood – Horror writer Richard Kinnell (Tom Berenger) buys a disturbing painting at a yard sale in this small town on the Massachusetts border. The artist hanged himself after burning all of his other paintings. Every time Kinnell looks at the painting the picture has changed, and it appears to be following his route, leaving a real life bloody trail behind it. When Stephen King's "The Road Virus Heads North" was adapted into an episode of *Nightmares & Dreamscapes* (1:05), certain liberties were taken, most notably moving Rosewood into New Hampshire.

Salem – Jimmy Paulsen's intended bride has lied to her father and now Jimmy's being accused of child molestation. Granted, she's only 14, but that's pretty close to the age of consent. The trouble starts when his dead and dismembered future father-in-law shows up and wants revenge in "The Janitor," Tracy Carbone's short story debut in the anthology *Nobody (2006)*.

Salem, Canobie Lake Park – UNH student Devin Jones takes a summer job in North Carolina at Joyland amusement park. Looking for an older, smaller park to base his Joyland on, Stephen King decided that Canobie Lake was about the right size, visiting the century-old park and relying on its guide map for details. Canobie Lake's "Mine of Lost Souls," one of the few dark rides remaining in New England, was used to help develop Joyland's "Horror House." The major difference, geography aside, is that Joyland's dark ride is haunted by the ghost of a murdered park guest. King's *Joyland* (2013) does include additional features not found at Canobie Lake, such as the serial killer. See also **University of New Hampshire**.

Salem, Grand China Restaurant – As *God of Vampires* (2010) begins, hit man Frank Ng (Dharma Lim) has been hired to take out a rival crime lord. Unfortunately, Frank was not told the crime lord is a *kiang-shi*, the legendary Chinese vampire. After the first encounter ends badly, Frank heads into the heart of Boston's Chinatown to find answers. Indie film budgets being what they are, the venerable Grand China was used instead of Boston. The fact that leading man Dharma Lim's family owns the restaurant didn't hurt either.

Salem, The Mall at Rockingham Park – Timmy returns a birthday present and finds himself in the mall with a gift card. After being turned away from a teddy bear store, Timmy finds an alternative store and builds himself a zombie. Of course, now he has to figure out how to get it home in "Build-A-Zombie" by Scott T. Goudsward. The story of excessive customization first appeared in *Epitaphs* (2011).

Sandwich, Little Pond Road – The Lower Corner National Historical District, a collection of architecturally and historically significant of buildings along State Route 109, is the site of the original settlement of Sandwich. It includes the 1850s Greek Revival farmhouse at the junction of Little Pond Road and NH 109 North that was the final home of actor Claude Rains. One of his final roles was as Professor Challenger in *The Lost World* (1960). He retired to Sandwich in 1963 where he lived until his death in 1967. See also **Moultonborough**.

Sandwich, Vittum Hill Cemetery – Vittum Hill Cemetery is the final resting place of Dr. Norbert Wiener (1894 - 1964), considered the father of cybernetics starting with his first book on the topic in 1948. Cybernetics, the study into ways to extend human capabilities by interfacing with mechanical and electronic augmentations gave rise to the cyborg, a staple of science fiction, as noted by Daleks and Cybermen from *Doctor Who*, Darth Vader, and RoboCop. However, the horror genre anticipated the merging of man and machine before Wiener was even born with such tales as "The Man That Was Used Up" by Edgar Allan Poe. The satire about a reassembled war hero was first published in 1839 in *Burton's Gentleman's Magazine*.

Seabrook – Grammer Weare is on her way to Ting Seaver's shanty. Ting's daughter Doll is about to give birth and old Grammer is the village midwife. Alan Marshall's "Death and Transfiguration" is a tale of birth and death among the poor saltmarsh farmers. It was critically acclaimed when it first appeared in the October 1933 issue of *Story* but remains forgotten today. H. P. Lovecraft read the story in 1933 and in a letter to J. Vernon Shea, admits the dialect Marshall used perplexes him, claiming he knew Portsmouth and the surrounding area and didn't recognize it. Considering the obscure dialect Lovecraft himself used in "The Dunwich Horror," he might not want to start that discussion.

Sheppard Beach – A small coastal town is rocked by two unsolved murders. Two local boys, Derrick and Caleb, are fascinated by the murders and attempt their own investigation. They name the killer "the Ragman" because of his tattered clothes and his similarity to a ghost tale Derrick's grandfather told them about a junk and rag collector. It's believed the Ragman is hopping trains to commit his grisly murders up and down the eastern seaboard. Decades later, the killings start up again, this time in Sheppard Beach, a thinly disguised Hampton Beach. Derrick and Caleb resume their childhood investigation to distract them from their lives - Derrick is on the edge of a divorce and Caleb is a full-out junkie. Just like back when they were children, they have no plan as to what to do if they actually find him in *Dreams The Ragman* (2011) by Greg F. Gifune.

Smokey Hollow – As *Loonies* (2015) by Gregory Bastianelli opens, reporter Brian Keays and his pregnant wife decide to choose a quieter life in small-town New Hampshire to raise a family after years of Brian covering the police beat in Boston. As he settles in as editor of the weekly newspaper, the rural tranquility is shattered when Keays discovering a trunk with the skeleton of a child in their attic. Suddenly, a murder rocks the town, with the victims strangled and pillowcases placed over their heads. This is the MO of a string of unsolved serial murders from the town's past. Has the original serial killer returned after a long hiatus or has someone else decided to continue the grisly tradition?

Somersworth – Cathy's Roadhouse was a popular local spot on Route 9, right up until the day it burned down, just as Johnny Smith predicted, in Stephen King's *The Dead Zone* (1979). See also **Ridgeway**.

Stark Corners – In John Bellairs' young adult novel *The Eyes of the Killer Robot* (1986), Professor Childermass and Johnny Dixon travel to this "little bitty burg" in the shadow of Mount Creed in the White Mountains in search of the evil robot built by madman Evaristus Sloane that can only be animated by human eyes placed in the robot's head. Unfortunately, they do find it.

Stonewall – Phil is a long haul trucker going to Stonewall to get a load of tractor parts. He encounters three people standing in the middle of the road. A priest claims that the woman accompanying him is possessed by a demon and needs an exorcism. The other man is her husband, who keeps her restrained to silence her rantings. She claims they have kept her tied up and have been assaulting her. Aside from there being no tractor plant in Stonewall, Phil's night is about to get very odd in "Incident on NH Route 66" by Tony Tremblay. The story appeared in *Dark Passages 2* (2016).

Stratham – H. P. Lovecraft caught a ride to Dover with the Little family in May of 1922. From there he caught a train to Boston and then back to his beloved Providence, Rhode Island. The Littles were actually heading north on State Route 108 to a summer cottage. Knowing of Lovecraft's antiquarian interests, when the Littles reached Stratham, they went east on State Route 33. This route would still get them to Dover (via State Route 16) but the extended loop gave Lovecraft's his first glimpse of Portsmouth. It was love at first sight. See also **East Road, Hampstead; Portsmouth**.

Sudleigh – Alice Brown's short story "Old Lemuel's Journey" (*Atlantic Monthly*, June 1920) is a regionalist ghost tale with a twist. Miserly Lemuel Wood is dying and when he slips into a brief coma, he awakens a changed man, begging the question – Can a man haunt his future self? See also **Hawes Cemetery, Hampton Falls**.

Suncook, Buck Street Cemetery – On October 4, 1875, 17-year-old Josephine "Josie" Langmaid (1858-1875) disappeared. After she didn't arrive at school, a search party was organized. A day later, she was found: in two pieces. Someone had assaulted her on her way to school, beat her to death, and severed her head from her body. A week later, a woodcutter named Joseph Lapage, already a suspect in a similar sexual assault and murder in Vermont, was arrested, tried, and eventually hanged for the crime. Josie was laid to rest in Buck Street Cemetery on what is now Pinewood Road. A small stone in a family plot simply notes her name. That quiet and dignified burial stands in stark contrast to the grisly memorial offering all the gory details, erected at the scene of the crime. See also **Academy Road, Pembroke**.

Sunrise Lake – The Lakes region quiets right down after tourist season. So it's the perfect time to have a quiet talk with yourself. Especially when you and yourself agree it's also a good time to dispose of a body. "Sunrise Lake" by David Price appeared in *Sex, Drugs, & Horror* (2013).

Swanzey, Mount Caesar Cemetery – Allan Parrish (Robin Williams) escapes from the magical game *Jumanji* (1995) after decades. Although the town's economic downturn is sad,

Allan finally realizes his detached father's obsession with finding him cost him his factory, meaning he really did love him. The scene where Parrish visits his parents' grave was shot in Mount Caesar Cemetery. See also **Brantford**.

Tarleton Corners – At a secluded cabin on the shores of Lake Glory, psychiatrist Helen Myrer is forced to play mind games to survive against serial killer Kevin McCallum in *The Cave* (1997) by Anne McLean Matthews.

Thompson and Meserve's Purchase – The uninhabited township encompasses the northern slope of Mount Washington and is home to Marshfield Station, the home base of the Mount Washington Cog Railway. Usually displayed at the station is the Peppersass, the world's first cog locomotive, which was retired in 1929. On Saturday, August 27, 1927, Peppersass was still in use, carrying sightseers up to the summit of Mount Washington. Among the visitors that day was H. P. Lovecraft, on a package tour of the White Mountains. Lovecraft was impressed by the scenery on the way up but was rained out on the summit. To celebrate Peppersass's 150th anniversary in 2019, the locomotive is currently on a four-year tour of railroad museums.

Tilton – A nurse returning home after work encounters a young boy along the road. He and his parents were in a small plane that has crashed. She drives him to the nearest police station, in Tilton. After treating his injuries, he attempts to lead rescuers back to the plane. His knack at finding landmarks in the dark is almost supernatural in "Devotion" by John McIlveen. The story was first published in his collected works *Inflictions* (2015).

Trafton – On the edge of the White Mountains National Forest is the tiny town of Trafton, the nearest neighbor to the compound of Alex Hunter and his militia group First Step. Hunter is more than the leader of the group that detonated a bomb at Plymouth Rock, he is possessed by a demon determined to find and eliminate *lamedvovniks*, the hidden saints of Hasidic tradition whose righteousness keep evil in balance in *The Hidden Saint* (1999) by Rick Hautala, based on the TV series *Poltergeist: The Legacy*.

Trimbull – At a rally in the town park, Johnny Smith shakes hands with Greg Stillson and sees Armageddon in Stephen King's *The Dead Zone* (1979). See also **Ridgeway**.

Twinningham – Three gentlemen are staggering home from an evening at the local tavern when they encounter an ancient carriage that was not there several hours before. Opening it, a desiccated corpse emits a sulfurous smoke that eats the flesh of the first one. Now it's a footrace against the smoke for survival. "The Yellow Smoke" by Scott Thomas appeared in his 2012 collection *Urn & Willow*.

University of New Hampshire – UNH library is where Johnny Smith begins his research on Greg Stillson, learning the truth about the candidate in Stephen King's *The Dead Zone* (1979). See also **Ridgeway**.
Daniel Willoughby is a lecturer in applied mathematics and an expert on Antarctica. When the 1513 "Piri Reis map" comes to light showing the Antarctic coast without ice thousands of years ago, he formulates a theory of a lost civilization. Now his grandson is going to prove the theory. Unfortunately, he's also about to discover Lovecraft's *At the Mountains of Madness* may not be fiction in "The Tomb of the Old Ones" by Colin Wilson, first published in *The Antarktos Cycle* (1999). See also **Keene State College**.
In the summer on 1973, UNH student Devin Jones' soon to be ex-girlfriend Wendy Keegan moves to Boston to work for the summer. Rather than spend the summer on the UNH campus alone, Devin takes a job in North Carolina at Joyland amusement park. Between the serial killer, the ghost of a murder victim, and the little kid with psychic powers, Dev's

broken heart may be the least of his problems in *Joyland* (2013) by Stephen King. See also **Canobie Lake Park, Salem**.

Wammsport – Divinity student Venetia Barlow is spending the summer in the small harbor town of Wammsport, restoring St. John's Prior House, attached to the local cathedral. Hell is planning a new assault on the living world, and the virginal future nun Venetia is the key to the entire, lurid plan in *House Infernal* (2007), the third book in Edward Lee's "City Infernal" series.

Washington – Old Washington Center Cemetery on Faxon Hill Road is the final resting place of part of Captain Samuel Jones, Jr. In 1804, Jones had an accident that required his leg to be amputated. At that time, it was believed that if you properly buried a dismembered limb, you would experience less phantom pain. The difference is, most people didn't erect a headstone for the missing part and then later move to another state.

Weare – When director Ulli Lommel began shooting a film in southern New Hampshire loosely based on the true crime case of Canadian serial killer pig farmer Robert Pickton, he approached the largest hog farm in the state, McCauslin Swine Farm in Weare. Owner Don McCauslin readily allowed his future breakfast meats to be filmed. *Killer Pickton* (2005) finds Billy Pickton (Curtis Graan) luring prostitutes to his sister's home where he drugs and kills them, before feeding their remains to his pigs.

West Ossipee – Model T Fords were not equipped for the winter roads in the Lakes Region. In 1917, local Ford dealer Virgil D. White decided he needed a way to expand the use of his cars into a year-round activity. White designed a package of attachments to customize the Model Ts for winter driving – most notably swapping out the front wheels for skis and adding tank tracks for the back. He patented the modifications as a "snowmobile," creating a whole new industry that that would be helpful in horror movies for fleeing such hibernal terrors as Alaskan vampires in *30 Days of Night* (2007), West Virginian cannibals in *Wrong Turn 4: Bloody Beginnings* (2011), and even the occasional Finnish feral Santa Claus in *Rare Exports: A Christmas Tale* (2010).

Westover – Reporter David Storm is doing an article on the drought plaguing the western White Mountains. His editor suggested a local angle on the recent cloud-seeding experiments of Professor Cruickshank. Soon after, Storm discovers the unseasonably early flurries contain a poison. The deeper the reporter digs, the more obvious it becomes that Cruickshank's experiments threaten to wipe out life on the planet in *Snow Fury* (1955) by Richard Holden.

White Mountains – The White Mountains are a mountain range covering about a quarter of the state of New Hampshire and a portion of Maine. Their proximity to the urban areas to the south, most notably Boston, has made visits common for centuries. With those visits comes inspiration. See **Crawford Notch; Frankenstein Cliff; Jericho Falls; Lincoln; Mount Chocorua; Mount Washington; Plymouth; Romney Mountain; Stark Corners; Trafton; Westover**.

Whitney – After running into an old classmate at Logan International Airport, Boston MA, Zoe Manning is talked into attending a party with a group of mysterious actors. Soon Zoe awakens to find herself a captive in her dead parents' home in Whitney. To her horror, she realizes she is being put through a reenactment of her life's deepest fears and secrets in *Night Games* (1987) by Marilyn Harris.

Whittaker Intervale – The Orne Farmhouse has a poltergeist problem, or more specifically, their teen niece has one. A psychologist is called in as the spirit begins to take control of the girl. Exorcizing a poltergeist is easy. Sneaking up on one –

that's a different story. "Mr. Hyde – and Seek" by Malcolm Ferguson first appeared in *Weird Tales*, May 1950.

Whyndom – Thirteen-year-old Henry's parents have separated and he and his mother have moved to a new home. The previous owner left a box in the basement with something in it. Now Henry feels as if his essence is slowly eroding, replaced cell by cell by something else. To combat his terror, he recalls his childhood home in Whyndom and the idyllic days of his childhood. "Petrified Forest" by Gregory L. Norris appeared in *Pentagonal Sextet* (2016).

Whyndom, Armstrong Road – Best friends Lawrence and Warren go exploring the dark woods behind Armstrong Road. Behind the trees is an orchard and behind that is an old dump from where Lawrence thinks his sister disappeared. They discover the old cars in the dump are arranged in a sundial, still hosting their dead drivers. Soon construction vehicles move in and people start disappearing again. Strange lights and flying discs are seen above the house. A drunken walk through the woods at night reveals the truth in "The Enclave" by Gregory L. Norris. The story appeared in *The Fierce and Unforgiving Muse* (2012).

Willard's Mills – 172 witches were burned at the stake by the extremely dedicated colonial settlers of Willard's Mill. Unfortunately, all 172 are back as demons, and they remain rather unhappy at the town. Former sheriff Stan Miller (John C. McGinley) was hoping for a quiet retirement. Those hopes are dashed when he must join forces with his replacement, Sheriff Evie Barret (Janet Varney). They may kill each other long before the demons get a shot in the TV series *Stan Against Evil*, running on the IFC network.

Wilton – Thieves break into a McMansion after a snow storm. The unplowed driveway indicates the family is obviously not at home. In search of ill-gotten gains, they stumble across the mummified remains of the family in a hidden room covered in strange runes. The thieves will leave the house, but not with the expected bounty. "The Folks on the Hill" by Philip C. Perron appeared in *Canopic Jars* (2013).

Wilton, Laurel Hill Cemetery – Rod Price (1947-2005) a founding member and guitarist for the blues-rock quartet Foghat, is buried in Laurel Hill. Foghat has become a popular choice for background music in horror. Their hit "Slow Ride" appears on the *Bates Motel* TV series (2:08) as well as *Dexter* (1:08 and 1:09). But nowhere is their use as horror background music more evident than in Rob Zombie's *Halloween II* (2009). Laurie Strode (Scout Taylor-Compton), unaware her murderous brother Michael Myers (Tyler Mane) is not only alive but honing in on her, insists on going to the town Halloween party dressed as characters from *The Rocky Horror Picture Show* (Zombie is a self-admitted fan of the show). So while Laurie as Magenta, gets drunk, her friend Harley (Angela Trimbur) dressed as Doctor Frank-N-Furter, hooks up with a werewolf (Matt Bush). Naturally, when they slip into his shag rug lined van, the radio is playing Foghat's "I Just Want to Make Love to You." The song is overly optimistic, for when Michael Myers chaperones, nobody's getting lucky.

Wolfeboro – *Sixth Sense* (1979) by Ramona Stewart opens with young Nancy Parsons on the receiving end of a blow to the head. Now she has visions whenever the Greenwich Village Slasher claims another victim. First thought to be hallucinations caused by neurological damage, she is suddenly taken seriously after describing a victim before the NYPD even finds the body. And taking her most seriously is the slasher himself, who travels to New Hampshire to break the connection – permanently.

VERMONT

Stowe's haunted covered bridge, crossing Gold Brook, is
supervised by the ghostly Emily.
Photo courtesy of Joseph A. Citro

Adamant – Adamant is the "artsy little village" where Norman Spencer (Harrison Ford) would illicitly meet Madison Frank (Amber Valletta) in the film *What Lies Beneath* (2000). Adamant is noted for a historic music school, making it an artsy little village. Unfortunately, the scenes set in Adamant were actually filmed in nearby Waterbury Center. See also **Addison**.

Addison – In *What Lies Beneath* (2000), Norman and Claire Spencer (Harrison Ford and Michelle Pfeiffer) live in a stately home overlooking Lake Champlain. Claire is growing increasingly concerned that either the house is haunted or that she is losing her mind. The house exterior was specifically built for the movie in DAR State Park. The house was dismantled after filming, but the spectacular view of Lake Champlain remains. No word if the ghost remains on location. See also **Adamant; Chimney Point, Lake Champlain; University of Vermont, Burlington**.

Akeleyville – A passenger on a midnight bus for Brattleboro is horrified when a new passenger sits next to him. The new arrival reeks of decay and appears to be wearing a monster mask. The chatty cadaver explains that he's off to meet the wife in Akeleyville. She doesn't look much better. "Night Bus" by Donald R. Burleson first appeared in *Eldritch Tales* #11, 1985.

Aldenville – An ancient cave is discovered at a construction site. Special Agent Scott Embry of the FBI's Special Paranormal Investigative Research and Intelligence Team is called in to protect a team of speleologists sent to examine the cave system. Something evil has been given access to the surface, and it's hungry in *Hidden Demons* (2014) by Dawn Gray, part of her S.P.I.R.I.T. series.

Antrim – In Joseph A. Citro's *Shadow Child* (1987), an ancient stone structure behind the Whitcome house on Pinnacle Mountain could be a colonial root cellar or a pre-Columbian relic. Either way, it is the focal point of mysterious disappearances, brutal murders, and animal mutilations. Is it an ancient evil or is the Whitcome family's houseguest, cousin Eric, somehow involved? See also **Chester; Ludlow; South Royalton**.

The sequel *Guardian Angels* (1988) opens with Bostonians Will Crocket, his mother Sheila, and step-father Dan moving into the former Whitcome house to escape the city life. Sheila is a novelist, Dan runs the local paper and Will bored out of his skull. The idyllic rural life is shattered by sounds on the roof and strange faces in the windows. Is it the exonerated but still suspected murderer or does ancient evil still haunt the woods?

Arlington – Jim Payne is the great-grandson of pulp writer Cavanaugh Payne. He has received a generous offer to sell his relative's correspondence with H. P. Lovecraft, which is why the New Yorker finds himself in the woods of western Vermont. Unfortunately, the mysterious collector is looking for something a little more personal from Payne in "The Dude Who Collected Lovecraft" by Nick Mamatas and Tim Pratt. The story first appeared in *ChiZine* #36 (April-June 2008).

Barre, Hope Cemetery - Home to some of the largest granite quarries in the world, Barre is where immigrant Italian stonecutting artisans came to ply their trade. And as they died, Hope Cemetery became an 85-acre outdoor gallery of statuary. Considered some of the finest and most unusual tombstone carvings in America, the cemetery is home to everything from Michelangelo's Pieta to stock cars, tractor-trailers, and abstract art. Hope and nearby Elmwood Cemeteries are often called "the show places of the Barre Granite Industry."

Bellows Falls – Situated on the west bank of the Connecticut River at the base of the Great Falls are a collection of Indian petroglyphs depicting life-sized, circular "heads" with eyes and mouths. Some of the heads have horns or antennae.

Dating back anywhere from 300 to 1,000 years old, the meaning of the figures is unknown and probably always will be – the original appearance of the carvings was irreparably altered 75 years ago when the local DAR hired a stone carver to deepen the carvings with metal tools to make them more visible for the tourists. Current explanations for the carvings range from aliens to vision quest imagery.

Bellows Falls, Steamtown – Steamtown was moved to Scranton, PA in 1984 and became Steamtown National Historic Site in 1986. While still located in Vermont, the perpetually cash-strapped foundation leased Canadian Pacific Railway engine #1293 to use in filming *Terror Train* (1980) with Jamie Lee Curtis. The film company renumbered the locomotive to #1881 and painted it black with silver stripes to match the one used in Montreal during earlier scenes. The engine was subsequently restored to #1293 and painted black, gold, and red. The engine moved with the collection in Pennsylvania but never used, finally being sold in 1996 to a private collection in Ohio where it is the primary engine for catered events.

Bellows Falls, Union Station – Bellows Falls was a rail hub for trains running between Montreal and Boston and New York. Today Amtrak still stops at the same stately brick train station that an increasingly suspicious Henry Akeley used as an alternative method to ship evidence to Miskatonic University in H. P. Lovecraft's "The Whisperer in the Darkness," first published in *Weird Tales* (August 1931). See also **Townshend**.

Bennington - A group of college students is telling ghost stories around a campfire in the woods outside of Bennington. Halfway through a story, the campers hear something crashing through the woods and they discover that they have built their camp in the field of bones. And near the center is a hut. And the hut is occupied by a very unhappy urban legend. "Place of Bones" by Barry Lee Dejasu appeared in *Wicked Witches* (2016).

Bennington College – Shirley Jackson's second novel *Hangsaman* (1951) introduces us to Natalie Waite, a sheltered seventeen-year-old. Natalie leaves an unhealthy home life for a progressive college that, not accidentally, resembles a satirical version of Bennington. Now as Natalie struggles to establish her own identity unencumbered by her dysfunctional family, a creeping darkness seems to be growing. Is it Natalie or the world itself? See also **Main Street, North Bennington**.

Shirley Jackson returned to the campus setting in a number of non-genre stories such as "Gaudeamus Igitur," "Family Treasures," and "Still Life with Teapot and Students." Her description of campus life and the tensions between students and faculty over academic castes and social mores were not complimentary to the college, which may be why they were not published until 50 years after her death in *Let Me Tell You: New Stories, Essays, and Other Writings* (2015).

Beth is a recent graduate of Bennington College who finds work in New York City. Now she must learn how to survive the city itself in Harlan Ellison's "Whimper of Whipped Dogs," first anthologized in *Bad Moon Rising* (1973).

Bennington College, Dewey House – Bennington College sophomore Paula Welden left her dorm room in Dewey House and went on a walk along a trail through the woods toward Glastenbury Mountain on Dec. 1, 1946. She was never seen again, adding another tale to the legendary "Bennington Triangle." See also **Glastenbury**.

The disappearance occurred soon after Stanley Edgar Hyman began his tenure as a professor. Welden would never know it, but she served as inspiration for Professor Hymen's wife, horror icon Shirley Jackson. Her short story "The Missing Girl," from the collection *Just an Ordinary Day* (1995), features a girl who disappears from a summer camp. The missing girl has made so little impression on those around her that by the end of the investigation, those looking for her doubt she existed at all. See also **Main Street, North Bennington**.

Bennington alumna Margot Hartman also used the high-profile disappearance as the inspiration for the screenplay of *Psychomania* (1964), the first film of her husband, low budget filmmaker Del Tenney. Starring James Farentino and Dick Van Patten early in their careers, the story revolves around an artist who works with nude models and is the primary suspect in a series of murders at a girls' college. The film originally titled *Violent Midnight*.

Bennington College, Jennings Hall – Bennington College's Jennings Hall is the music education building. It also is alleged to be haunted from its earlier existence as a private mansion. The old, gray stone mansion, secluded from the rest of the campus certainly gives the vibe of a haunted house. English instructor Stanley Edgar Hyman repeated the stories of the building's otherworldly reputation to his wife. His wife Shirley Jackson then used the hall as part of the inspiration for her novel, *The Haunting of Hill House* (1959). See also **Main Street, North Bennington**.

Bennington Triangle – See **Glastenbury**.

Benson – Rufus Wilmot Griswold was born in Benson in 1815. A failed minister, a mediocre poet, and an opportunistic editor, Griswold's sole remaining claim to fame is as the character assassin of Edgar Allen Poe in an 1850 biographical "memoir" that reworked Poe's life into a series of scandals, including allegations of incidents documented by records forged by Griswold to bolster his case.

Berlin – Painted red, the gable-roofed, wood-frame Montpelier Junction Railroad station, just outside the city in Berlin, is still used for the stops of the Amtrak's Vermonter route from Washington, D.C. to St. Albans, VT. Director Walter Ungerer's *The Animal* (1976) begins at the snow-covered station as a couple meets on the platform and head out into the Vermont winter. See also **South Woodbury**.

Bethany – In *X-Files* episode "Chimera" (7:16), FBI Special Agent Fox Mulder is sent to investigate a series of murders in the "perfect little town" of Bethany. It soon appears that the disappearance of local resident Martha Crittendon coincides with the appearance of ravens, the mythical companions of evil.

Bethel – In 2012, Dr. Robert Neville (Will Smith) is the sole human in New York City among hordes of mutated human monsters in the 2007 film *I am Legend*. The most recent film allegedly based on Richard Matheson's 1954 novel *I Am Legend* ends with a much more upbeat future for mankind than the novel, with Dr. Neville isolating a possible cure that he sends to the only known human stronghold, up in Bethel.

Birch Mountain – An abandoned hospital in the Green Mountains is where the denouement takes place in the R. Patrick Gates novel *Deathwalker* (1996). Former police detective Bill Gage, crippled by his addictions, faces both his own demons and the serial killer known as the "Deathwalker."

Black Pond – In the film *Superstition* (1982), a minister and his family move into the old Sharack house, an abandoned farmhouse with a bad reputation. They soon find that the reputation is deserved — the property is the site where a priest and his parish drowned the witch Elondra Sharack in 1692. The witch's ghost still haunts the property and exacts her revenge on anybody nearby. She, understandably, holds a particular dislike of the clergy. The film was also released on DVD as *The Witch*. (Not to be confused with the unrelated 2016 film with the same title).

Bradford – Young Emmett is alone on his family farm. In the absence of his parents, he explores the family fields, the barns and is particularly intrigued by the orchard dotted with ancient cellar holes and an old family cemetery. But it is when Emmett returns to his home that he discovers the darkest secret of the house. Scott T. Goudsward's short story "Emmett" was first published in the anthology *Nobody* (2006).

Brattleboro – Brattleboro is the setting for Stephen Rynas' short story "The Apprentice Sorcerer," first published in *Fantasy Fiction*, November 1953. Ralph meets Marilyn, a witch who collided with his chimney on Halloween. After several years of wedded bliss, Ralph discovers he must duel the Class A Champion Sorcerer Bascombe to remain with his wife.

In *Dry Skull Dreams* (1995) by Michael Green, Dr. Molly Coughlin returns to Brattleboro from her clinic in the small African village of Mamadou, unaware that an evil tribal shaman has infected her with black "seeds" that are rooting deep within her. The seeds are extraterrestrial and are slowly taking control, forcing her to pass them to an increasing number of additional victims.

Sara Hazel, halfway through what would be her final concert, dropped the mic and walked off stage never to be heard from again. Years later, Christian, an up and coming reporter, has finally traced his musical idol to an old farmhouse outside Brattleboro. His dreams of a bestselling biography of the lost star vanish when the farmhouse door is opened by a withered crone surrounded by cats. Christian still recognizes her, and as he interviews her, Sarah seems to look younger. She reveals her secrets to him over tea, cookies, and a black ritual in "T.S. Eliot Burns in Hell" by GD Dearborn. The story appeared in appeared in *Wicked Witches* (2016).

Brattleboro, Elliot Street – In 1870, Charles Dickens' death interrupted the serialization of *The Mystery of Edwin Drood* at chapter 6. Soon after in Brattleboro, printer Thomas P. James, who had settled on Elliot Street, claimed that Dickens had contacted him through automatic writing. Between Christmas 1872 and July 1873, James continued to produce texts that he claimed were from Dickens trying to complete his unfinished novel from the other realm. The two sections were published together in 1874 as *The Mystery of Edwin Drood*, with Charles Dickens given as the sole author. James never published any further work and died in obscurity several years later.

Brattleboro, Fox Farm Road – In a field off Fox Farm Road, the production crew of film *Redbelly* (2008) constructed a ramshackle hut and waited for winter to film the shack in the snow. The shack belongs to a cannibal hermit who is trapped in eternal winter in the belly of a great bear. The shack's final scene is its death scene as the construction was burned to the ground. See also **West Dummerston**.

Brattleboro, Meetinghouse Hill Cemetery – The film *Blood Rites* (2003) opens by introducing viewers to both the terrified Jenny Greene (Marina Morgan) and the 1765 Meeting House Hill Cemetery. Unlike Jenny, the cemetery will survive to the end of the film as Rachel (Heather Dilly), her boyfriend Eli (Steve Buck) and Reverend Chester (Chip Washington) battle the phantom that terrifies the town among the colonial cemeteries distinctive headstones and obelisks. See also **White Cross**.

Brattleboro, Union Station - The Brattleboro Museum & Art Center is housed in the refurbished Union Station. It is at this railroad station that Miskatonic University Professor Albert Wilmarth traveled to meet Henry Akeley in H. P. Lovecraft's "The Whisperer in the Darkness," first published in *Weird Tales* (August 1931). See also **Townshend**.

Bread Loaf Mountain – See **Ripton**.

Buckton – Christopher Golden's sequel *Laws of Nature* (2001) unfolds after the evolved feral beasts known as "Prowlers" have been thwarted in Boston. Now the beaten remnants of that pack have retreated to the woods of Vermont and threaten to expose a Prowler community that has peacefully coexisted with humans for generations.

Buel's Gore – Vermont Route 17 twists its way through this tiny town (population 12) in the Appalachian Gap, part of Camel's Hump State Forest. A snowy stretch of heavily wooded Route 17 is the filming location where Jack Nicholson is bitten by a lycanthrope in the film *Wolf* (1994). Now back in New York, an increasingly aggressive attitude is doing wonders for his career.

Burke Flats – Anna Neuville has returned home to the Flats at the urging of an old friend, one who died years before. Anna has a gift – she can talk to the dead. And the dead want her back to assist the FBI's Special Paranormal Investigative Research and Intelligence Team investigation of the moors. For 200 years, something has claimed lives in the swamp, and whatever it is, the body count is escalating in *Malevolent Gateway* (2012), part of Dawn Gray's ongoing S.P.I.R.I.T. series.

Burlington – Rod Steiger terrorizes his pregnant, next-door neighbor Linda Koslowski in *The Neighbor* (1993). Apparently, she reminds him of his mother, and he's determined to remain an only child at any cost.

Jason Tanner is a sales rep for a pharmaceutical company. He's on his way to a small clinic in Burlington when he stops for the night. He's had a fight with his wife and slapped her around. He was going to call to apologize again but is distracted when he discovers his finger can pass through solid objects. And it seems to be slowly spreading. "Penetration" by Joseph A. Citro first appeared in *Thunder's Shadow Collector's Magazine*, February 1994.

It is a decade after the worst of the global zombie pandemic that wiped out billions. Author Max Brooks is interviewing survivors, including the former Vice-President of the US, retired and living in Burlington in *World War Z – An Oral History of the Zombie War* (2006).

Burlington is also the 1955 birthplace of award-winning author and comic artist Stephen R. Bissette. Best known for his work on the *Swamp Thing* comic book, Bissette was a co-founder and editor of the adult horror comic book anthology *Taboo* (1988-95). He has illustrated horror anthologies and novel per year for such luminaries as Nancy Collins, Douglas E. Winter, Joseph A. Citro, Rick Hautala, Neil Gaiman, Christopher Golden and Joe Lansdale. With his son Daniel, Bissette wrote and illustrated a faux-Christian comic tract for the film *Head Trauma* (2006). The two also collaborated on "An Alphabet of Zombies" for the anthology *Zombies* (2007). A horror film critic and horror comics historian, he is the author of *We Are Going to Eat You!* (1989), an overview of cannibal horror movies. Bissette co-authored of *The Monster Book: Buffy the Vampire Slayer* (2000) with Christopher Golden and Thomas E. Sniegoski. He also co-authored *The Neil Gaiman Companion* (2008) with Christopher Golden and Henry Wagner.

East of Burlington, nestled in the woods, is a small village that is best left unnamed. Ally has come to the village to be a live-in caretaker, helping elderly Stan tend to his wife Eleanor who suffering from Alzheimer's. Problem is, Ally is not a native, and hasn't learned that the locals have their own approach to recycling in "Up in Old Vermont" by Scott Smith. The story appeared in the 2015 anthology *Seize the Night*.

Burlington, Coach Street – *The Spirit of Ethan Allen* runs a number of tours along Lake Champlain's shoreline daily from the Burlington Boat House on Coach. On July 30, 1984, as many as 86 passengers were aboard a chartered sightseeing cruise ship, *The Spirit of Ethan Allen*, for a private party. The cruise neared Appletree Point when the largest group sighting of the Lake Champlain monster took place. Champ remained visible for about three minutes. The estimated 30-foot long serpent swam parallel with the boat for 1,000 yards until a speedboat's approach frightened it off. See also **Lake Champlain**.

Burlington, Ethan Allen Homestead Museum – Ethan Allen, Revolutionary War hero and leader of the Green Mountain Boys, settled down on the edge of Burlington. Late in his life, he became interested in metaphysics and metempsychosis (the transmigration of the soul), much to the horror of local clergy. If transmigration was true, Allen hoped to return as a wild horse, free to wander the Vermont hills. B.A. Botkin's *Treasury of New England Folklore* (1944) records that shortly after Allen's 1789 death, a large white stallion was seen roaming the hills around Burlington.

Burlington, Main Street – In 1947-48, Bela Lugosi was touring the country performing a series of dramatic readings, including Edgar Allan Poe's "A Tell-tale Heart." He stopped by the studios of WCAX radio in Burlington on Main Street, and without music or effects, sonorously read the story into a microphone for possible promotional use. Recorded onto two 12-inch 78 RPM disks, the performance was later given to Forrest Ackerman. The vinyl disks were misfiled and forgotten until rediscovered in 2002 when the Ackermansion was being packed up for a move. This recording was used as the narration by Raúl García for his Alberto Breccia inspired version of *Tell Tale Heart* (2005).

Burlington, Medical Center Hospital of Vermont – In 1973, ravaged by alcoholism and hepatitis, Veronica Lake died in this hospital. Lake's films include *I Married a Witch* (1942) and *Flesh Feast* (1970). The facility is now referred to as the Medical Center Campus at Fletcher Allen Health Care.

Burlington, Perkins Pier - South of the ferry landing on King Street along Burlington's waterfront is Perkins Pier. There you will find a monument to the cryptid species *Belua aquatica champlainiensis*, better known as the Lake Champlain monster. The granite marker commemorates the lake serpent first recorded in 1609 by explorer Samuel de Champlain. See also **Lake Champlain**.

Burlington, Shelburne Road – 346 Shelburne Road is the former site of the Elizabeth Lund Home. A refuge for unwed mothers, a Philadelphia teen fled there in 1945 to give birth to Theodore Robert Cowell. Mother and son moved to Tacoma Washington, where in 1951, she married. Her son was adopted, taking his step-father's name. By the time he was executed in Florida, January 24, 1989, everyone knew him by that name: Ted Bundy.

In 1999, 308 Shelburne Road was home to the Panda Inn restaurant and the scene of a double homicide. It took a decade before the vacant building was demolished and replaced with a nondescript drugstore, but by 2002, locals were tired of looking at the eyesore it had become. So local newspaper *Seven Days* asked area authors to imagine scenarios about the shunned building for the December 18, 2002, issue. "The Last Fortune Cookie" was Joseph A. Citro's contribution, telling of arsonist for hire who doesn't complete his job, but at least departs with a full stomach. The story was collected in Citro's *Not Yet Dead* (2009).

Burlington, University of Vermont – In *What Lies Beneath* (2000), Harrison Ford plays a genetics professor at the university whose extracurricular dalliances have started to become a problem. The UVM campus appears in several scenes. See also **Addison**.

Real-life UVM professor of English Tony Magistrale is an authority in gothic and horror film and fiction, particularly that of Stephen King and Edgar Allan Poe. In addition to Professor Magistrale's writings, he also teaches such courses as "Films of Stephen King," "The American Horror Film," "Poe's Children," and "The Literary Vampire."

Burlington, Vermont District Court – Dr. Julian Olcott (Carl Schell) was tried for homicide in the death of a young girl patient. He was acquitted but his medical license revoked. Now he has arrived at an experimental girls' reformatory in

England to teach science. Coincidentally, a werewolf has begun attacking the young girls of the campus. *Lycanthropus* (1962) was filmed in Italy and set in England. The English dubbed version was released in the US as *Werewolf in a Girls' Dormitory*.

Burlington International Airport – See **South Burlington**.

Camel's Hump State Forest – See **Buel's Gore**.

Camel's Hump Mountain – See **Duxbury**.

Canaan – Sam Winchester (Jared Padalecki) and his brother Dean (Jensen Ackles) have split up to follow different leads. Dean is in Canaan, looking for Bela Talbot (Lauren Cohan). Bela, a con artist and procurer of supernatural objects for profit, had previously stolen a mystical revolver that might prevent Dean's impending death. Bela no longer has the gun and has her own problems – her deal with demons runs out soon, and completion will be unpleasant and permanent for Bela in "Time Is on My Side," episode 3:15 of *Supernatural*.

Canaan, Northland Restaurant – In 2008, a research team will go into the New Hampshire wilderness to solve the mystery of why and how the citizenry of Friar vanished without a trace in 1940. As the film *Yellowbrickroad* (2010) opens, the intrepid expedition is assembling at a Canaan landmark, the Northland Restaurant and Lounge on Gale Street, using the parking lot to pack the last of the supplies into their vehicles. Crossing the Connecticut River into New Hampshire will be the least unpleasant thing to happen to them.

Canaan, Prince Farm – Rodney Prince's pasture has a cave in it, with a history of odd noises and missing persons. The locals are divided about the cave – some believe it is the burrow of subterranean monsters, while others simply feel it's the back door to hell itself. The short story "The Cave of the Splurgles" by Edward Page Mitchell was first published anonymously in *The New York Sun*, July 1877.

Carson Corners – See **Lake Pocumtuc**.

Castleton – The "Ancient Vermont" exhibit on the second floor of the Calvin Coolidge Library at Castleton State College houses large stones alleged to have been modified by ancient Celts to create ritual symbols of animals and phalli in association with stone structures such as those at **South Royalton, VT** and **North Salem, NH**.

Cavendish – Phineas P. Gage (1823–1860), in a freak blasting accident, had a 3-foot long, 13-pound iron rod driven into his skull, through his brain, and out of the top of his head. Gage survived and gained immortality in medical journals. 1998 was the 150th anniversary of the accident, and the town has erected a memorial plaque to commemorate Gage's accidental lobotomy. In addition to the facts and a timeline, the plaque also includes a map to the location of Gage's date with destiny, roughly a ¾ mile walk. Gage's skull, the iron rod, and a death mask are in the collection of Harvard University's Warren Anatomical Museum. The rest of his remains are buried in San Francisco.

Center Hollow – In Jack Scaparro's *The Dollkeeper* (1987), a woman that is a pillar of the community hides a deadly secret that may be related to the disappearance of a dozen local children.

Center Rutland – As *Zombie Town* (2007) begins, a truck has jackknifed across the only road into Otis, taking out a telephone pole with it, cutting the town off from the rest of the world. The Rutland Town Fire Department, headquartered in Center Rutland, plays itself at the scene of the accident, which gives them a front row seat to the beginnings of a zombie apocalypse. See also **Otis**.

Chadbury – In *Son of the Endless Night* (1985) by John Farris, Richard Devon commits a brutal slaying at the Davos Chalet Resort on Hermitage Mountain. The murder trial at the Haden County Court becomes a battle between the forces of light and the ancient demon that possesses Devon.

Charles – *Welcome Home, Johnny Bristol* (1972) opens with Johnny Bristol (Martin Landau) returning home after captivity as a POW in Viet Nam. His only respite in captivity was telling stories about the farms, the swimming hole, and the first girl he kissed. Released from the military hospital, Johnny sets off on a trip to his childhood home, only to discover it's gone and no one has heard of it. Did he make everything up as a coping mechanism in the cage? Was the town wiped out in a secret government experiment? Or is something darker going on?

Chelsea – Jon Lansdale (Michael Caine) is a successful cartoonist who whose drawing hand is amputated in a car accident. He blames his wife (Andrea Marcovicci), who was driving during the accident that ends his career. As his life collapses around him, he begins to suspect, in a perpetual alcoholic haze, that the hand survived and is haunting him. As he descends into madness, so does the disembodied limb's body count. *The Hand* (1981) was Oliver Stone's second directorial effort, based on his adaptation of *The Lizard's Tail* (1979) by Marc Brandel. The book was re-released in 1981 using the film's title.

Chester – Chester is the childhood home of horror writer novelist and folklorist Joseph A. Citro. While in high school Citro discovered a small stone structure in the woods behind his home, one of hundreds that dot hillsides of Vermont. The builders and function of these stone huts, beehives, and chambers remains a topic of debate. Whether these drystone masonry constructed buildings are proof of ancient explorers or colonial farmer buildings, the one on Citro property resonated with the future author. It would be the nexus of his first novel *Shadow Child* (1987) with the Whitcome family moving into an old farm house with a similarly mysterious chamber on the property. See also **Antrim**.

Cherryfield – A Ranger has disappeared, his last letter postmarked Cherryfield. He was warning an anthropologist that there was a cult operating in the Vermont woods. Concerned, the professor contacts a former student and then also disappears. And so adventurer Kate Furyaka and her sidekick Donat Cartier rush to Vermont and find themselves in a town controlled by a mysterious ancient evil known as Yog-Yoteth the White Worm. Unfortunately for the cultists, outnumbered and outgunned is exactly how Miss Fury likes the odds in "Fury in Vermont." Done in the classic pulp style by Ron Fortier, the story first appeared in *Dark Furies* (2005).

Chittenden – Six nights a week, brothers William and Horatio Eddy conducted séances in their farmhouse. The brothers would summon spirits recognized as deceased friends and relatives. The specters moved freely around the room and interacted with the audience. If the brothers were charlatans, no one ever uncovered the fraud. Henry Olcott, a respected attorney and war hero, investigated the brothers in 1874. After 9 weeks, he left a believer. It was at the séances that Olcott also met spiritualist Madame Helena Blavatsky. The two would return to New York and found the Theosophist movement.

Coker Creek – Frank Black (Lance Henriksen) decides to take his daughter Jordan (Brittany Tiplady) on a Christmas vacation. Instead of tranquility, they discover a dead Mafia hit man who appears to be unusually alive for someone supposedly dead for nine years. Add two mysterious healers in the woods, and you understand why Frank rarely takes a vacation in the *Millennium* episode "Omerta" (3:09).

Connecticut River Valley – In *A Return to Salem's Lot* (1987), anthropologist Joe Weber (Michael Moriarty) drives from New York to his hometown and the house he has inherited in

Jerusalem's Lot, Maine. His hope is that small town life would straighten out his son Jeremy (Ricky Addison Reed). That quickly becomes the least of his problems when he learns his hometown is a vampire sanctuary. And they want Weber to write their history. Footage was shot in various locations on the Vermont side of the Connecticut River Valley, notably near Newbury, Peacham, and St. Johnsbury, to establish the image of an increasingly rural and justifiably isolated countryside leading to the vampire refuge. See also **Strafford**.

Corriveau – Benny Martini always wanted to be a clown, elevating "class clown" into an art form. Benny, however, he didn't want to be a mere birthday party entertainer. Benny wanted to be a circus clown, so when the Macintosh Traveling Circus rolled into town, Benny went every day until they hired him. Now he's the low clown in the circus totem pole. He finds a clown history in a bookstore and reads a chapter on the *darker* side of clowns. He prays to the god of clowns Polichinelle to be higher on the circus's food chain. What happens next is not the least bit funny in "Put on a Happy Face" by Christopher Golden. The story first appeared in *Blood Lite III: Aftertaste* (2012).

Craftsbury Common – Alfred Hitchcock used the town common in his black comedy *The Trouble with Harry* (1955). Since the village is a National Historic Site, the location is mostly unchanged from the 1954 filming. See also **Highwater**.

Crown Point Bridge – See **Lake Champlain Bridge**.

Dark Mountain – A small community in Windham County named after the nearby mountain, Dark Mountain is home to Ezra Noyes of the Vermont UFO Intelligence Bureau. The town first appears in Richard Lupoff's "Documents in the Case of Elizabeth Akeley," a sequel to H. P. Lovecraft's "The Whisperer in the Darkness." Lupoff's story was first published in *The Magazine of Fantasy & Science Fiction*, March 1982. See also **Townshend**.

Deering – A couple moves from New York to Vermont to find a simpler life and to salvage their marriage in *Hangman* (1991) by Christopher Bohjalian. The house needs to be completely rehabilitated, starting with its reputation for evil and the noose in the attic from a century-old suicide.

Dorset – Outdoorsman, author, and magazine editor Tony Atwill lived in Dorset. When his mother died in 2002, He decided it would be fitting to reunite her with his father, who had died in 1946. Loading his dogs in a camper, he drove to Florida, retrieved his mother's urns, and then drove cross-country to the Chapel of the Pines Crematory in Los Angeles where his father's cremains rested. And that is how the ashes of horror great Lionel Atwill came to rest with his wife in the woods of western Vermont in an anonymous forest glen. Atwill's horror resume includes *Doctor X* (1932), *The Mystery of the Wax Museum* (1933), *The Vampire Bat* (1933), *Son of Frankenstein* (1939), and *Frankenstein Meets the Wolf Man* (1943).

Dove's Landing – In Judith Kelman's *The House on the Hill* (1992), a child-killing sociopath goes blind in prison and is placed under house arrest in a deserted home in the woods on the outside of a small rural town. Now a killer may be stalking the streets. Is a blind man under constant electronic surveillance once again on the prowl or is there a new menace to the children of Dove's Landing?

Dummerston, East-West Road – Dummerston Center Cemetery is home to six graves of the children of Revolutionary War veteran Lieutenant Leonard Spaulding (1728-1788). Spaulding's family was being decimated by a mysterious ailment that slowly drained the life from them, killing 9 members of the family in 16 years. It was believed that an evil root had grown from coffin to coffin, and each time it reached the end of the row, another family member died. The only cure for this vampiric curse was to break the root's progress by exhuming the most recent victim and burning his vital organs. The fact that Lt. Spaulding himself died of consumption (tuberculosis) before half his afflicted children similarly wasted away may be a more pragmatic cause of the deaths. Then again, Spaulding isn't buried in the same cemetery – he's a mile and a half down the road in East Dummerston's Bennett Cemetery. See also **Village Green, Woodstock**.

Dummerston, Middle Road – Dummerston Congregational Church, built in 1842 is a photogenic example of transitional Greek Revival/Gothic Revival architecture. It is so picturesque that it was used in the film *Blood Rites* (2003) as the church in White Cross where Reverend Chester (Chip Washington) maintains a rare sanctuary against the spectral presence terrorizing the town. See also **White Cross**.

Dummerston, Naulakha – Named after *Naulahka* (1892), a book he co-authored with his late brother-in-law Wolcott Balestier, Naulakha is the house designed and built by Rudyard Kipling (with the proper spelling of Naulakha, a Hindi word meaning "priceless jewel"). A long, tall building in the American Shingle style, it overlooks the Connecticut River Valley. While living here, Kipling wrote some of his most popular books, such as *The Jungle Books* (1894-95), and some of his many poems and stories of the supernatural, such as "The Lost Legion," first published in *Strand Magazine*, May 1892.

Duxbury – The base of Camel's Hump Mountain is the setting of Daniel Pierce Thompson's *May Martin, or, the Money Diggers* (1835). The tale of lost treasures, occult divinations, and ghosts was an immediate bestseller when it was released in 1835. There was a widespread belief that lost treasure, protected by the supernatural, could be found through the regional. The most famous of the crystal-gazing treasure hunters was Joseph Smith, Jr., who found golden plates that gave rise to the Mormon religion. See also **Green Mountain Cemetery, Montpelier**.

East Burke – In Joseph A. Citro's short story "Soul Keeper," Carl Congden crashes his car after driving away from a fight with his wife about her tithing. Now, he finds himself immobile and at the mercy of a religious zealot, in a story first anthologized in *Lovecraft's Legacy* (1990).

East Corinth – Although the film *Beetlejuice* (1988) is set in Connecticut, the exterior footage was shot in East Corinth. The Maitlands, a recently deceased couple (Geena Davis and Alec Baldwin) find their beloved house has been infested by the Deetz family, (Jeffrey Jones, Catherine O'Hara, and Winona Ryder), self-proclaimed aesthetes who are redecorating in modern kitsch. Unable to scare the family out of their house, they hire Beetlejuice (Michael Keaton), a ghost specializing in the removal of the living. But the cure may turn out to be worse the disease.

East Corinth, Chicken Farm Road – The covered bridge where the Maitlands (Geena Davis and Alec Baldwin) have their fatal crash in *Beetlejuice* (1988) was a nondescript wooden plank bridge over the Tabor Branch, given a Hollywood makeover. The actual bridge beneath the faux covered bridge no longer exists either. It was replaced by a new bridge parallel to the former location.

East Corinth, Jewell Lane – The rambling Victorian house that the Maitlands loved beyond death in *Beetlejuice* (1988) was a façade built for the movie, and was dismantled after filming. The hill where it was built, off of Jewell Lane, gave it a commanding view of downtown.

East Corinth, Northeast Slopes – The faux covered bridge where the Maitlands (Geena Davis and Alec Baldwin) have their fatal crash in *Beetlejuice* (1988), in frugal Yankee tradition, was repurposed. It is now in use at the Northeast Slopes ski area, where it serves a picturesque but functional purpose as a shed housing the rope tow engine.

East Corinth, Village Road – The main street through town passes most of the locations still recognizable from *Beetlejuice* (1988). The archetypical white-steeple of the East Corinth Congregational Church (645 Village Road) is easily recognized from aerial shots of the town. It is also next door to the building which was turned into the local hardware store. At the end of the film, Lydia Deetz (Winona Ryder) has enrolled in school. The building Ryder is shown exiting, Miss Shannon's School for Girls, is the local Masonic Lodge (778 Village Road).

East Craftsbury – Alfred Hitchcock used the spectacular fall foliage of East Craftsbury as exterior shots in his black comedy *The Trouble with Harry* (1955). See also **Highwater**.

East Dummerston, Bennett Cemetery – See **East-West Road, Dummerston**.

East Gruesome – See **Norwich**.

East Lupton – Murray Leinster's whimsical short story "The Devil of East Lupton" was first published in *Thrilling Wonder Stories*, August 1948. A hobo stumbles across alien technology, only to be hunted down as a supernatural evil.

East Montpelier – In the 1982 film version of Ray Bradbury's 1962 novel *Something Wicked This Way Comes*, Jason Robards battles the evil Jonathan Pryce. East Montpelier was briefly used for the film's establishing shots, even though the movie itself is set in the mid-west.

Easton – Easton is a small, quiet town, the perfect to start a family to ex-city folks like Dave and Carol Stern. That was until they met the Poacher and his murderous dogs in Brian McNaughton's *The Poacher* (1978). The novel was significantly reworked by the author and released as *Buster Callan* (2002) with a more human but no less menacing hunter.

Eden – Ritual slayings are being discovered across the nation - all in towns with religion-derived names. The trail leads investigator Matt Senacal to Eden where Biblical names and Old Testament law mask an Old Testament ritual to initiate a New Testament Armageddon in *Cult* (1990) by Edward J. Frail.

Eden Falls – In Joseph A. Citro's short story "Kirby," first anthologized in *After the Darkness* (1993), 10-year old Terry is the new kid in town and Kirby is his new best friend. Has Terry created an imaginary friend or does Kirby have the ability to transform himself as needed?
In Richard Mindell's novel *Eden Falls* (2003), tensions between native Vermonters and flatlanders erupt in a violent confrontation that returns years later to haunt the farming community in the guise of a serial killer.

Eureka – Eureka is the town nearest a patch of unclaimed woodlands, or a "gore" with a bad reputation. Now, ex-reporter Roger Newton must discover why the burnt ruins of a hotel in the gore seem to attract Bigfoot reports amid disappearing locals in Joseph A. Citro's *The Unseen* (1990). The novel was re-released in 2000 as *The Gore*. See also **Glastenbury**.

Falmouth – A mysterious fungus has taken control of the village, exerting a strange influence over the recently interred. The local doctor must determine how to defeat it, assuming it is even possible. The living citizens have a strong opinion on the topic too. "Dust from a Dark Flower" by Daniel Mills first appeared in the mycological-themed horror anthology *Fungi* (2012). See also **Rockingham**.

Falmouth Toll Road – A grief-stricken father walks aimlessly from the gravesite of his son. He wanders onto the toll road, abandoned since the arrival of the trains. As he is haunted by his memories, so to the road is haunted by its past – abandoned homes, and dying villages. As night falls, he comes across an old inn, still struggling to survive. He will find kindred spirits within – literally and figuratively in "The Wayside Voices." The story by Daniel Mills first appeared in the September/October 2012 issue of *Black Static* (#12).

Fenwick – John Driver's *Hunger of the Beast* (1991) finds Diana LaBianca's vacation at the secluded Wilkinson Inn is interrupted when the owners suspect she is actually there to investigate them. Now, she is imprisoned in the basement of the inn at the mercy of Esau, their deformed, half-witted, and thoroughly evil son.

Ferrisburg – A colonial town on the shores of Lake Champlain is where miserly John Grindall was cursed to physically feel the cold held in his heart, as recorded by William Austin in the short story "The Man with the Cloaks." The tale's first appearance was in *The American Monthly Magazine,* January 1836.

Friars Island – See **Lake Champlain**.

Gibbington – Melanie Blaime (Cindy Sampson) returns to her hometown when her estranged father (Bruce Dern) becomes the primary suspect in a murder. 17-years ago, a mysterious encounter in the swamps killed Blaime's wife and drove him to send Melanie away. Now the ex-sheriff is a hermit in the swamps. Problem is, Blaime isn't the killer. The bigger problem is the killer isn't human in *Swamp Devil* (2008).

Glastenbury – The local Indians considered the heavily wooded Glastenbury Mountain to be cursed land. Folklorist Joseph A. Citro coined the term "Bennington Triangle" after a rash of documented disappearances between 1945 and 1950, with additional mysterious disappearances noted as early as 1892. Add strange lights in the skies, unidentifiable sounds from the woods, and reported Bigfoot sightings to the mix and you'll understand why the town never prospered. See also **Bennington College; Eureka; Hobston**.

Glendon – In Duffy Stein's *Ghost Child* (1982), the Talmans move from New York to their dream house in central Vermont. The house needs a little work, but it comes with a toy room – a room filled with puppets and dolls from the original owners. The longer the Talmans stay, the more events begin to resemble the events leading to the grisly deaths of the original owners.

Granbury – Sydney Madison is a successful writer of historical novels who decides to write his next novel in peace and quiet. That's how he ended up at the Kempton hunting lodge. Unfortunately, he's sharing the space with a Lovecraftian god in "The Feaster from Afar" by Joseph Payne Brennan. The story first appeared in the 1976 edition of the anthology *The Disciples of Cthulhu*.

Granville – South Hollow Cemetery is the final resting place of actor, writer, and director Henrik Galeen (1881-1949), who played a key role in the development of the German Expressionist movement in cinema. That movement's influence on American directors led to the stylistic fluidity of scenes in horror films such as James Whale's *Frankenstein* (1931). Among Galeen's credits are *The Student of Prague* (1913), *The Golem* (1915), and *Waxworks* (1924). His most important contribution was the script for *Nosferatu, Eine Symphonie des Grauens* (1922), released in the US as *Nosferatu the Vampire* (1922), starring Max Schreck as Graf Orlok and directed by one of Germany's most distinguished filmmakers, F.W. Murnau. There is no headstone and the grave location is unknown. The most likely burial spot is in the plot of fellow expatriate Austrians Franz and Ilona Branschofsky.

Green Manors – Alfred Hitchcock's *Spellbound* (1945) begins as Green Manors Sanitorium awaits the new director. Dr. Anthony Edwardes (Gregory Peck) arrives to replace retiring Dr. Murchison (Leo G. Carroll). Soon Dr. Edwardes has fallen in love with Dr. Constance Petersen (Ingrid Bergman), a brilliant but aloof psychoanalyst. When it is discovered that the new director was murdered, the amnesiac masquerading as him is the chief suspect. He flees with Dr. Petersen close behind, convinced if she can cure his amnesia, he can clear his name. Look for dream sequences by surrealist artist Salvador Dalí. The script was based on *The House of Dr. Edwardes* (1927), written by John Palmer and Hilary A. Saunders under the pseudonym Francis Beeding.

Greenfield Center – Dr. Cook, the only doctor in Greenfield, is revered by nearly everyone in his idyllic little town. Those that disrupt the status quo have a habit of dying unexpectedly. *Dr. Cook's Garden* was a 1970 made-for-TV movie starring Bing Crosby, adapted from a 1967 Broadway play by Ira Levin starring Burl Ives. Establishing shots were filmed in Woodstock.

Greenwich – Mr. John Philip Johnson wanders around New York City all day, doing good deeds. One such act of kindness is to watch a child while his mother supervises their furniture being packed for a move to Greenwich. Mr. Johnson has no ulterior motives – it's just his turn to be the good one in "One Ordinary Day, with Peanuts" by Shirley Jackson. The story first appeared in *Fantasy and Science Fiction* (January 1955). See also **Main Street, North Bennington**.

Greenwood – Twenty years ago, Jana Mercer (Brigitte Bako) witnessed the murder of her family by serial killer Calvin Hawks (Larry Drake). Today, she is a photophobic recluse who discovers that Calvin has been released from prison, has hacked her computer, and is coming to finish the job. So she flees to her hometown in Vermont in *Paranoia* (1998). See also **Jacksonville; Wilmington**.

Guilford – In June of 1928, H. P. Lovecraft spent two weeks at a farmhouse recently purchased by his friend Vrest Orton. Two years later, the house and the visit became the foundations of "The Whisperer in the Darkness," first published in *Weird Tales* (August 1931). In 1925, Orton founded Countryman Press, publishing books on traditional Vermont crafts, such as fireplace building. Often operating the press himself, he invited Lovecraft to move to Guilford become his editor. Lovecraft, with his aversion to the cold, deferred on the grounds that the winter temperatures would kill him. See also **Townshend; Weston**.

Hampden – At Hampden College, an elite group of gifted classics students stages a Greek bacchanalia in the woods. When the frenzy ends, they discover they have ripped a local farmer to pieces. Now someone is blackmailing them, per *The Secret History* (1992) by Donna Tartt.

Harmony – Fifteen years ago a girl named Lisa went missing in the woods outside Harmony, in the ghost town of Reliance. There were no clues to her disappearance, just convoluted memories of Lisa's fascination with Teilo the Fairy King. Now, memories and small clues are starting to resurface as her brother Sam and cousin Evie begin to search anew for Lisa. People from fifteen years ago are showing back up in town as part of an elaborate game carefully orchestrated to uncover the true cause of Lisa's disappearance in *Don't Breathe a Word* (2011) by Jennifer McMahon. See also **Reliance**.

Harrington Falls – Construction at the old Blake mansion in the sleepy hamlet of Harrington Falls has uncovered a hidden tunnel in Joseph Nassise's *Riverwatch* (2003). Now the last surviving Nightshade, an ancient race of demons that feed on blood and terror, is on a rampage after he is accidentally freed from his prison.

Hartmore College – In Wendi Lee's detective novel *Habeas Campus* (2002), Bostonian detective Angela Matelli heads to Vermont. Her client is an anthropology professor with any unusual problem. One of his students died unexpectedly the week before, and now he thinks he's seen her wandering around the campus. His field of specialty? Haitian voodoo.

Hatfield Corners – Dr. Smith (Jonathan Harris), Will (Billy Mumy), Penny (Angela Cartwright), the Bloop, and the Robot stumble across an alien teleporter. Will triggers the device to return to Earth planning to stay just long enough to direct a rescue mission to the Jupiter 2 in the *Lost in Space* episode "Return from Outer Space" (1:15). Unfortunately for Will, he arrives in a small town where no one believes he is from outer space and he is running out of time.

Hazelville – Hikers and campers are turning up dead, and Park Ranger Cody (Kevin McCauley) suspects the killer of the forest – a Great White Pine. And so begins director/writer Michael Pleckaitis's parody of *Jaws*, right down to the "We're going to need a bigger axe" quote in the film *Trees* (2000).
A 2004 sequel *Trees 2: The Root of All Evil* finds our intrepid Park Ranger dealing with an entire crop of coniferous killers that have been sold to the unsuspecting residents as Christmas trees. Both films were shot in Watertown, CT.

Hermitage Mountain –See **Chadbury**.

Highgate – Chucky, the doll carrying the soul of serial killer Charles Lee Ray (Brad Dourif), arrives at the home of Sarah Pierce (Chantal Quesnelle) and her daughter Nica (Fiona Dourif). Chucky then does what he does best, terrorizes and kills the family one by one. This time, it's a little more personal

– Sarah was the one who called the cops on him, pre-doll days. *Curse of Chucky* (2013) is the sixth in the Chucky franchise.

Highwater – The trouble with Harry Worp is that he's dead but won't stay in one place. And half the town thinks they may have been the one who killed him, in Alfred Hitchcock's *The Trouble with Harry* (1955). See also **Craftsbury Common; East Craftsbury; Morrisville**.

Hillport – Otis Morks is struck by lightning and now the stubborn Yankee is able to disbelieve things out of existence in Robert Arthur's short story "Obstinate Uncle Otis" first published in *Argosy*, July 19, 1941.

Hilly Vale – Hilly Vale is a small town and nearest railroad stop to the deep woods that surround Shadowlands, the secluded mansion of legendary stage magician Coleman Collins. Collins's nephew Del Nightingale and his friend Tom Flanagan take the train to spend the summer there in Peter Straub's *Shadowland* (1980). As time passes, however, Tom begins to suspect that what Collins is teaching his nephew is not harmless sleight of hand, but very real, very dangerous sorcery.

Hinsdale - A botched robbery finds a gang of would-be robbers on the lam. With nowhere to go, the getaway driver decided they should hide at his grandmother's abandoned house in the woods of Vermont. It sounds like a good plan, assuming any of them survive that long. "The Getaway" by Paul Tremblay appeared in *Supernatural Noir* (2011).

Hobston – Mysterious things happen in Hobston, leading paranormal researchers to suspect it is a gateway between worlds similar to the Bermuda Triangle. Now a psychologist, a priest, and a physicist must battle beings from an alternate dimension trying to open a portal into our world in Joseph A. Citro's *Deus-X* (1994). See also **Glastenbury**.

Hubley's Gore – Thomas Mordane's *Blood Root* (1982) brings Mark and Laura Avery to the gore, giving up the city life as their first child's birth approaches. Now they must cope with Laura's pregnancy, recalcitrant Yankee farmers, and the Druids who worship the oak trees around the gore.

Hunter's Hollow – Frank and Joe Hardy head into the Vermont countryside to investigate a Revolutionary War Hessian zombie who may be trying to chase a family out of their colonial house by burning it down. Does this local folk figure have anything to do with the sabotage at the traveling circus in Burlington? *Track of the Zombie* by Franklin W. Dixon, the 71st Hardy Boys mystery first appeared in 1982.

Jacksonville – The picturesque Candlelight Bed & Breakfast was used for scenes of a nursing home in the film *Paranoia* (1998). Jana Mercer (Brigitte Bako) has fled to her hometown in the wake of serial killer Calvin Hawks' (Larry Drake) release from prison. Police officer Mark Daniels (Robert Floyd) accompanies her to visit her aunt (Mary Jane Wells) at the nursing home. Jana and Mark share a moment on the B&B's gazebo by the pond in the yard. Scenes between Jana and her aunt were shot in the B&B's Halifax Room. See also **Greenwood**.

Jeffersonville – In *Something Wicked This Way Comes* (1982), Jason Robards battles the evil Jonathan Pryce. Jeffersonville was among several small towns used briefly for the film's establishing shots, even though the movie is set in the mid-west.

Jeremiah's Lot – Stephen King, while attending the University of Maine, had a weekly column in the school newspaper. In a December 18, 1969, column, he mentioned a Shaker village named Jeremiah's Lot. As King recalled the story, the entire population simply disappeared one day and the town was now a ghost town. The concept of a vanishing population seems to have some appeal to the future novelist. See also **Momson**.

Killington Ski Resort – The resort has closed for the season and the staff is cleaning up. A small plane crashes into the mountaintop, triggering an avalanche that buries the lodge. The plane, it turns out, was carrying a recently discovered Ice Age woman whose biology must be kept warm to keep her dormant. Johnny (Harmon Walsh) must now battle the cold, a limited air supply, and a million-year-old bloodthirsty creature (Ami Veveers-Chorlton) who can freeze you from the inside out. Assuming, of course, his girlfriend (Noelle Reno) doesn't kill him first in *The Ice Queen* (2005).

Lake Alban – In Paul Zindel's young adult novel *Loch* (1995), Loch and his sister Zaidee are on an expedition with Sam Perkins, their marine biologist father. They work for a ruthless media mogul Anthony Cavenger. A bloody encounter on remote Lake Alban has Cavenger in search of proof that lake monsters exist – in the form of a carcass. Perkins must try to prove the lake is home to a colony of plesiosaurs before his boss can exterminate them. Unbeknown to the adults, Loch, Zaidee, and Cavenger's daughter have befriended a baby plesiosaur with an overprotective parent.

Lake Bomoseen - Alexander Woollcott, critic, author, and Algonquin Round Table member had a summer home on Neshobe Island. Woollcott's *While Rome Burns* (1934) popularized the urban myth of the vanishing hotel room, which he rewrote as a screenplay for the "Into Thin Air" (1:5) episode of *Alfred Hitchcock Presents*. Woollcott also appeared with Noel Coward in the supernatural melodrama *The Scoundrel* (1935). See also **Lake Pocomtuc**.

Lake Champlain – Separating New York and Vermont and entering Quebec Province, Lake Champlain is a freshwater lake with a rich history in the development of the US. It is also home to North America's most famous lake monster. The Lake Champlain Monster, or "Champ" for short. A fixture in Native folklore, Champ has been spotted over the centuries by hundreds of witnesses. Be it a hoax, a surviving dinosaur, or a misidentified known species, Champ has become a tourist attraction as well as the occasional fodder for horror writers. See also **Coach Street, Burlington; Perkins Pier, Burlington; Chimney Point, Lake Champlain; Friars Island, Lake Champlain.**

In 2012, *Shadow Show: All-New Stories in Celebration of Ray Bradbury* was published as a tribute to the master. Inspired by Bradbury's "The Foghorn," Joe Hill's contribution to the anthology was "By the Silver Water of Lake Champlain." Little Gail London heads down to the lake one morning and meets up with her buddy Joel Quarrel. They suddenly realize that the large rock they have been playing on is not a rock but the body of Champ washed up on the shore. Gail and Joel make plans on how to proceed and how to spend the money when they sell the carcass. Unfortunately, their plans are a tad premature.

Lake Champlain, Chimney Point – The Champlain Bridge (also known as the Crown Point Bridge) was a bridge across Lake Champlain between Crown Point, New York and Chimney Point. This is the bridge that Michelle Pfeiffer is on when attacked by Harrison Ford in *What Lies Beneath* (2000). This bridge was also the location of numerous sightings of the Lake Champlain monster looking toward Bulwagga Bay in Port Henry, NY. The bridge in the movie was demolished in 2009. The current bridge opened in 2011. See also **Addison; Lake Champlain**.

Lake Champlain, Friars Island – The fictional island used by author Joseph A. Citro in his novel *Dark Twilight (1991)* is where Harrison Allen relocates to rebuild his life. He discovers the residents have a dark secret involving the creatures of the lake. The book was subsequently re-released as *Lake Monsters* (2001). See also **Lake Champlain**.

Lake Groton – In the May 1951 issue of *National Geographic,* author F. Barrows Colton recalls a story from his youth. His father and uncle went to their fishing camp on Lake Groton, bringing Joe LeBlanc, a local French Canadian handyman to chop firewood. When his father returned from a day of fishing, the axe was there but LeBlanc had vanished. They later found him at a local town, terrified. He claimed to have seen a *loup-garou* in the woods and fled for his life. Colton explained the *loup-garou* was the traditional French Canadian form of a werewolf where a man transforms fully into a wolf. Colton notes there had been no additional werewolf reports from the area since LeBlanc's encounter.

Lake Memphremagog – Although predominantly in Quebec, Lake Memphremagog extends down into Vermont. Over 38-square miles large, the lake is both deep and cold, much like Loch Ness. And like Scotland's Nessie, Memphremagog is home to Memphre, one or more long-necked serpents with reported sightings dating back two centuries. The Canadian side of the lake takes the sightings of a 30-foot-long lake monster a tad more seriously than Vermont, with the Royal Canadian Mint issuing a commemorative quarter coin in 2011 that featuring the beast as part of a Canadian Mythical Creatures series.

Lake Pocomtuc – It's a year after the 2017 nuclear war that sealed mankind's fate. Peter Robinson lives alone with his dog Gandalf. His nearest neighbor is Howard Timlin, a 2-hour walk away in the former wealthy summer enclave of Woodland Acres. Timlin and Robison reminisce about the past while radiation poisoning continues to slowly kill them. As the effects worsen, they decide to go out on their own terms in "Summer Thunder" by Stephen King, which first appeared in *Cemetery Dance* #72 (January 2015).

King places the fictional lake as 60 miles from Bennington, along the NY border. This roughly places the Lake on top of Lake Bomoseen, home to a wealthy summer enclave whose residents included famed raconteur and dramatist Alexander Woollcott. Woollcott co-authored a 1933 Broadway drama with George S. Kaufman that has a familiar name to King fans – "The Dark Tower." And the date the bomb destroyed the world, 2017, is also the year King's book series *The Dark Tower* is due to be released as a film, which even if a bomb, should be less radioactive. See also **Lake Bomoseen**.

Ludlow – Consisting of a sequence of three waterfall drops into pools, Buttermilk Falls, just outside Ludlow, has been one of southern Vermont's most popular swimming holes for centuries. In the 1952 prologue to Joseph A. Citro's *Shadow Child* (1987), Brian and his younger brother Eric are brought by their grandfather to the old man's secret fishing hole. Neither boy has ever been there before, yet Brian is disturbed by how familiar it seems. If the description of the grandfather's fishing spot seems familiar, it is because it Buttermilk Falls was also a childhood swimming destination of author Citro. See also **Antrim**.

MacKinac Lodge – On their way to a ski vacation, the gang meets Laurel and Hardy, the guests of the week in "The Ghost of Bigfoot" the 10th episode of season one of *The New Scooby-Doo Movies*. Laurel and Hardy are heading to the same lodge to find work. But the MacKinac Lodge is empty – the ghost of Bigfoot has scared off most of the skiers. This looks like a job for Fred, Velma, Daphne, Shaggy and Scooby Doo!

Manchester – Hulda Burton, the second wife of Captain Isaac Burton, began wasting away in a manner similar to that which killed his first wife, Rachael. Vampirism was immediately suspected. So, in 1793, Rachael Burton's corpse was exhumed and the organs were removed from the remains. The organs were carried to the local blacksmith and burned to ashes on the forge. Unfortunately, poor Hulda kept right on dying – she had a less supernatural affliction – consumption, now known as tuberculosis. See also **Village Green, Woodstock**.

Marion – Ambrose Bierce pens the tale of three stalwart citizens who spend the night "At Old Man Eckert's." First anthologized in *Can Such Things Be?* (1909), the three investigate reports that Eckert has disappeared and that his house is now haunted. Unfortunately, only two stalwart citizens return the next day.

Marriot – In the film *The Jacket* (2005), Gulf War soldier Adrien Brody is drugged, straight-jacketed, and trapped inside a morgue drawer as part of his PTSD "treatment" at the Alpine Grove Hospital. His treatment causes him to jump around in time and each journey into the future brings changes when he returns to the present. Although the film takes place in Vermont, it was actually filmed in Scotland and Canada.

Mayerville – A blasphemy committed in a Tibetan monastery returns to face explorer Jason Ford as he summers in the isolated Vermont countryside in "Carrion Crypt" by Leroy Yerxa writing as Richard Casey. It was first published in *Fantastic Adventure*, July 1947.

Middlebury – In West Cemetery rests the mortal remains of Amun-Her-Khepesh-Ef who died in 1883 BC. The two-year-old mummified son of Sun Woset, third King of Egypt and his wife Hator-Hotpe, the remains were purchased by local collector Henry Sheldon in 1866 for his home/museum, but never displayed it because of its poor condition. In 1945, the museum director took pity on the ancient toddler's corpse, had him cremated and then gave him a decent Christian burial. The Mummy's tombstone still stands, carved with the hieroglyphs for Life and Soul, and, of course, a Christian cross.

Middlebury College – Between Warner Hall and Painter Hall is a stone marker commemorating one man's war against gravity. Roger W. Babson (1875–1967) made millions in the stock market by applying Newtonian Physics principles to financial decisions. He also considered gravity to be his personal enemy. He became obsessed with gravity at the age of 18 when his younger sister Edith drowned. When his grandson also drowned in 1947, it became a personal vendetta for the rest of his life. He created the Gravity Research Foundation to conquer the force he held responsible for the deaths of his kin. In the 1960s, in return for financial donations, Babson was allowed to erect monuments on college campuses along the East Coast, placed to remind students of the benefits soon to be forthcoming when gravity was harnessed.

Milburn – In the 1981 movie version of Peter Straub's *Ghost Story* (1979), the village of Milburn is relocated from upstate New York to Vermont as a deadly secret comes back to haunt four octogenarians. See also **Dedham Pond, Milburn; Ottauquechee River; Sykes Mountain Avenue, White River Junction; Woodstock; Elm Street, Woodstock**.

Milburn, Dedham Pond – The Chowder Club decides to hide Eva Galli's body in the film *Ghost Story* (1981). They place the body in a car and send it to the bottom of Dedham Pond. See also **Milburn**.

Misty Meadows – Pierre Comtois' short story "The Country of the Wind," moves Ithaqua the Windwalker, August Derleth's interpretation of Algernon Blackwood's "Wendigo," from the frozen north to an abandoned village in the Vermont woods. The story first appeared in *Cthulhu Codex #6*, Autumn 1994.

Momson – In the summer of 1923, all 312 citizens of Momson simply vanished. Fifty years later, the houses and buildings still stand uninhabited, mysteriously abandoned in the middle of day-to-day activities. This is not an isolated incident according to Stephen King. In his novel *'Salem's Lot* (1975) and the novella "Jerusalem's Lot," first anthologized in *Night Shift* (1978), he notes that the exact same thing happened in Maine; In October of 1798 and October of 1975, the villagers of Jerusalem's Lot simply disappeared. See also **Jeremiah's Lot**.

Montpelier, Green Mountain Cemetery – Green Mount Cemetery is the final resting place of Daniel Pierce Thompson (1795-1868), folklorist, antiquarian, and author. All but forgotten today, Thompson was New England's most successful and famous novelist prior to the arrival of Nathaniel Hawthorne. Most of his books are histories and romances, but he could not resist adding a touch of local folklore. *Lucy Hosmer, or, The Guardian and Ghost* (1848), supposedly based on real events, features evil uncles, ingénue heiresses, and of course, a ghost. See also **Duxbury**.

Montpelier Junction Railroad Station – See **Berlin**.

Moriah – Silas Flood was an army chaplain who lost his faith in the carnage of the Civil War. Ten years later, he is a reporter in New York, still struggling to rebuild his life. He is sent to the village of Moriah in the Green Mountains to investigate the Lynch brothers, who claim to summon spirits and talk to the dead. Flood arrives to find Moriah is a haunted village – widows, grieving parents, even the Lynch brothers bear their own ghosts. In the evenings, Flood joins the town at a nightly séance where the spirits rise to offer solace to the living. Flood questions his ability to write this story when he is just as a haunted by his own past. *Moriah* (2017) was written by Daniel Mills.

Morrisville – Alfred Hitchcock had originally planned to shoot his black comedy *The Trouble with Harry* (1955) entirely in Vermont. A soundstage was built in tiny Morrisville at in the American Legion Barracks (which also doubled as the local school gym). But after fighting cold autumn rains on the tin roof for over a month, the idea was abandoned and the production was returned to sunny California. See also **Highwater**.

Mount Garnet – Stephen King's 1979 novel *Dead Zone* was turned into a television series in 2002. The US Government's Remote Viewing Unit is an intelligence gathering team of psychics hidden beneath a warehouse in Mount Garnet. Johnny Smith (Anthony Michael Hall) encounters the project in two episodes: "The Hunt" (2:16) and "Total Awareness" (3:05).

New Brecon – Jim and Judy Thornton have bought their dream house. Unfortunately, the realtor neglected to mention the poltergeist. "A Friendly Exorcise" by Talmage Powell was first published in *Alfred Hitchcock's Mystery Magazine*, March 1968.

New Haven – Evergreen Cemetery is the final resting place of Dr. Timothy Clark Smith (1821-1893), a 19th-century physician, suffered from severe taphephobia, the fear of being buried alive. This was a real concern among Victorians and driven by such tales as Poe's "Premature Burial," a new industry sprang up - "safety coffins," with various devices and signals to signal the outside world that the coffin's inhabitant had revived. Dr. Smith took the concept one step further. Not only was he buried with a bell to ring should he revive, the grave has a window. A 14x14 inch square piece of glass, now opaque with age, offered a view of Smith's head so his bereaved family could check up on him and make sure he remained dead. So far, so good.

New Thetford – Brion McKibben adopts an abused puppy and names it Whisper. The two become inseparable until Whisper dies. Now, the heartbroken boy brings Whisper's remains to a local Iroquois medicine man named Eleazar who mystically resurrects the dog. Unfortunately, Old Eleazar has miscalculated and Whisper is now controlled by demons known as the Yaksha who go on a killing spree in *Whisper* (1991) by Raymond Van Over.

Neshobe Island – See **Lake Bomoseen**.

Newbury – See **Connecticut River Valley**.

Newfane – Ezra Noyes of the Vermont UFO Intelligence Bureau first meets Elizabeth Akeley at the Newfane Bus Station in Richard Lupoff's "Documents in the Case of Elizabeth Akeley," first published in *The Magazine of Fantasy & Science Fiction*, March 1982. See also **Townshend**.

North Bennington, John G. McCullough Free Library – *We Have Always Lived in the Castle* (1962), the final novel by Shirley Jackson, is narrated by 18-year-old "Merricat" Blackwood, telling the story of the Blackwood family. Six years ago, Merricat's family was poisoned with arsenic. The scandal made the surviving sisters, Merricat and Constance, outcasts in the town. Each week, Merricat reluctantly walks into town to buy groceries and visit the library. That path would echo that of the author, who would walk down the hill from her home on Main Street to the John G. McCullough Free Library at 2 Main Street, and then stop for groceries at Lincoln Square. See also **Main Street, North Bennington**.

North Bennington, Lincoln Square – When Shirley Jackson needed groceries, she would put her youngest child in the stroller and walk down the hill from their home on Prospect Street to Powers Market in Lincoln Square, the intersection of Prospect, Main, and three other streets. It was on a return walk that Jackson came up with a story idea about a small town and the village square. That story was "The Lottery," first published in the June 28, 1948, issue of the *New Yorker*. See also **Main Street, North Bennington**.

A 1996 made-for-television movie version of *The Lottery* was filmed in North Carolina with Veronica Cartwright as the "lottery winner" and Keri Russell as her daughter with a surprisingly strong pitching arm.

North Bennington, Main Street – Author Shirley Jackson lived at 66 Main Street from 1953 to her death in 1965. North Bennington was divided between locals and the transplants who arrived to work at the college, and the two social castes rarely interacted. Many of her works were written in these walls, including her novels *The Bird's Nest* (1954), *The Sundial* (1958), *We Have Always Lived in the Castle* (1962), and *The Haunting of Hill House* (1959) (regarded by Stephen King as one of the important horror novels of the twentieth century). The last three all feature the shared concept of a house that is isolated from the neighboring community. See also **Bennington College; Dewey House, Bennington College; Jennings Hall, Bennington College; Greenwich; John G. McCullough Free Library, North Bennington; Lincoln Square, North Bennington; Prospect Street, North Bennington; Ricket's Landing**.
The Bird's Nest was made into the film *Lizzie* (1957), starring Eleanor Parker as the schizophrenic heroine.

North Bennington, Prospect Street – Shirley Jackson and her family lived at 12 Prospect Street from their 1946 arrival in town until the 1949 move to Main Street. It was here Jackson wrote the early short stories works that established her as a gifted writer and exacerbated the usual "townies vs. academia" tension of college towns with "The Lottery" (1948), "Charles" (1948), and similar stories that suggested small towns hid a dark underside that appeared at unexpected times. See also **Main Street, North Bennington**.

North Montpelier – North Montpelier was the final home of Driftwood Press, where W. Paul Cook, a close friend of Lovecraft, wrote and personally printed a tribute to his departed friend. *In Memoriam, Howard Phillips Lovecraft:*

Recollections, Appreciations, Estimates (1941) is considered one of the finest memoirs written about Lovecraft.

Northfield – As if lake monsters and Sasquatch weren't enough for one state, Northfield has its own contribution: "The Pigman." Since 1971, sporadic reports still come in of encounters with a man-sized creature, covered in white hair with the facial features of a pig. Usually spotted around a rugged wooded area outside of town called the Devil's Washbowl, he seems to specialize in scaring the hell out of romantically inclined teenagers parked along the secluded road.

Norfolk – Sergeant Kensin Cook is recruited to join the FBI's Special Paranormal Investigative Research and Intelligence Team. Norfolk is his hometown and his familiarity with the area is needed. It turns out Cook is well aware of what has caught the attention of S.P.I.R.I.T. – and he knows who summoned it so many years ago. Now he and a childhood friend's expertise in the occult, they must stop the return of pure evil. *Deadly Resurrection* (2016) by Dawn Gray is part of her S.P.I.R.I.T. series.

Norwich – Modernist poet Ramon Guthrie (1896-1973) is buried in Hillside Cemetery. One of the major poets of the mid-20th century, Guthrie made a rare visit to the horror genre with his poem "Springsong in East Gruesome, Vermont." The juxtaposition of horror and rustic life creates both verse and cognitive dissonance. The poem was first anthologized in *Asbestos Phoenix* (1968).

Old Bennington Cemetery – Old Bennington is a village located within the town of Bennington. The Old Bennington Cemetery, behind the Old First Church, is the resting place of Poet Laureate Robert Frost, his wife Elinor and their children, all buried in a family plot. See also **Ripton; South Shaftsbury**.

Otis – Local mechanic Jake (Adam Hose) is struggling to keep the family business running when parasites begin turning the citizens of Otis into bloodthirsty zombies. With the only road out of town blocked off, Jake, his ex-girlfriend Alex (Brynn Lucas), and his trigger happy rival Randy (Dennis Lemoine) must survive small town zombie apocalypse without killing each other in the 2007 film *Zombie Town*. See also **Center Rutland; Proctor; Marble Street, West Rutland.**

Ottauquechee River – Historic Elm Street Bridge crosses the Ottauquechee in Woodstock. It is from this bridge that Edward Wanderley (Douglas Fairbanks Jr.) falls to his death after an encounter with Eva Galli (Alice Krige) in the film version of *Ghost Story* (1981). See also **Milburn.**

Owlsfane – In Duffy Stein's *The Owlsfane Horror* (1981), an engaged couple rent a vacation ski house across from a locally notorious haunted house, which they ill-advisedly decide to break into at midnight.

Palacestone – Mick Longston moves into the perfect little house in a charming little town in *Eyes of the Doll* (1999) by R. E. Prichard. Soon, he is jailed for the gruesome murders of his neighbors, a local couple that dabbled in voodoo. It seems that several of the town's leading citizens incurred the wrath of a voodoo demon several years before and the demon was imprisoned in Mick's house until he and his deceased neighbors inadvertently released it.

Panton – The railroad ticket agent of Newburyport, Massachusetts was born here in H. P. Lovecraft's *The Shadow over Innsmouth* (1936). To celebrate his coming of age, the story's narrator has begun traveling New England researching his genealogy. The agent suggests that the bus is less expensive than the train to travel from Newburyport to Arkham, MA. However, the bus requires a visit to Innsmouth, Massachusetts.

Passumpic – Passumpic is a small town in Windsor County where Elizabeth Akeley meets her great-grandfather Henry Akeley on his return from Yuggoth in Richard Lupoff's "Documents in the Case of Elizabeth Akeley," first published in *The Magazine of Fantasy & Science Fiction*, March 1982. See also **Townshend**.

Passumpic River – According to H. P. Lovecraft in "The Whisperer in the Darkness," first published in *Weird Tales* (August 1931), severe flooding of the Passumpic, and West Rivers in November of 1927 evoked whisperings of odd things found in the floodwaters, particularly in Caledonia County above Lyndonville. Vaguely human in shape, but more crustacean than anything else, the stories are dismissed as folklore by Professor Albert Wilmarth of Miskatonic University. See also **Townshend**.

Peacham – See **Connecticut River Valley**.

Peru – Annie Trumbull Slosson's "Dumb Foxglove" first appeared in *The Atlantic Monthly*, April 1895. It tells of the ghost of a crippled child who returns to her tiny farming village to do that which she couldn't in life.

Pinebridge – In *Good Night, Sweet Angel* (1996) by Clare McNally, Jenn Galbraith's ex-husband tried to kill her and their four-year-old daughter, Emily. He succeeded only in killing himself. Now Emily's invisible friend Tara protects her from the vengeful ghost of her father, who still tries to abuse her, even from the grave. But does Tara have her own agenda? Soon Emily's mother is fighting for her daughter's very soul against forces she doesn't believe exist.

Pinnacle Mountain – See **Antrim**.

Preston – Each day young Matthias Worsham sees demons sleeping in the trees. He has only seen them with their eyes open twice. Neither time ended well in "Where Demons Sleep in the Trees." The story appeared the collection of Scott Thomas's work *Urn & Willow* (2012).

Proctor – LaFond's Auto Sales straddles Main Street. One side is a gas station with a vintage Mobil red Pegasus logo, and the other side is sales and service. It plays itself in the 2007 film *Zombie Town*. Jake LaFond (Adam Hose) is struggling to keep the family business running. He's a lousy mechanic, his ex-girlfriend (Brynn Lucas) is back in town, and just to top off a lousy day, his brother (Phil Burke) is turning into a zombie. Jake will return to his family business to plan a counterattack as things continue to get worse. See also **Otis**.

Province – Three hundred years from now, the fastest form of transportation is "jaunting," teleporting great distances almost immediately. The first tests on humans were conducted at Province, now a historic site as important as Kitty Hawk was in the days of aviation. There are drawbacks, such as the immediate death and/or madness if you jaunt while conscious, which is why general anesthesia is mandatory when preparing to travel. And, why you always make sure everyone in your party actually takes the gas in "The Jaunt" by Stephen King (*Twilight Zone* Magazine, June 1981).

Reliance – The rumor is that everyone in town just up and vanished in 1918. The only thing certain is that all that's left are stone walls, cellar holes, and a small cemetery. It is in Reliance that Lisa and her friends try to contact the Fairy King Teilo. They leave him presents and sweets and in return, he gives them an ancient book on fairies and how to cross over the fairy realm. It is also in Reliance that Lisa disappears. Has she crossed into the fairy world or is there something more sinister afoot in *Don't Breathe a Word* (2011) by Jennifer McMahon. See also **Harmony**.

Ricker Basin – See **Little River State Park, Waterbury**.

Ricket's Landing – Miss Harper is traveling by bus. She dislikes bus travel under normal conditions. Compounding her discomfort is the fact that the driver is surly and the bus is filthy. She dozes off and is rudely awakened and pushed off the bus before she realizes that it's the middle of the night, it's raining and it's the wrong stop. That's when things start getting odd in Shirley Jackson's "The Bus," first published in *The Saturday Evening Post,* March 27, 1965. See also **Main Street, North Bennington**.

Ripton – The Homer Noble Farm was the summer home of Poet Laureate Robert Frost. The National Historic Site in the shadow of Bread Loaf Mountain in the Green Mountain National Forest is maintained as a memorial to Frost by Middlebury College and is open seasonally. See also **Old Bennington Cemetery**.

Rockingham – The old Rockingham Meeting House was erected in 1787, making it one of the two oldest public buildings in the state and the one closest to its original condition. The building and burying ground were the inspiration for the Falmouth Meeting House and cemetery in "Dust from a Dark Flower" by Daniel Mills. The story first appeared in *Fungi* (2012), as the local doctor fights a battle he's going to lose. See also **Falmouth**.

Round Hill – See **Townshend**.

Route 108 – Abra Stone is drugged and kidnapped by the Crow, one of a group of psychic vampires called the True Knot. Abra's shining is so powerful the group thinks it will help reverse the disease decimating their ranks. But as the Crow drives through the Vermont night, Abra launches a secret weapon. She and Dan Torrance can swap minds, and Dan Torrance has much better control of his shining, as the Crow will soon discover in *Doctor Sleep* (2013), Stephen King's sequel to *The Shining* (1977).

Rutland, New Miskatonic University – According to Brian Lumley, in his second Titus Crow novel *The Transition of Titus Crow* (1975), the Wilmarth Foundation detonated a nuclear device beneath Devil's Reef in Innsmouth, Massachusetts to kill Cthulhu's daughter. Cthulhu's rage was such that Innsmouth, Miskatonic University, and parts of Arkham are totally destroyed. The new campus was wisely built further inland in Rutland.

St. Johnsbury – See **Connecticut River Valley**.

St. Johnsbury, Stonkers Farm – Just north of the city, doomsday prophet Harry Stonkers and his wife own a small farm where they and faithful followers await the return of flying saucers that will mark the rapture. Johnny Smith's mother Vera joins this cult in Stephen King's *The Dead Zone* (1979).

Shelburne – In the 1998 film *Urban Legend*, folklore professor Robert Englund invites co-ed Rebecca Gayheart to eat Pop Rocks and then drink soda. She refuses because she "knows" it would cause her stomach to explode. Chemist William Mitchell (1911-2004) was the inventor of Pop Rocks and by proxy, is the father of the urban myth. He is buried in Shelburne Village Cemetery.

Shelburne Falls – In Rick Hautala's *Winter Wake* (1989), John Carlson, his wife Julia and stepdaughter Briana are forced to give up their comfortable life in Shelburne Falls to move to John's childhood home on Glooscap Island in Maine. The family's opinion on the relocation does not upon arrival.

South Burlington – In Richard Laymon's *Blood Games* (1992), the five protagonists fly into Burlington International Airport to begin their annual reunion. This year, they will drive out to the abandoned Totem Pole Lodge, scene of a massacre 12 years before. Unfortunately, the lodge isn't quite deserted.

South Royalton – A complex series of standing stones and chambers known collectively as "Calendar One" appear to have astronomical alignments and ancient European inscriptions. Calendar One is one of the largest of these stone sites scattered across New England that appear in the work of such authors as H. P. Lovecraft, Joseph Payne Brennan, Karl Edward Wagner, Rick Hautala, and Joseph A. Citro. See also **Antrim; Castleton; Calendar II Site, South Woodstock.**

South Shaftsbury – The Robert Frost Stone House Museum was Frost's home from 1920-1940. In 1923, his Pulitzer Prize-winning volume of poems, *New Hampshire* was published, including "Two Witches" and "In a Disused Graveyard" saw print from this house. See also **Old Bennington Cemetery.**

South Woodbury – Director Walter Ungerer's award-winning film *The Animal* (1976) tells of a couple who meets at a train station and goes to an isolated farmhouse deep in the inhospitable winter woods. Director Walter Ungerer's South Woodbury home serves as the farmhouse as he explores what happens when fate and loss blur the line between the mundane and the supernatural. The wife begins to see children and animal tracks that the husband cannot or will not see, leading to a climactic, unexplainable schism between them. See also **Berlin.**

South Woodstock – In 1817, Frederick Ransom's body was exhumed by his father. The corpse's heart was removed and burned on a blacksmith's forge as a remedy to the vampirism that struck the family. It was an unsuccessful cure, as Frederick's mother, sister and two brothers soon followed him to the grave. See also **Village Green, Woodstock.**

South Woodstock, Calendar II Site – Calendar II in central Vermont is the most well-known of the Vermont pre-Columbian, astronomically-aligned stone chambers scattered across the state. CIA spy Ward Hopkins and FBI agent Nina Baynam are in hiding, hunted by the Straw Men, a centuries-old, worldwide cabal of killers. The ancient stone structures indicate how long the Straw Men have been in America, but still no clue as to how to stop them. *Blood of Angels* (2003) is the final installment in the "Straw Men" series by Michael Marshall.

Stillwater – When the state highway to Rutland is closed, travelers are forced to take the Stillwater Road. According to "The Horror in the Burying-Ground" by Hazel Heald with major revisions by H. P. Lovecraft, this decrepit farming town hides a ghastly secret of revenge and premature burials. It was originally published in *Weird Tales*, May 1937.

Stockton – Joseph A. Citro's first published short story, "Them Bald-headed Snays," appeared in *Masques III* (1989). The tale finds young Daren Oakley being sent to live with his anachronistic grandparents in Vermont. There he discovers the fastest way to cure an ill is to hurt a Snay.

Stony Hill – In Madeline Yale Wynne's short story "The Little Room," two spinster aunts have a house with a mysterious room that may or may not actually exist, depending on whom you ask and when you look. The story first appeared in *Harper's Monthly*, August 1895.

Stovington – The Torrance family lived in this town prior to becoming winter caretakers at the Overlook Hotel in Colorado, according to Stephen King's *The Shining* (1977).
The 1997 TV mini-series version of *The Shining* is more specific. Now that Jack (Steven Weber) is unemployed, they live in the run-down Poplar Apartments where Wendy (Rebecca De Mornay) keeps a watchful eye on their psychic son Danny

(Courtland Mead). The exterior shots of the apartments were filmed at similarly named apartments in Denver, Colorado. See also **Stovington Academy**.

Arnie Cunningham often drove through the town on his fireworks runs for Will Darnell in Stephen King's *Christine* (1983).

Undersecretary of Defense William Unger, a Stovington native, was targeted for death by Dink Earnshaw in Stephen King's novella "Everything's Eventual," first anthologized in *Everything's Eventual*, 2002.

Stovington Academy – The prep school where Jack Torrance formerly taught in Stephen King's *The Shining* (1977) is also the school Johnny Smith's student Chuck Chatsworth attends in King's *The Dead Zone* (1979).

The academy bookends the 1997 King-produced TV mini-series version of *The Shining*. In the beginning, Jack Torrance (Steven Weber) is seen punching a student, leading to the unemployment that sends the family to Colorado. The ending finds Dick Hallorann (Melvin Van Peebles) and Wendy Torrance (Rebecca De Mornay) reuniting 10 years later as Danny Torrance (Wil Horneff) graduates from Stovington. See also **Stovington**.

Stovington CDC – In Stephen King's *The Stand* (1978), containment at the Center for Disease Control in Atlanta is breached. Attempts to find a cure to the plague are moved to the Stovington CDC facilities, which is also where Stu Redman is imprisoned.

Stowe – In Stephen King's *Cycle of the Werewolf* (1984), paraplegic Marty Coslaw is sent to spend the remainder of the summer with relatives in Stowe after his encounter with the werewolf in his Maine hometown. Only his Uncle Al believes Marty is still in danger and makes contingency plans.

Stowe, Gold Brook Bridge – Spanning Gold Brook on Covered Bridge Road, the 50-foot truss bridge is typical of the picturesque covered bridges of New England. And like most of the covered bridges, it is haunted. Known in tourist and ghost hunter circles as "Emily's Bridge." It is one of the more widely known haunted bridges, as popularized by Joseph A. Citro in his 1997 *Passing Strange: True Tales of New England Hauntings and Horrors*. The story, as ghost tales are wont to do, is a little vague on specifics, other than someone named Emily died on the bridge after being spurned by her beloved. Built in 1844, the bridge was added to the National Register of Historic Places in 1974. Sightings continue to this day.

Stowe, Main Street – Illustrator Sal DeVito (J. J. Barry) moves to Vermont from New York City after his divorce. His career and life are back on track until he accidentally kills a young girl (Karen Lewis) when she runs out in front of his car. Exonerated by the police, the girl's grandfather (William Robertson) is less forgiving and places a curse on him. To break the curse Sal goes to a local psychic named Adrianna (Kim Hunter). Adrianna is used to dealing with tourists – she may be out of her league in *Dark August* (1976). The film, set in Stowe, was filmed in various locations in town with the shops and church spires of Main Street particularly recognizable.

Stowe, Round Hearth – Attorney Mike Kirxby has left a trail of wives and lovers behind him. A chance meeting with ex-wife #3 ends in a one-night reunion. Now Kirxby is suddenly meeting, sleeping with, and bidding a final farewell to all the women he's had relationships in reverse order. To his horror, realizes this countdown will lead back to his first wife, who was so crazy she nearly drove him insane as well. To avoid the countdown of exes, he first flees to a ski lodge in Vermont, where he meets another ex. Maybe he'll have better luck fleeing to the Caribbean because he's running out of old girlfriends. "All the Birds Come Home to Roost" by Harlan Ellison first appeared in *Playboy*, March 1979.

Stowe, St. Angelo's Hospital – Teenager Tara has awakened in a hospital room in Vermont with no idea how she got there. The last thing she recalls, she was heading home from school in Connecticut in the "Fair Haired Child" (1:9) episode of the *Masters of Horror* television series. Things are about to get worse – there is no such hospital in Stowe.

Strafford – The historic Strafford Meetinghouse becomes the abandoned 'Salem's Lot church. Such a sanctuary is very much necessary when anthropologist Joe Weber (Michael Moriarty) decides writing the requested vampire history was a poor career decision in *A Return to Salem's Lot* (1987). Look for a 12-year-old Tara Reid in her first movie role. See also **Connecticut River Valley**.

Sutton – Aaron Bailey inherits the ancestral property in Sutton, unaware that this small town has an ongoing pact with the demon Moloch. Unfortunately for Aaron, his ancestors were part of the coven, and he is the key to fulfilling the pact that will free Satan in *Evil Agreement* (2012) by Richard L. Hatin.

Tashmore – Andy McGee and his pyrokinetic daughter Charlie hide in a cottage in Tashmore Pond on the Vermont side of Tashmore Pond. They are fleeing a secret government agency simply known as "The Shop," which is looking to exploit Charlie in Stephen King's novel *Firestarter* (1980). In both the novel and the 1984 film version, the cabin on Tashmore Pond is where the Shop's hired gun John Rainbird (George C. Scott) finally catches up to and captures the McGees (David Keith & Drew Barrymore).

Thompson's Valley – The town has been abandoned and is going back to nature. Only John Staples remains, living in the grist mill his ancestors built centuries before. But now Staples is not alone. Something is grinding its way through the solid rock the mill is built upon. Something big and relentless in "The Worm" by David H. Keller. The story first appeared in *Amazing Stories*, March 1929.

Tilton – Annie's husband James died in a plane crash. Two days after the tragedy, she gets a call from her late husband, in some sort of afterlife waiting area where time is fluid. He warns her about two future tragedies. The first prediction is confirmed by the quarterly newsletter from the librarian in Tilton, where Annie and James had a summer cottage, noting the passing of their handyman, as James forewarned. The second warning takes longer to be fulfilled but may save her life in "The New York Times at Special Bargain Rates" by Stephen King. The story was originally published in the October/November 2008 issue of *The Magazine of Fantasy & Science Fiction*.

Torchester – Christine and Nick Marino flee to the tiny ski hamlet of Torchester to escape vengeance-seeking trolls in the novel *The Vengeance* (1983), Robert C. Sloane's sequel *A Nice Place to Live* (1981). The plan is unsuccessful.

Townshend – H. P. Lovecraft's "The Whisperer in the Darkness," first published in *Weird Tales*, August 1931, finds Henry Akeley living at the old Akeley place south of Townshend Village, on the side of Dark Mountain. At nearby Round Hill, he discovers a mysterious black stone with hieroglyphs similar to markings found in the *Necronomicon*. He believes it is another piece of evidence that the aliens he calls Mi-Go are already on the planet and have begun a plan to harvest mankind. See also **Union Station, Bellows Falls Union Station, Brattleboro; Dark Mountain; Guiford; Newfane; Passumpic; Passumpic River; Wickenden**.
The old Akeley place and the inscribed stone return in "Envy, The Gardens of Ynath, and the Sin of Cain" by Darrell Schweitzer first published in *Interzone*, April 2002.
Townshend Woods – The woods south of Townshend are where Winthrop Hoag's briefcase was inexplicably found. Hoag had

disappeared several months before from a cabin outside of Arkham, Massachusetts which he inherited from his occultist cousin. Coincidentally, that cousin had disappeared from that same cabin seven years before. Lin Carter's "Strange Manuscript Found in the Vermont Woods" was first published in *Crypt of Cthulhu* #54, 1988.

Tyburn – Dr. Ambrose Perry has retired to a home in the deep woods of Vermont, miles from the nearest town. There he has begun experiments in accessing primal ancestral memory in "The Ancestor," a posthumous collaboration of H. P. Lovecraft and August Derleth that was first anthologized in *The Survivor and Others* (1957).

Vergennes – An elderly man recalls a terrifying encounter from his earlier days as a railroad man. He was on his way to Vergennes on business, but in this earlier time, the trains only go as far as Rutland, forcing him to travel the last 50 miles on horseback across rough terrain. He stumbled across an isolated village not listed on his map. Even odder, all of the residents were blind. There is a cause for this phenomena – it is not natural in "The Naked Goddess" by Daniel Mills. The story debuted in his collection *The Lord Came at Twilight* (2014)

Vernon – Vernon is home to the former Vermont Yankee Nuclear Power Plant, the state's only dalliance with nuclear power. It was the target of continual protests until finally shut down in December 2014. In Stephen King's 2011 novel *11/22/63*, the shutdown was a little more abrupt. Jake Epping, a Maine school teacher, is tasked by a dying friend to prevent the Kennedy assassination. It seems his friend has a time portal to 1958 in his diner's pantry. The changes Jake makes in the past ripple through time, changing the future and causing earthquakes, one of which triggers a core meltdown at Vermont Yankee. Fortunately, Jake can return to 2011 and reboot the changes but subsequent attempts make things even worse.

Washington – Simon Phillips (Omid Abtahi) lives in a secluded cabin on the outskirts of town. Phillips, like Olivia (Anna Torv), was also a Cortexiphan test subject as a child in the ongoing story line in *Fringe*. Phillips now reads minds to the point that human contact is painful and incapacitating. Walter (John Noble) needs him to read the mind of a comatose prisoner to prevent a bioterrorism attack in "Concentrate and Ask Again" (3:12)

Ben & Jerry's "Flavor Graveyard" of discontinued ice cream flavors. Photo courtesy of Ben & Jerry's Homemade, Inc

Waterbury – One of the oddest, albeit beloved, graveyards in New England is behind the Ben & Jerry's Ice Cream Factory in Waterbury. There you will find the "Flavor Graveyard," a cemetery dedicated to discontinued ice cream flavors, each with a dignified headstone.

Waterbury, Little River State Park – Above the Waterbury Dam in the Little River State Park is the ghost town Ricker Basin. All that remains of the town are a few cellar holes, several family cemeteries, and a few rusted pieces of old farm equipment. One notable piece of abandoned equipment is the decaying remains of a sawmill furnace. Author Daniel Mills used the rusted hulk as a local landmark in his story "The Hollow," the story of an abandoned boy who grows up around the ruins of the failed village of his childhood. Loneliness and his father's abandoned library are his sole companions. The story appeared in the author's collected stories, *The Lord Came at Twilight* (2014).

Waterbury Center – See **Adamant**.

Weathersfield – Clarissa Bleeker hates the portrait of her husband's grandmother Eliza that hangs in the parlor. She also hates Eliza's gravestone, which coincidentally, seems to be moving toward the house ever since Clarissa had the portrait moved. "The Restless Gravestone of Weathersfield, Vermont" by Scott Thomas appeared in his 2012 collection *Urn & Willow*.

Wenton – Jessica Fletcher (Angela Lansbury) travels to Vermont at the behest of a former student (Thom Bray). He is a poetry teacher who needs to impress the dean, whose daughter he is wooing. His competition is the equestrian instructor (Barry Williams), who likes to dress up as the headless horseman. At least until they find him headless and horseless in *Murder, She Wrote* episode "Night of the Headless Horseman" (3:11).

West Dummerston – Director John DiGeorge's original fantasy film *Redbelly* (2008) transforms the West Dummerston woods into a mythical medieval land with a princess (Erica DeMilio) trapped in a stone tower. The 18' diameter, 8' tall circular stone structure was built specifically for filming the scenes of the Princess in isolation struggling against her personal phantasms.

Also in the film, an abandoned mute prince (Justin Allen) with an externalized glass stomach has been enslaved since childhood by an evil moonshiner. The moonshine set was built in the woods from a 1000-gallon propane tank. The set was realistic enough to convince hikers they had stumbled across a real still.

West Hall – In 1908 Sara Harrison Shea was found dead in the fields behind her home, just months after her daughter Gertie had been found dead in the same area. Now the town claims Sara's ghost walks the town. A century later Ruthie Washburn and her sister Dawn awaken to find their mother missing. As Ruthie searches the old house for clues, she finds a secret compartment with Sara Harrison Shea's diary. Ruthie begins tracking her mother with the information in the wallets and soon finds links between the diary's horrors and her mother's disappearance. To her growing horror, it appears Shea's death and her mother's disappearance are connected in *Winter People* (2015) by Jennifer McMahon.

West River – See **Passumpic River**.

West Rutland – Writer/Director Brett Piper returns his stop-motion animation roots in *Arachnia* (2003). A freak meteor shower forces a plane to crash in the Arizona desert. The characters seek shelter in an abandoned farmhouse only to discover that the meteor strike has brought a giant subterranean spider in search of live food. Piper used the facilities of Edgewood Studios in Rutland for the film and West Rutland stood in for scenes of the Arizona desert with explosions carefully monitored by the volunteer West Rutland Fire Department.

West Rutland, Marble Street – The Downtown Laundry Basket on Marble was a filming location for *Zombie Town* (2007). Our heroes are preparing for one last desperate attempt to stop the zombie plague from spreading beyond the town. Billy (Jon

Norman Schneider) wants to stop at the family laundromat to check on his father. The bad news is Billy's father is a zombie. The good news is he was also a gun nut, so the team now is once again fully armed. See also **Otis**.

West Windsor – Brownsville Cemetery is the final resting place of actor Charles Bronson. Although best known for tough guy roles, Bronson, under his real name of Charles Buchinski, was Vincent Price's mad assistant Igor in *House of Wax* (1953), the first horror film in 3D produced by a major studio.

Westfield – Olivia (Anna Torv), Peter (Joshua Jackson), and Walter (John Noble) are called in to investigate a series of odd events in Vermont in the "Welcome to Westfield" (4:12) episode of *Fringe*. They discover a strong electromagnetic field affecting the town and driving the townsfolk mad. Walter concludes that those infected have somehow been merged with their doppelgangers from the parallel universe.

Weston – Maple Grove Cemetery is the final resting place of Vrest Orton (1897-1986), author, artist, historian, and founder of the Vermont Country Store. Orton met Lovecraft when both lived in New York and soon became a travel companion and correspondent. Lovecraft spent several weeks with Orton's family in Guilford, which would be the inspiration for "The Whisperer in the Darkness," first published in *Weird Tales*, August 1931. Orton also illustrated the cover of the only edition of publisher Paul Cook's *The Recluse* (1927), which featured the first appearance of H. P. Lovecraft's famous long essay, "Supernatural Horror in Literature." See also **Guilford**.

Whistler's Gore – Taking a page from Edgar Lee Masters, author Daniel Mill's tale "Whistler's Gore" uses the epitaphs in the village graveyard to tell the story of how a minister's sermon triggered a sweeping religious revival in town. Let it suffice to say that as far as Whistler's Gore was concerned in 1798, you were going to find God, one way or another. The story first appeared in *The Lord Came at Twilight* (2014).

White Cross – The film *Blood Rites* (2003) finds teenager Rachel Zimmerman (Heather Dilly) and her father (Bill Hickok) moving to isolated White Cross. Rachel tries to fit into her new surroundings, but between classmates obsessed with sex, an unusually high murder rate, and a white specter that demands virgin sacrifices, the transition is not going well. See also **Meetinghouse Hill Cemetery, Brattleboro; Middle Road, Dummerston**.

White River Bridge – See **East Corinth**.

White River Junction – In a bar in White River Junction, aspiring artist Carlo Duarte agrees to a job as the keeper of a lighthouse on the White River. He looks forward to the isolation as a way to concentrate on his art. But it's hard to paint when you discover your job is hell in "Lux et Veritas" by Thomas F. Monteleone (*Lighthouse Hauntings,* 2002).

White River Junction, Sykes Mountain Avenue – In the film *Ghost Story* (1981), the Vermont Transit Busport in White River Junction doubles for the bus terminal in Milburn when Don Wanderley (Craig Wasson) returns home for his twin brother's funeral. See also **Milburn**.

Whitehall – Artist Leslie Abbott lives in remote Whitehall to stay as far away from people as she can in an attempt to keep her psychic abilities under control. Now, she is telepathically seeing other psychics being hunted down and strangled. And Leslie knows she is the next victim in *Night Screams* (1981) by Bill Pronzini and Barry N. Malberg.

Wickenden – In August 2011, a tropical storm hit Vermont, drenching the state so severely that it was compared to the floods of 1927. The 1927 floods triggered the events recorded in H. P. Lovecraft's "The Whisperer in the Darkness," and the 2011 flooding similarly inspired events in Kristin Dearborn's *Whispers* (2016). The Mi-Go continue their insidious encroachment on humanity, and they have taken control of Wickenden. Sarah Sorrell is under siege in her cabin an hour outside of town, with the Mi-Go attempting to convince her to join them. Sarah has rescued Neveah, a hitchhiker who turns out to be a prostitute and drug mule fleeing her pimp. Sarah thought holding out against the aliens was bad, but now her Mi-Go minion neighbors have brought Neveah's psychotic pimp to the cabin for a climactic battle between good, evil, and ET. See also **Townshend**.

Wickham – Keomany Shaw, confectionary shop owner and Earthwitch, fights back the powers of evil with Peter Octavian the ex-vampire. Shaw leaves her tranquil mountain town to battle demons in Christopher Golden's *The Gathering Dark* (2003), book 4 in his "Shadow Saga" series.

Williams Crossing – Tabloid reporter Savvy Skye heads to Vermont to interview self-professed vampire Count Yorga. Before the interview begins, the immortal count bites her on the arm and drops dead. Now she's feeling anemic and light sensitive and Yorga has disappeared from the morgue. *Vampires of Vermont* (1999) by Mark Sumner is part of his "News from the Edge" series. The books were adapted into the 2001 cable television series *The Chronicle*.

Wilmington – In the film *Paranoia* (1998), Calvin Hawks (Larry Drake) is stalking Jana Mercer (Brigitte Bako) and stops to buy a new knife for the project. The scene where Calvin tries out the new knife on his hand was shot in one of the quaint gift and cutlery shops along Main Street in Wilmington. See also **Greenwood**.

Wilmington, Pettee Memorial Library – In the film *Paranoia* (1998), Calvin Hawks (Larry Drake) has discovered potential future victim Jana Mercer (Brigitte Bako) is back in Vermont.

A quick trip to the Pettee Library provides her address and an opportunity to demonstrate his knife technique on the librarian. See also **Greenwood**.

Winooski – In 1962, four teens accidentally release the Ne-Wa-Ta, a cave-dwelling cannibal cursed by the Native gods. Now in their sixties, the boys must reunite when the monster is released again, this time, to face the terrors from their youth to save their families in *Deadly Whispers* (2013) by Richard L. Hatin.

Winooski River – See **Passumpic River**.

Wintersend – In the1996 short story "Moonlight in Vermont" by Esther Friesner, an odious teen tourist discovers the colonial founders of the town are currently both undead and respected civic leaders. And now, even worse, he wants to join the undead. The story was first anthologized *in Sisters in Fantasy 2.*

Woodstock – Woodstock has been used for location shots for a number of films, but is most recognizable as Milburn, both in 1981 and 1929, in *Ghost Story* (1981), with scenes shot in the Windsor County Courthouse, North Chapel Universalist Church, and the Central Vermont Public Service Corporation Offices (which became the Village Pump Restaurant). See also **Milburn**.

Gwen Verdon (1925-2000) died at the home of her daughter in Woodstock. One of the major musical comedy stars of all time, one of her four Tony awards was for the role she originated on Broadway in 1955 – the devil's cohort, the damned soul Lola in *Damn Yankees!* A middle-aged sports fan sells his soul to the devil (Ray Walston) to become the baseball superstar who can lead his beloved Washington Senators to beat the Yankees in the World Series. But despite the devil's best attempts, including overtures from the gorgeous Lola, the man just wants to return to his wife. Verdon and Walston would reprise their roles in the 1958 film version as well.

Woodstock, Elm Street – In the film *Ghost Story* (1981), there is a Civil War statue on a pedestal in the middle of Elm Street at Central Street. Because the existing "traffic dummy," a cement slab with a blinking warning light, would be an anachronism in flashback scenes, the film crew camouflaged it with the statue. See also **Milburn**.

Woodstock, Village Green – In 1830, when another member of the Corwin family began to waste away, the family had his dead brother's body exhumed. The body was reburied and the heart carried to the middle of the village green where it was burned to ash in an iron pot. The pot was then placed in a 15-foot deep hole in the middle of the square. A block of granite was placed over the pot, the hole refilled and fresh blood from a slaughtered bull sprinkled over the hole, ending the outbreak of vampirism in Woodstock. See also **East-West Road, Dummerston; Manchester; South Woodstock**.

These cases of tuberculosis misdiagnosed as vampirism were collectively the inspiration for such diverse works as Amy Lowell's poem "A Dracula of the Hills" first anthologized in *East Wind* (1926), H. P. Lovecraft's "The Shunned House" (*Weird Tales*, October, 1937), *The Case of Charles Dexter Ward* (*Weird Tales*, May, 1941) and Edgar Allan Poe's "Ligeia" (*American Museum*, September 18, 1838).

During the "Year without a Summer," A farmer, seemingly unaffected by the frost and cold in the summer, takes in a wanderer, known in folklore as Bridget. Her presence speeds the crops and makes the weather seasonal. But her assistance comes with a price. The farmer balks at the price and breaks off the relationship using the tried and true methods used in Woodstock in years past. "In the Wake of Bridget" appeared in *Midnight Call and Other Stories* by Jonathan Thomas.

INDEX

GOUDSWARD

79, 80, 85, 91, 92, 93, 94, 97, 98, 99, 100, 101, 102, 103, 106, 111, 117, 118, 120, 121, 122, 124, 125, 127, 128, 130, 133, 150, 219, 271, 272
Haven (series) – 64
Hawkey, Raymond – 109
Hawthorne, Nathaniel – 57, 149, 152, 205, 207
Heald, Hazel – 84, 273
Hill, Betty and Barney – 160, 183, 186
Hill, Joe – 129, 150, 155, 159, 164, 172, 185, 208, 210, 257
Hirshberg, Glen – 157, 184
Holden, Richard – 221
House of Dark Shadows (1970) – 38, 111
Howard, Kat – 190
Hughes, Ted - 110
Hyde, Christopher – 181
Hynd, Noel – 174

I am Legend (2007) – 232
The Ice Queen (2005) – 256
Ice Scream (1997) – 21
In Dreams (1999) – 198
In the Mouth of Madness (1995) – 177
Innsmouth (2015) – 211
The Incredible Hulk (series) – 198
Ipcar, Gahlov – 111
The Iron Giant (1999) – 110
IT (2017) – 43
IT (series) – 43

The Jacket (2005) – 260
Jackson, Shirley – 230, 231, 251, 264, 265, 270
Jackson, Winifred V. – 105
James, Thomas P. – 233
Janghwa, Hongryeon (2003) – 75

Jewett, Sarah Orne – 42, 51, 85, 116
Jumanji (1995) – 145, 182, 217

Kaplow, Robert – 13
Karloff, Boris – 14, 100, 181
Keene, Brian – 96
Keller, David H. – 277
Kelman, Judith – 244
Kennard, Jr., James – 211
Kenyon, Nate – 131
Keohane, Daniel G. – 187
Ketchum, Jack – 42, 85, 133
Kiernan, Caitlín R. – 172
Killer Pickton (2005) – 220
King, Stephen – 4, 5, 6, 7, 8, 9, 10, 11, 12, 13, 16, 17, 18, 19, 21, 22, 24, 25, 27, 28, 29, 30, 31, 32, 33, 34, 35, 36, 37, 39, 40, 41, 43, 44, 45, 46, 47, 48, 49, 50, 51, 52, 54, 55, 57, 58, 59, 60, 62, 63, 64, 65, 66, 70, 71, 72, 73, 74, 76, 77, 78, 79, 80, 81, 82, 85, 88, 89, 90, 92, 93, 94, 97, 98, 105, 106, 108, 112, 113, 114, 117, 118, 120, 122, 123, 126, 131, 132, 138, 139, 143, 145, 151, 156, 157, 160, 162, 163, 177, 180, 183, 184, 187, 189, 196, 199, 200, 212, 213, 216, 219, 238, 255, 259, 262, 263, 265, 269, 271, 273, 274, 276, 277, 278,
King, Tabitha – 8, 66, 89, 90
Kingdom Hospital (series) – 33, 76
Kipling, Rudyard – 245
Klein, T. E. D. – 212

Lacey, Patrick – 176
Laimo, Michael – 128, 139
Lake, Veronica – 237
Lake Champlain Monster – 236, 237, 257
Lake Placid (1999) – 69
Lake Placid 2 (2007) – 70

Horror Guide to Massachusetts is a map to geographical
locations, real and fictional, utilized in horror tales set in New
England. It is hard to say which is more disquieting, terror
amidst staid Yankees in a familiar setting or horror in obscure,
forgotten corners of the Commonwealth. Both have their uses as
weapons in the battle to scare you out of your wits.

Horror Guide to Florida

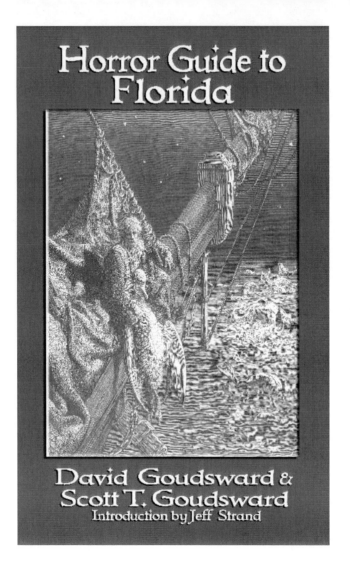

David Goudsward &
Scott T. Goudsward
Introduction by Jeff Strand

Horror Guide to Florida is a map to geographical locations, real and
fictional, utilized in horror tales and films set in the Sunshine State.
And just for good measure, they've included some true stories and
events that should be horror stories, or lest the inspiration for future
ones. Florida scares many people for many different reasons, be it the
alligators and giant snakes in the Everglades, sharks with a taste for
tourists, hurricanes with a taste for trailer parks, or giant mice wearing
pants. But where else, outside your nightmares, can you find giant
prehistoric penguins, exploding clergymen, mutant vampire were-
turkeys, and the Bermuda Triangle all in the same geographic area?
Come with the brothers Goudsward and explore the mysterious, the
macabre, and the downright bizarre world hidden in the shadows of
Florida.

POST MORTEM PRESS
www.postmortem-press.com

About Post Mortem Press

Since its inception in 2010, Post Mortem Press has published over 100 titles in the genres of dark fiction, suspense/mystery, horror, and dark fantasy. The goal is to provide a showcase for talented authors, affording exposure and opportunity to "get noticed" by the mainstream publishing community. Post Mortem Press has quickly become a powerful voice in the small genre press community. The result has been five years of steady growth and successful endeavors that have garnered attention from all across the publishing world.

Made in United States
North Haven, CT
13 March 2025

66751525R00190